TEACH YOURSELF BOOKS

PSYCHOLOGY

PSYCHOLOGY

Nicky Hayes

TEACH YOURSELF BOOKS

For UK order: please contact Bookpoint Ltd, 39 Milton Park, Abingdon, Oxon OX14 4TD. Telephone: (44) 01235 400414, Fax: (44) 01235 400454. Lines are open from 9.00 – 6.00, Monday to Saturday, with a 24 hour message answering service. Email address: orders@bookpoint.co.uk

For U.S.A. & Canada order queries: please contact NTC/Contemporary Publishing, 4255 West Touhy Avenue, Lincolnwood, Illinois 60646 – 1975 U.S.A.. Telephone: (847) 679 5500, Fax: (847) 679 2494.

Long-renowned as the authoritative source for self-guided learning – with more than 30 million copies sold worldwide – the *Teach Yourself* series includes over 200 titles in the fields of languages, crafts, hobbies, sports, and other leisure activities.

British Library Cataloguing in Publication Data
A catalogue for this book is available from the British Library

Library of Congress Catalog Card Number: 93-86268

First published in UK 1994 by Hodder Headline Plc, 338 Euston Road, London NW1 3BH.

First published in US 1994 by NTC/Contemporary Publishing, 4255 West Touhy Avenue, Lincolnwood (Chicago), Illinois 60646 – 1975 U.S.A.

The 'Teach Yourself' name and logo are registered trade marks of Hodder & Stoughton Ltd.

Typeset by Multiplex Techniques Ltd, St Mary Cray, Kent.
Printed in Great Britain for Hodder & Stoughton Educational, a division of Hodder Headline Plc, 338 Euston Road, London NW1 3BH by Cox & Wyman Ltd, Reading, Berkshire.

Impression number   16 15 14 13 12 11
Year   2004 2003 2002 2001 2000

CONTENTS

ACKNOWLEDGEMENTS

My thanks are due to Usha Patel, Colin Smith, Graham Gibbs and Christine Sefton, whose different kinds of support have helped me so much during the writing of this book.

This book is dedicated to

Professor Steven Rose

who first introduced me to levels of analysis
as an alternative to <u>reductionism</u>

1
WHAT IS PSYCHOLOGY?

What is psychology? There are a lot of ways that I could try to answer that question. The most straightforward answer, though, is to say that psychology is about understanding people: how they think, what they say, and why they do what they do. That is not the whole answer, of course, because there are some psychologists, like those who work with dolphins and chimpanzees, who are interested in understanding animals as well. But most psychologists are mainly interested in people.

The problem with trying to understand people, though, is that people are complex, and change all the time. We learn from our experiences, we form good intentions, and we are acted on by circumstances. So what we do can be influenced by a great many different factors. Also, everyone has their own ideas and opinions about what people are really like. These ideas can influence what we do, and also how we interpret what other people are doing. And since we each have had different lives, and learned from our experiences, these ideas can be very different from one person to the next.

What all this adds up to, of course, is that there are not any easy answers. You will not find, after reading this book, that you know everything there is to know about people. But you will find, I hope, that after reading this book you know a great deal more about people than you knew before; and that knowledge may help you to understand the people around you a little better.

The first part of the word 'psychology' comes from the Greek 'psyche', which means the soul, or the essence of life, and was sometimes portrayed as a female figure representing the mind; the second part also comes from the Greek language, and indicates

— 1 —

knowledge or science. So combining the two gives us the idea of psychology as being the science of the mind.

This idea of psychology has been through a couple of transformations over the past 150 years or so. In the first half of the twentieth century, for instance, a kind of psychology developed which took the view that if psychology was to be a proper science, then it must be objective, dealing only with information which could be directly observed and measured — in other words, with people's behaviour, not their minds. After all, you cannot directly see into someone's mind. All you can really see is what they do or say, and that is their behaviour.

Gradually, though, psychologists became better at studying experience as well as behaviour, and at conducting research which let them test out their theories about how people do make sense of their experience. They do not do it in the same way as those early philosophers, of course, and we will be looking at how psychologists do their research later in this chapter. But psychologists nowadays are as interested in understanding the mind as they are in understanding people's behaviour.

A modern definition of psychology would probably refer to it as **the scientific study of both experience and behaviour.** We are interested in what people experience as well as what they actually do, and we need to put them both together in our attempt to understand human beings.

Psychologists, of course, are not the only people who are trying to understand human beings. But where a sociologist, say, will try to understand human beings from the point of view of people in society, and how groups of people and social trends emerge, a psychologist is mainly interested in the individual person. That does not mean that we can ignore society, though: as we will see in the next chapter and elsewhere in this book, it simply is not realistic to try to understand an individual person as if their society or culture had nothing to do with what they were like. But it means that in psychology we take the individual person rather than society as a whole, as our starting point.

———— Levels of explanation ————

So where do we begin in the attempt to understand the person? One of the most important lessons that we have learned from the history of psychology is that just looking at one single aspect of experience or behaviour is not enough. People do things for lots of different reasons, and usually for several reasons at once. If we try to single out just one of those reasons, as if that were the only explanation, then straightaway we hit problems. Just saying, 'oh, they're really intelligent', to explain why someone became a research physicist does not answer the whole question, because it does not tell us why they became interested in science in the first place – or even why they went into an academic career at all, instead of becoming, say, a politician or trader. Instead, we have to look at what people do from several different angles, to see how all the different factors and influences work together to produce the final outcome.

One of the most useful ways of thinking of this is to think of it in terms of **levels of explanation**. Anything that we do can be studied from several different levels. Imagine, for instance, that you came across someone reading this book. If we wanted to understand what was going on there, we could look at it from a number of different levels. We might ask what is going on in the actual process of reading. For example, how we can look at a set of marks on a printed page, and respond to them as if they were words that someone has spoken to us. And that would be part of an explanation of what was going on.

But it would not be the whole answer. There would also be the question of why the person was reading this particular book, rather than, say, a book about car mechanics. That would lead us again into questions about their own personal experience and why they had developed some interests rather than others. We might also ask why they were reading in the first place, rather than, say, cultivating rice or watching TV. That would lead us again into a different set of questions, which would include questions about their particular culture as well as questions about personal habits, beliefs and moods.

In other words, we can look at the same thing using a number of different levels of explanation. We might use a very general level, such as looking at cultural influences on human behaviour. We might decide to approach a question from the point of view of social influences, by looking at how the people close to us affect what we do and how we conform to social expectations – or do not, as the case may be. We might look at it from the point of view of personal habits and past experiences, or we might look at it from the point of view of understanding how people process information in their minds. All of these, and many others, are levels of explanation which we can use in our attempt to understand human beings, and no single level of explanation is going to be enough in itself.

The reason for this is that each level of explanation is more than just the sum of the lower level. Sometimes, for instance, you hear people saying that once we know about all the different nerve cells in the brain, then we will know all there is to know about how the brain works. But this is not true, because there are often entirely new properties which emerge when the different parts are combined into a whole system. And these **emergent properties** can make all the difference.

Perhaps this will be clearer if I take an everyday example. A cake is made up of common ingredients: flour, eggs, butter, and so on. To understand what a cake was, you would have to know about these. But knowing about them would not tell you everything about the cake, because a cake has properties which the single ingredients on their own do not have. At the simplest level, it has a taste and texture which are not present in the single ingredients. At higher levels, it may have cultural or symbolic significance, like the way that it can be given to someone on their birthday. None of these can be deduced simply by studying the ingredients.

It is the same with a human being. We can learn a great deal about people by studying the brain and how it works. But we cannot learn everything. We may be able to trace which nerve cells in the brain are active when we are solving a problem; but that does not tell us how we are working out a solution, or why we are thinking about the problem in the first place. We need to look at human beings using as many levels of explanation as possible, if we are really to begin to understand what is going on.

Table 1.1 shows something of the range of levels of explanation which we can use in analysing problems. As you can see, psychologists use a wide range of levels of explanation in their work, choosing those ones which seem to be most appropriate for

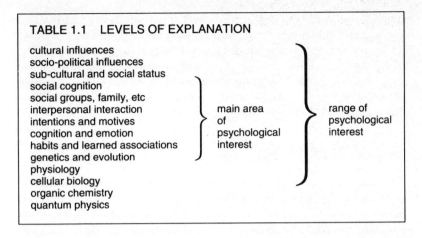

TABLE 1.1 LEVELS OF EXPLANATION

cultural influences
socio-political influences
sub-cultural and social status
social cognition
social groups, family, etc
interpersonal interaction   main area   range of
intentions and motives   of   psychological
cognition and emotion   psychological   interest
habits and learned associations   interest
genetics and evolution
physiology
cellular biology
organic chemistry
quantum physics

the questions that they are trying to answer. So the study of psychology involves looking at human beings from a number of different angles. A professional psychologist would have to be aware of each of these levels of explanation, and be able to use insights from each of them when trying to solve a particular problem. An academic psychologist, though, generally conducts research within one single specialist area, and so often uses a more limited number of levels of explanation at any one time.

Areas of psychology

Studying psychology, then, involves studying experience and behaviour in terms of different levels of explanation. This implies that it also means knowing something about each of the main areas of psychology. There are six of these, roughly speaking, and each one gives us a different kind of information, which we can use in our attempt to understand people.

Cognitive psychology

One of the central areas of psychological knowledge is known as cognitive psychology. This is to do with gathering and using information – taking in information and making sense of it (a process we call perception) – with remembering things, or recognising them, and with thinking and reasoning. These mental processes are known as cognition, which is how cognitive psychology gets its name. Psychologists studying cognition have discovered a great deal about how people's minds work, and that information is often useful when we are trying to understand why someone is acting in a particular way.

Social psychology

Another branch of psychology is concerned with understanding how people act when they are with other people. This ranges from looking at body language to understanding why people obey those in authority, or when they may or may not help someone who seems to be needing it. Social psychologists are also interested in how we make sense out of our social experience. This part of social psychology is known as social cognition, because it is about the mental side of social life.

Individual psychology

Some psychologists have been concerned with studying what makes people different from one another. Some people, for instance, seem to be more intelligent than others, some people are highly creative while other people are not, and each of us has our own special personality. We also differ in motivation: some people are keen to get ahead in life, while others are mainly concerned with establishing a happy home and family life. Individual psychology is concerned with what motivates people, as well as with how people are different from one another.

Physiological psychology

All this makes it seem as though understanding people is really just about looking at what they do, or how they process information. And that *is* a large part of it. But sometimes what we do or how we think is also influenced by our physical state. If we are tired or stressed, for instance, we often do not make decisions very well, or we can become irritable with the people around us. So an important part of psychology is concerned with understanding how our physiological state influences us. The research of a physiological psychologist might be about studying the effects of brain damage or how drugs work, or it might involve studying sleep and dreaming, or looking at the physiological effects of stress and how they can be reduced.

Developmental psychology

Some psychologists are particularly concerned with studying how people grow and change throughout life. Each year that passes adds to our store of experience and knowledge, but how do we use that knowledge? And do we inevitably decline as we get older? Developmental psychology is concerned with understanding how changes in childhood, adolescence, adulthood, and old age affect us, and what those changes actually involve. Interestingly, the picture which emerges when we really begin studying the processes of maturity and ageing is much more optimistic than the one which society often supposes – but we will look into that in more detail in the appropriate chapter.

Comparative psychology

Comparative psychology, as its name suggests, is all about making comparisons. But what are we comparing ourselves with? With other animals. As we know from evolutionary biology, human beings are a kind of animal – even if rather a special one. So that leads us to some very interesting questions about how close we are to other animals, and whether we have anything in common with them – or whether they have anything in common with us. Comparative psychologists are interested in animal behaviour in its own right, of course, but we are also interested in studying how animals interact with one another because that might give us some clues to understanding human beings.

5/14/02

— Obtaining evidence —

Gathering psychological evidence is a bit like detective work. It is always easy to jump to conclusions about an answer. If a crime has been committed, you can always find someone who is certain who is responsible. But sometimes they are completely wrong. In the same way, whenever we are studying something in psychology, it is easy to jump to conclusions about it. After all, we all think we know about human beings. But sometimes, as with the crime, our conclusions are simply wrong.

So the psychologist, like the detective, has to put in hours of painstaking work collecting evidence, to find out what is really going on. Sometimes all that evidence will lead to the same conclusion that we might have obtained by guessing, or from 'common sense'. But even though our conclusions might not be earth-shattering, at least we know that they are based on a solid foundation. Quite often, though, what we discover is totally unpredictable. Without collecting the evidence in the first place, we would never have known.

Psychologists collect evidence in many different ways. Psychology as an academic discipline has been around for nearly 150 years, and during that time it has passed through several phases. Each of these phases has left us its methods of research. As a general rule, these phases occurred because a particular group of psychologists believed that they had the best starting-point for studying human beings. The methods that they used for doing that study, therefore, can be helpful in giving us some kind of insight into that particular level of explanation.

Introspection

Psychology began life as a special branch of philosophy, so in its early days the approaches which it used were very similar to those used by the philosophers of the time. For the most part, this involved **introspection** – trying to understand the mind by analysing one's own thoughts, feelings and experience. Although this method fell out of favour for a time, because it did not seem to be scientific enough, in a more systematic form it is used in psychology again today. Cognitive psychologists, for instance, sometimes use a method called **protocol analysis** to give them some ideas as to how people solve problems. This involves asking people to talk aloud about what they are thinking as they do a task, and analysing what they say. Some psychologists have found it a helpful way of gathering evidence about problem-solving, or even quite complex tasks like musical composition.

The early introspectionist psychologists, however, were eventually overtaken by a new approach to psychology which developed round about the beginning of the twentieth century. This approach was known as **behaviourism**, and those who supported it argued that psychology needed to become more objective and scientific. As we saw earlier, they tried to do this by restricting psychology to the study of behaviour.

Experiments

The behaviourists brought with them a rigorous scientific method, with which they tried to look at the 'pure' elements of behaviour, cutting out what they saw as 'contaminating' influences. They did this by conducting tightly controlled laboratory **experiments**. An experiment involves manipulating a situation to bring about an effect. The behaviourists, in particular, tried to control their experiments very carefully. They would try to rule out all other possible influences, and then see what happened if the one factor that was left was altered.

This method of study has remained in psychology. Some research into attention, for example, has involved asking people to identify a single message or concentrate on identifying a signal on a screen, while different factors in the message have been adjusted. These experiments are carefully carried out under laboratory conditions, so that the researchers can be sure that their results really were caused by the factor they were studying.

Action research

There are also other kinds of experiments, which are much more loosely controlled. Research in organisational psychology, for example, often consists of **action research**, in which working conditions or communication systems are changed and researchers observe how the change affects the people working in that particular place. Although field experiments like this cannot be as carefully controlled as formal laboratory experiments, they can still tell us a great deal about people at work, and have done so, over the years.

Animal experiments

Unlike a modern psychologist, many of the early behaviourists believed that one single level of explanation could provide the key to understanding all human behaviour. This level of explanation was to do with habits and learned associations. They believed that all human behaviour was really just chains of learned associations combined together, in the same way as atoms combine to form animals, plants or minerals.

This led them to look for the 'atom' of psychology, or the simplest unit of learning which they could find. To do this, they spent a great deal of time studying animal learning, because they believed that this was a 'pure' form of learning. Unlike humans, they believed, animal learning was 'uncontaminated' by memories, ideas or imagination, so to study it would help them to identify how the basic units of learning combined to produce complex behaviour.

Other psychologists, too, used animals to study basic units of human experience. In the 1960s, for instance, many animal experiments were conducted to investigate visual perception, and animal studies are still used to investigate some aspects of brain functioning. But animal experiments are now much less common than they used to be in psychology. Nowadays, psychology is much more concerned with the ethics of animal research, which fortunately has meant that only studies which are serious scientific research and likely to be of real value in adding to knowledge are likely to be permitted.

Observation

The behaviourist school of thought, as we have seen, emphasised rigorous experimentation as the main research method for psychology. Gradually, however, psychologists with wider interests began to have more influence, and people began to use non-experimental methods for studying human behaviour. For example, nobody in their right minds would suggest experimenting on children, but there was a lot of interest in psychological aspects of child development throughout the twentieth century. Those psychologists had to come to their conclusions by observing children, not by experimenting with them.

There are lots of different ways of performing scientific

observations, but just looking at what is in front of you is not one of them. Researchers need to know what they are looking for, and how they will know if they do actually observe it. Psychologists conducting observational research also need to make sure that their own unconscious biases do not affect how they make sense out of what they see. So many observational studies are conducted in a very systematic way, and sometimes under quite controlled conditions — like watching children play in a specially equipped playroom.

Alternatively, psychologists sometimes conduct observational studies of behaviour in the natural environment. This approach is known as ethology, and is one of the main methods of studying animal behaviour, at least nowadays. It is also very useful when we are looking at families — for example, we have learned a lot about how parents interact with their babies by doing ethological observations.

Surveys

Sometimes, psychologists want to make large-scale observations of what people do or think, and they do this by conducting surveys. A survey involves a special questionnaire, which is given to a large number of people. By analysing their answers, the psychologist can observe general tendencies, or trends in what people are doing or thinking. Surveys about AIDS, for example, have helped psychologists to understand more about people's attitudes towards it — although they still do not tell us very much about what people actually do, only what they think they might do — which is not always the same thing.

Psychometrics

Another special type of observation which psychologists use is known as **psychometrics**. Psychometric tests are tests which are designed to tell us something about the person's mind. They usually take the form of special kinds of questionnaires, which have been carefully constructed and tested, and they can sometimes give us useful clues about someone's personality, skills or abilities. But it is important to remember that these are only clues – psychometric tests do not have all the answers, and they do not give the whole picture. They can be useful in supplementing other information, but they are not complete in themselves.

Case studies

Experiments and observational studies, for the most part, tend to deal with information from large numbers of people. This approach dates back to the first half of the twentieth century, when it was generally assumed that people, as a whole, were pretty similar. The general approach in society at that time involved understanding 'the masses', and the masses were not really seen as individuals. During the second half of the twentieth century, though, attention became much more focused on the individual person, and this in turn affected psychological research methods.

One outcome was that psychologists began to ask much more detailed questions about individuals and their experiences. To do this, they began to concentrate on just a few individuals, or single cases. **Case studies** were not new to psychology: many famous case studies had taken place in the past. But they were often regarded as somehow being less scientific than large-scale studies. More recently, though, psychology has begun to accept the case study as a regular research method which can give us useful information.

For example, we have learned a lot about how the mind works through case studies of people with cognitive problems. One case study, for example, was of a respected academic who was completely unable to recognise people's faces. She was above average intellectually, and in all other respects her mental functions were normal. Studying this single person in detail gave the psychologists undertaking the case study some useful evidence about how the mental skill of face-recognition is organised in the brain.

Accounts and interviews

As we have seen, psychology in the twentieth century was deeply influenced by the behaviourists' insistence that studying behaviour was the only truly scientific approach. But in the later part of the twentieth century it was increasingly apparent that this simply was not good enough. Two people can be in similar situations, but each of them can interpret what is going on quite differently. Their interpretation will influence how they react, and that will influence what happens in the end. So if we really want to understand people, we also need to study how they make sense out of the world that they live in.

Account analysis

Towards the end of the twentieth century, psychology became increasingly concerned with social and personal meanings and experiences. Clearly, it is difficult to get at this kind of information using laboratory experiments or observations, and so a different research method became popular. This became known as account analysis, because it is all about analysing the accounts which people give of their own experiences.

Interviewing

Psychologists collect accounts by conducting **interviews**. Interviewing is a skilled affair, because the person doing the interview needs to make sure that the other person feels relaxed and confident. After all, if you did not trust someone, you would not be prepared to tell them much about your feelings or thoughts, would you? So an interviewer has to be good at encouraging people to speak, and at striking up a good rapport with the person they are interviewing.

There are lots of ways of analysing accounts. Some psychologists look at the ways that people express their ideas, and the metaphors and assumptions which they use. This is known as **discourse analysis**. Other psychologists look at the types of reasons, or attributions, which people give. And some concentrate on identifying the main themes which emerge from what people are saying. Each of these methods is a type of **qualitative analysis** - a way of looking at the meaning of the information, rather than just collecting information about the numbers of people who reacted in particular ways.

We can see, then, that the psychologist has a wide range of tools to help in their detective work. Incidentally, I have presented these research methods as if they were only developed at certain times during the century. That is not really true. If we look back, we find that individual psychologists have used almost all of these methods at some time or other. But different methods are seen as important at different times, by psychology as a whole, and this is the process which I have been describing.

It is important, because it affects how much influence a particular piece of research can have – both in psychology, and in society as a whole.

—— What do psychologists do? ——

As we have seen, academic psychologists generally work within a small area of psychology. Their task is to conduct research into that area, identifying the underlying mechanisms and processes which are taking place, and how they can contribute to our understanding of people. Professional psychologists, on the other hand, draw from the work of academic psychologists, and put it to use. They also conduct research of their own, and many of the areas of psychology contain important theories and evidence which have been drawn from professional psychology.

Professional psychologists can be found at work in almost any area which involves dealing with people. Forensic psychologists, for example, work with police and with prison staff in tackling many different aspects of crime: the rehabilitation of criminals as well as finding the perpetuators of single crimes. Sports psychologists work with coaches and competitors, developing stress-reduction techniques, better training systems and ways of maximising competitive performance. Consumer psychologists are at work in advertising and market research, studying how people respond to consumer pressures and working out how suppliers can approach different markets.

One of the largest areas of professional psychology is concerned with people at work. Occupational psychologists are involved in helping to select and train people for different jobs, whereas organisational psychologists are concerned with the human side of management, and with things like managerial decision-making and occupational stress-reduction. There are also health psychologists, at work in the health service and as consultants, many of whom are concerned with organisational aspects of the health industry. Other health psychologists study issues like doctor-patient communication, or health education campaigns.

Some psychologists, too, are concerned with mental health. Clinical psychologists often work in the psychiatric service, dealing with people who are mentally ill or strained in some way. They are not the same as psychiatrists, who are doctors and tend to use physical treatments like drugs. Instead, clinical psychologists develop programmes to teach people better ways of coping with their lives, or help to train psychiatric nurses in dealing with their patients. Some clinical psychologists work in the community, alongside a general practitioner; and counselling psychologists help people to deal with the stresses and strains of everyday life.

Environmental psychologists are specialists in how people are affected by their environments, and they will often act as consultants for new architectural developments, or in approaches to reducing crime through the design of city environments. Educational psychologists apply psychological knowledge to the child in school, not only in terms of how it learns, but also by diagnosing sources of educational disadvantage.

There are many other types of work that psychologists do – this list only gives us a small sample. And there are even more people who have studied psychology to A-level or as part of a degree and who have found it useful in their work. They include policemen, social workers, doctors, nurses, personnel officers and many others. As these people have found, knowing about psychology may not give you all the answers, but it does help you to ask the right questions!

2

5/19/02

—SELF AND OTHERS—

This chapter is about who we are and how we come to be that way. We each have had different lives, and we were each born with our own particular kind of temperament and physique. These things all help to make us different from one another. Even very newborn babies differ in their likes and dislikes. But we also live in society, and amongst other people who matter to us. And that is crucially important in who we are.

——— The first relationships ———

All over the world, babies are brought up in different ways. The experiences of an Inuit child, living in a traditional community in the Arctic regions of northern Canada, are widely different from the everyday experiences of an infant growing up in Papua New Guinea; and both of these are different from the experiences of a child growing up in Britain. In some communities, babies are kept tightly wrapped up (swaddled), in others they wear few if any clothes; in some communities they are carried around continuously, while in others they spend most of their day in cots or beds. And in some communities, they spend all their time with their mothers, while in others they are looked after by relatives, friends or older children.

Yet despite all these different conditions all over the world, babies grow and, if they survive, generally develop into mature, balanced adults. Human babies can adapt to a tremendous range of different environments and conditions. These differences in how they are looked after do not really matter, as long as a baby gets what it really needs for healthy development. And what it needs most of all, is other people to care for it.

Human infants, when they are first born, are physically totally helpless. They have to be fed, cleaned and carried around by other, older humans, and without this they would not be able to survive. This physical helplessness continues for a very long time – far longer than in any other animal. On the face of it, it would seem as if luck, as much as anything else, is what helps babies to get through. But nature does not really work that way. As we will see in Chapter 14, the process of evolution means that we would only develop in a certain kind of way if it gave us an increased chance of surviving. And the human infant is actually a long way from being as helpless as it looks.

Sociability

Human infants are born supremely adapted for sociability. Being unable to move themselves, and also unable to cling to their mothers, as many animals do, they depend completely on other people. Because of this, they are very strongly predisposed to interact with people – and this is true of babies all over the world. For example, when an infant is first born, it is unable to change the focus of its eyes. But those eyes have a fixed focus, and it is fixed at just the right distance to allow the child to look at its mother's face while she is breast feeding. And this is from the first day after birth.

Smiling

Human infants also begin to make facial expressions very soon. Often these are quite tiny movements, but their parents, who are used to the baby's face, can recognise them. A human infant inherits a tendency to smile when it sees something which resembles a human face – and as it gets older, the resemblance needs to be more and more exact. Ahrens (1954) showed that very young babies, in their first month or so, would smile just when they saw an oval shape with two dots in it for eyes; but as the baby grew older, more detail was needed, until by four months the infant would only smile at a real human face, or a very realistic picture.

For a parent, of course, being looked at by your baby, and smiled at, is an extremely special experience. It is likely to be very rewarding, and so it means that the parent is more likely to want to spend time with the baby, playing with it and talking to it. And that interaction, as we shall see, forms a strong foundation for the future relationship between a parent and their child.

Crying

Babies also have a very good way of summoning help when they
need it. Since the human infant cannot run for help itself, it needs to
have a way of summoning help from its caretaker quickly. And it
has. A baby's crying can penetrate for a very long distance, and
people quickly learn to recognise the sound of their own baby's
crying as opposed to any other infant.

Some psychologists believe, too, that there are special harmonics in
a baby's cry which activate the autonomic nervous system, so that
adults find it particularly disturbing. This means that they are
particularly likely to hurry to the baby and try to calm it down. It
might also account for the intense degree of frustration on the part
of parents who are living with a continuously crying child, and who
may sometimes become so frustrated and upset that they injure the
child. We do not know whether this is really the case. We do know
that people find baby cries extremely disturbing — that is not really
under question — but it is possible that they disturb us because
they are associated with pain and distress, and not because of the
harmonic qualities of the sound.

In either case, though, the fact is that very few people can really
ignore a baby crying. It is a very good way for the infant to
communicate the fact that it needs help. Moreover, infants can
communicate more than one message through crying. Wolff (1969)
recorded baby cries and analysed them using a sound
spectrograph, showing that there were at least three different types
of cry, with three different patterns of sound: one for pain, one for
hunger and one for anger. And the mothers were perfectly able to
recognise the message in their own baby's crying.

So even an apparently helpless infant is equipped to be sociable. It
responds to the sound of people's voices, it shows pleasure when
people are nearby, and it can summon help if it needs it. The baby's
physical survival depends on the people around it, and so the baby
needs to be able to interact with people too.

Parent–infant interaction

As it grows older, the baby's tendency towards sociability becomes
even more apparent. Babies delight in even the simplest repetitive

games with another person. As any parent knows, they will play games like 'peek-a-boo', or 'throw-your-teddy-out-of-the-cot-and-see-daddy-pick-it-up' for as long as the adult is prepared to carry on playing, but they rarely show so much persistence with games that they play on their own, with rattles or toys.

Parents and other adults almost automatically seem to adapt themselves to these baby games. Psychologists have conducted many observations of paren–child interaction, and found that most of the things which parents and infants do when they are playing help the baby to learn skills it will need in childhood and later life. But for many people this is almost entirely unconscious: we do it automatically, without thinking.

One thing which people do when they are playing with a baby, for instance, is that they make faces. Carefully analysed video-tape of these games shows that the babies, too, make faces. Parent and infant imitate one another, and these exchanges can go on for some time. It is games like these which set the foundation for later social experience. Infants learn how to take turns, and how to wait for the other person to respond before doing their action — which is like the turn-taking that goes on in conversation, and even involves the same kind of timing. Moreover, they learn it very quickly: we are strongly predisposed to learn that kind of thing.

Infants are also strongly predisposed to learn to communicate, and again we help them automatically. Psychological studies of baby-talk have shown that the special way that human beings talk to babies, which is so often ridiculed by comedians, actually helps the baby to notice speech. The softened tones and higher notes that we use are particularly easy for the baby to hear, and the repetition of vowel sounds ('baa-baa') draws attention to the part of the language which the child learns to produce first.

A human baby, then, may be physically helpless, but it is not at all helpless in terms of social abilities. It is already equipped with some social skills, and learns new ones even faster than it learns physical co-ordination. What all this adds up to is that other people are the most important thing in the child's world.

People are also the most important thing in an adult's world, at least for all of us except a few very exceptional individuals. And what infant sociability does, is to form the foundation for the personal attachments and relationships which we all need in later life.

Developing attachments

It used to be believed that infants developed attachments to the people who looked after them; and this led to a number of debates about whether mothers should go out to work, and similar issues. But as a result of these debates, psychologists began to study how relationships develop very carefully, and they found that things were not nearly as simple as that.

For one thing, many babies develop special attachments to more than one person, and sometimes they will develop a special relationship with someone that they only see for a relatively short period each day. In the pioneering study by Shaffer and Emerson, conducted in 1964, the psychologists found that many of the infants in the families that they were studying had special attachments with their fathers, who were out at work all day, as well as with their mothers, who in this particular study were at home. Other babies, though, did not form attachments with their fathers. And some formed attachments with the fathers, but not with their mothers, even though it was the mother who was with them most of the time.

So what made the difference? Shaffer and Emerson found, as have many psychologists since, that it was the quality of social interaction between parent and child which affected the infant's response. Babies become especially fond of parents (and other people) who are sensitive to the signals they are giving out – smiling and other facial expressions, movements and so on – and who are prepared to interact with them in their playing. They do not develop attachments very easily to people who just care for them physically but do not play with them or talk to them.

Even though parents become attached to their infants very quickly, it takes longer for the infant to develop its own attachment. Although infants often prefer to be with one person rather than someone else, in the first few months they are rarely distressed if their special person is not present. But psychologists found that full attachment would appear at about seven months. Then, the baby would cry if the person had to leave – although, of course, babies can usually be distracted quite quickly.

This attachment forms the basis of the loving relationship between parent and child, which persists throughout life, if it is not actively disrupted. And it, in its turn, is based on the quality of the interactions between the parent and the small baby. Of course, this does not mean that an attachment has to be based on that — as adopted children know, a relationship which begins later in life can be just as special. But a predisposition to interact with people, and to form relationships with the people who respond with you in a sensitive way, is one which is common to human infants all over the world. It is, quite literally, part of our heritage as human beings.

—————— The self-concept ——————

In later life, too, other people are more important to us than we sometimes realise. Each of us has our own, personal idea of ourselves — something which is known as the **self-concept.** On the surface, it seems as if we should develop that idea from our own personal experiences of what we can do, and what we like. But when psychologists have studied the self-concept, they have found that one of the most important factors in how we see ourselves is how other people see us.

Social relationships

As early as 1902, Cooley described the self-concept as the 'looking-glass self'. What Cooley meant was that we see ourselves as if we were reflected in the eyes of other people. We do not just think of ourselves in terms of our own personal knowledge: we judge what we are like the by the way that other people respond to us, and what we think they may think.

Guthrie (1938) related an story about a group of students who decided to play a joke on a class member — a girl, who was very plain and unattractive. The male students in the class took it in turns to ask her out, and treated her as if she were attractive and interesting. Guthrie observed that the students who were fifth and sixth on the list were actually very keen to take the girl out, because by that time she had changed considerably. The extra interest that she was receiving had raised her self-confidence, and now she was interesting to talk to, and took pains to make herself look attractive.

The self-fulfilling prophecy

What this also means is that sometimes other people's ideas about us become a **self-fulfilling prophecy**. In other words, what we think about someone may come true simply because we think it. One of the most striking illustrations of this mechanism was reported by Rosenthal and Jacobson, in 1968. They had gone into an ordinary high school in America, ostensibly to test out a new kind of intelligence test. On the basis of the test which they gave (which was really just a standard one) and class marks, they chose a number of ordinary children, whose performance in class was only average. They did not speak to the children directly. Instead, they let the teachers 'overhear' a conversation in which these children were named as being likely to show a sudden spurt in their academic work over the next year.

When Rosenthal and Jacobson returned to the school a year later, they found that the children they had chosen were up at the top of their classes. Because the teachers believed that they would do well, they had given them extra encouragement. The children did not know anything about the beliefs, but they had felt the encouragement, and had worked harder. They had also become more confident about their ability to learn. So the prophecy which Rosenthal and Jacobson had made — that the children would improve during the course of the next year — had come true simply because they had said it.

Self-image and self-esteem

Many other psychologists, too, have found that the self-concept depends on the type of interaction that we have with other people, and on the expectations that they have of us. The self-concept is often thought of as having two different parts. One of these is a descriptive part, which is just about what we are like: tall, being good at languages, liking sport, and so on. That part is known as the **self-image**. The other is an evaluative part, which makes judgements about whether we are good, bad, worthwhile and so on. That part of the self-concept is known as our **self-esteem**.

Personal relationships

Carl Rogers, the famous psychologist who is known as the father of counselling psychology, argued that our level of self-esteem depends on the type of personal relationships that we have had. People, Rogers argued, have two basic psychological needs – and will suffer psychological damage if those needs are not met. One of those needs is the need for **positive regard** from other people – affection, love, trust and so on. Everyone, Rogers argued, needs positive regard of some kind. Even people who avoid close relationships find it important that other people should respect them. To have some kind of positive regard from other people is a very fundamental need, which has to be satisfied.

But we have another fundamental need, too, which also has to be satisfied. That is the need for **self-actualisation**. Self-actualisation means making real ('actualising') the different parts of the self — in other words, exploring and developing our ideas, abilities, interests and talents. This is a fundamental need in people too: without any way of developing our abilities or skills, we can become psychologically damaged.

People self-actualise in many different ways. Many people have a hobby or an interest which takes up some of their leisure time, and this usually involves some kind of skill, or problem-solving. Fiddling with a car engine, playing video games or darts, baking, sewing clothes, or conducting a successful children's party are all highly skilled activities. We enjoy doing them, and doing them well gives us a sense of achievement and satisfaction. It helps us to feel good about ourselves.

So far, so good. Most people have family, friends and working colleagues who provide them with the positive regard which they need, and hobbies, interests and, if they are lucky, challenging jobs to satisfy their need for self-actualisation. And for that reason, Rogers argued, most people have a reasonably high level of self-esteem. While they do not see themselves as being perfect, they are reasonably content with being who they are.

But Rogers was working as a clinical psychologist, and so he came across a lot of people who were not in that position. In these patients, Rogers found that the two needs contradicted one another. Their need for positive regard, or approval from other people, was in direct conflict with their need for self-actualisation. These people had come to Rogers because they were suffering with neurotic problems. From his clinical observations and treatments, Rogers concluded that these problems occurred because they were suppressing such an important psychological need.

Conditional positive regard

When Rogers explored the childhoods which these people had experienced, he found that they all had one thing in common. They had all grown up with parents or others who had made their positive regard conditional on good behaviour. In other words, when they were naughty or had misbehaved — as children often do — they had received a very clear message that they were unloved and unwanted. 'Normal' people, though, had parents who, even if they were strict, always made it clear that they still loved their child.

Those children who had grown up with conditional positive regard were actually being given a message that it was not really them who was loved — it was some ideal, perfect child who was never naughty. So they grew up believing that they had to be ideal and perfect, and that if they were not, nobody would like them. What this meant was that they needed approval from other people so much, that they would not risk exploring their own interests, in case other people did not like it or did not approve. They stifled their own personal ambitions, interests or talents — in other words, their need for self-actualisation — in order to be sure of social approval.

These people, as we can see, had very low self-esteem. They had developed unrealistic **conditions of worth** – in other words, unrealistic ideas about what they needed to do to gain social approval or respect. And they applied these unrealistic conditions of worth when they were judging their own behaviour. Even if they were really quite successful, they still thought of themselves as failures, or as inferior to other people. Naturally, all this had made them very anxious, and eventually neurotic.

Unconditional positive regard

The solution which Rogers found was very simple. He argued that everyone needs some kind of secure psychological base from which they can develop. That base will be found in a relationship which gives them **unconditional positive regard** — positive regard which does not depend on how the person acts. If you really love, trust or like someone, then you accept the decisions which they make about how they are living their life. That does not mean, of course, that we have to condone things which are morally wrong, but we can dislike what someone does, and make that clear, without disliking that particular person. As parents do all the time.

But Rogers found that it is not only parents who can provide this kind of relationship. In fact, we can experience this kind of relationship at any age, and it can provide us with the security that we need to begin to self-actualise. Many people in adult life find relationships which give them that security, and begin to explore aspects of themselves which they have ignored before — like people who go to college for the first time in their thirties or forties. The important thing is to have a relationship of that kind at all — it does not have to be in childhood.

Rogers developed an approach to psychotherapy based on this principle. The role of the therapist, he argued, should be to provide an accepting and warm relationship for the client (he did not approve of the word 'patient') — in other words, a relationship based on unconditional positive regard. This would give the client the psychological freedom to make their own life-decisions, and to develop solutions to their own problems, because they would not be risking disapproval. Rogers called this **client-centred therapy**, because it is entirely based on what the client wants and does, not on what the therapist thinks they should do. Many counselling psychologists still use this approach today.

5/10/02

—— Cultural and social influences ——

We can see, then, that both our social interaction and our personal relationships can have a considerable effect on how we see ourselves — on the self-concept. But our ideas about ourselves, and how we are linked with other people, are also shaped by the social groups and cultures that we belong to. And different cultures can make very different assumptions about individuals, and what it is to be an individual human being.

Cultural contexts of self

In the Western world, it is quite common to see each person as a separate individual, who may choose to link themselves with some kind of social group if they want to. This model of the individual person has a long history: ultimately, it goes back to the philosophical systems of the ancient Greeks, and was reinforced by later philosophers such as Descartes, in the seventeenth century. The idea is also apparent in European history. The Protestant reformation, for example, emphasised the individual's own direct responsibility and conscience in religion, rather than the responsibility of the priesthood to interpret religion for the community.

It is open to question, though, whether any human being really can be such an entirely separate individual as all that. Most of us exist within a network of communities and social expectations: family, friendship groups and occupational groups. Many people seek out communities to belong to: religious groups, communes, volunteer groups. In other words, we do not really exist as independent individuals: we live within social networks and groups. As we will see later in this chapter, belonging to these social groups can form a very important part of our sense of identity.

We do, though, tend to believe that it is important to be an individual. Being an individual involves making one's own decisions about one's life, partners, friends and career. And it is this belief which makes the Western approach rather different from most of the other cultures in the world.

Self embedded in community

For example, in most of the traditional African cultures, and in Native Australian cultures as well, the person is seen as being primarily a member of the community. That does not mean that they are not seen as being an individual person. But it does mean that how they live their life concerns the rest of the community as well, and is not just their own responsibility. Individualism which does not concern itself with the community as a whole is seen as being irresponsible, and pretty well uncivilised.

When the Native Australian rock group Yothu Yindi began to have commercial success with their records, for instance, the decisions about how the group's career should go were all taken by the group's tribal community, and as spokespeople for their culture, the members of the band had no wish to do anything else. The prominence of the band had brought increased acknowledgement and recognition of Native Australian culture to white Australian audiences (and later to world-wide ones), and to the members of the group, it was important that they remained a part of their culture, rather than abandoning it and chasing success as individual musicians.

In other words, they regarded being part of their community an important part of being themselves – not just as an optional extra. To people from such cultures, the idea of acting as an individual, separate from family, community and social group, is simply unrealistic – and selfish, too. According to Mbiti (1970), the individual self is firmly located within the collective self of the tribe or people, and to try to separate them is to mean that the person only operates with half an identity.

Layers of self

A different idea of the self is apparent in Hindu belief systems. Bharati (1986) described how Hindu belief is centred around the idea of the self – but not the individual self-concept as it is in Western cultures. Instead, according to Hindu thinking the innermost self, or *atman,* is at one with God: it is a central, spiritual self which everyone possesses, but which can only be reached through meditation and other techniques. Other, more superficial parts of the self also contain more superficial qualities, like personality, and negative emotions such as jealousy or greed.

For the most part, therefore, what someone sees as their self-concept is really these outer layers of personality, and not their true, inner self. Only those who have disciplined themselves, through yoga or meditation, have access to the *atman* and can experience the true unity of the self and God.

So this idea of the self, too, is very different from the idea of the individual which is maintained by Western cultures. Although this view is not based on the importance of the culture and community, it still maintains the idea that there are other dimensions to the self: that there is more to being human than simply our own individual wishes and emotions.

The private self

Even within highly industrialised societies, there are different ideas of the self. Japanese people, for example, see the self as operating within a social context – but not a context of traditional family or tribe. Like city-dwelling Westerners, Japanese people may be meeting strangers all the time. But Japanese society places a great deal of emphasis on social consideration and social harmony. In order to maintain this, people are expected to keep inner emotions private, and to act in a socially acceptable manner at all times. Azuma, Hess and Kashiwagi (1981) described how this idea is apparent even in the experiences of a very young child in Japan.

At the age of 2 or thereabouts, as many parents know to their cost, children often become very wilful, insisting on getting their own way at every opportunity — or trying to. It is at this time that they have to learn social responsibility — or, at least, that they cannot always have their own way in everything. Different cultures go about teaching this in different ways. Among traditional families of the Shona people of Africa, for instance, children of this age go to live with their grandmother, and stay with her until they are about 5. So the more experienced family member is the one who tackles this difficult part of child-rearing. Western parents tend to confront their children, refusing to co-operate until the child eventually learns that it must moderate its behaviour.

A Japanese mother, though, does not tend to confront an egocentric 2-year-old directly. Instead, she 'suffers' her child, making it very clear that its behaviour is causing her pain and distress. In this way, the child is brought to realise that its actions have social and emotional consequences for other people, even from a very early age. It is encouraged to feel responsible for the suffering that it has caused, and also guilty, so it learns self-control as a way of not causing the suffering and not having to feel the guilt. These messages are consistent throughout childhood, and leave powerful influences on the adult's behaviour.

A Japanese person, then, is still regarded as an individual, but the self is essentially private. An individual has extremely important social responsibilities which cannot be avoided, and this means that, for the most part, personal wishes, emotions, and impulses need to be kept in check. The self is not independent of other people, because it is easily able to cause grief or pain to them, through inconsiderate behaviour. So social interaction has to be managed in such a way as to minimise that grief or pain, and so minimise the guilt which the individual would feel for having caused it. The self is seen as existing in a social context, with social requirements meaning that it often has to be kept private.

We can see, then, that people in different parts of the world – and also in different subcultures within Western countries – have very different ideas of what it is to be an individual person. The idea of the individual as entirely separate from others is really quite an uncommon one. And even in Western cultures, we are not quite as immune from the influence of other people as all that.

Social identity

There is another way, too, in which other people affect the way that we see ourselves. We are all part of society, and each of us belongs to some of the social groupings in society. Social groups can be large-scale, like what gender or ethnic background we have; they can be medium-scale, like being an accountant or a machinery tuner in a mill; or they can be small-scale, like being a member of a local astronomy club. But whatever size they are, belonging to different social groups has an influence on our sense of identity.

Social identity theory began in psychology with the work of Henri Tajfel, and has become a very useful way of understanding many important things about how human beings act. Essentially, what Tajfel pointed out was that the social groups which we belong to exist in the real world, and vary in terms of things like how powerful they are, how widely known they are, and how much prestige there is in belonging to them. Because we all live in the real world too, we are aware of these differences. So, for example, if we belong to a local astronomy society and are aware that, in that local town, the astronomy society is quite respected, then we would feel proud of belonging to it.

Moreover, belonging to that particular social group would be part of our own identity — part of who we are. And at times we would interact with other people as a member of that group — like speaking up for the group, or giving the members' point of view when we were talking with someone who did not belong to it. We would be able to slip into that particular social identity when it seemed to be relevant.

At other times, a different social identity might be the relevant one. An argument about who should do the washing-up might begin as just a discussion between two partners. But if one of them makes a remark which seems to be about gender, it can rapidly change from being a personal argument to a confrontation between men and women. Each person would be arguing as a representative of their own group, not as just their individual selves.

Categorisation and self-esteem

We all, then, have a number of different social identities. According to Tajfel, social identities come from our basic human tendency to sort the things into different categories. We categorise other people as well as other things: this person is a typical Volvo driver, that person is a heavy rock fan, and so on. And we include our own groups in the classification.

But there is more to it than that, because it is also a basic human tendency to look for sources of positive self-esteem. In other words, it is important for us to feel good about our own groups – we need to be able to feel proud of belonging to them. If the group does not have much status, then we often try to redefine it, so that we can see it as more important than it might seem. But if we cannot do that, then we will try to leave the group, or at the very least, pretend that we are not like the others.

For example: imagine that as a child you have a particular hobby — trampolining, say — which you really enjoy doing. Moreover, you are really getting quite good at it, and have passed various certificates. But then you join a new school, and it becomes apparent that your new friends there see it as an inferior kind of sport. What would you do?

Actually, there are several possibilities which are open to you — and all of them amount to ways of keeping positive self-esteem. You might leave the trampolining group altogether, and look for some other hobby which will be a bit more respected. You might claim that you only go because of parental pressure, or because your younger brother likes to go and you have to take him, or something like that. That would be distancing yourself from the group — saying that you are not really like the others.

Changing the status of the group

Alternatively, you might try to get your friends to change their view of it, for example by pointing out that it actually involves a very high level of skill. Or you might argue that it is a great deal better than other kinds of recreational activity that some people do. Both of these are attempts to change the perceived status of the group, so that it becomes more respected. Or you could change your friends, and only associate with other people who also do trampolining, and know how skilled it is.

This is a fairly small-scale example, but exactly the same processes take place in larger social groups too. It is now much easier for a black child, for example, to grow up being proud of being black than it was 50 years ago. There are far more black people with responsible, professional jobs, or holding highly respected positions in society than there used to be, which helps. There are also many people in the public eye who are proud of being black, and ready to say so.

This is because, over the past 50 years, a great many black people have been deliberately changing the perceived status of their group, by challenging stereotypes and discrimination whenever they encounter it. This has had its effect. There is still racism, of course, and still a lot to do, but the general view in Western society is very different from the view which was commonly held — even by black people — 50 years ago.

We can see, then, that who we are, and how we see ourselves, is very much linked with how we interact with other people. We all have our own personal likes, dislikes, talents and personalities. But we also exist in a network of social interaction, and have done so since we were very small babies. Other people's reactions and ideas matter to us, and they influence how we go about acting in life. Our cultural background also shapes how we see ourselves, and so do our social identities. None of us is totally patterned by these social influences — after all, everyone is different — but we are not totally independent of them either.

3

——————EMOTION——————

If you were to do a survey, asking what makes a human being different from a computer, the chances are that most of the replies would mention the same thing: emotion. Human beings, as we all know, do not just act like machines. We have another dimension to our experience as well — we feel things. We become happy, or upset, or thrilled, or furious — and we are not always particularly rational about how we do it. In this chapter, we will look at the psychology of a number of different emotions, and at how psychological knowledge has been used to help people to cope with anxiety and stress.

———————— Happiness and love ————————

When we think of emotions, it is generally the unpleasant ones which come to mind: fear, anger, anxiety and so on. Partly, that is because we live in a society which tends to emphasise pessimistic ideas more than optimistic ones: films, news and TV dramas all dwell on negative emotions and ignore positive ones. So we tend not to notice the positive emotions that we feel, or to dismiss them as not really happening. People who give up smoking, for instance, often notice that they become more easily irritated. But they overlook the fact that they also become more able to smile, and they laugh more easily. Both of these have the same physical origin — they are to do with getting the nicotine out of the system — but we only talk about the unpleasant consequences.

Positive emotions

In reality, though, the positive emotions which we experience are just as rich and varied as the negative ones — if not more so. Argyle and Crossland (1987) explored some of the dimensions of positive emotions, by asking people to imagine themselves in each of 24 different situations (Table 3.1). They were asked to describe how they would feel if they were in that situation, and to say whether the feeling produced by the situation was like the feelings produced by any of the other situations on the list.

TABLE 3.1   SITUATIONS PRODUCING <u>POSITIVE EMOTIONS</u>

Spending a good social evening with friends
Receiving an unexpected compliment which means a lot to you
Getting involved in a thriller on TV
Feeling overwhelmed by the beauty of nature
Getting on well with your loved ones
Solving an important personal problem
Listening to a beautiful piece of music
Engaging in a favourite hobby (not sports)
Having a rewarding conversation
Doing some sort of commitment activity (e.g. charitable work, etc.)
Feeling popular at a social gathering
Being a success at something important to you
Being absorbed by your work
Meeting an interesting new person or people
Engaging in a favourite sporting activity
Being successful at work
Reading a good book
Doing some enjoyable physical work
Buying yourself something you have wanted for ages
Spending some time thinking about the good things in life
Being given a valuable present by someone dear to you
Having a long hot bath, or pampering yourself some other way
Spending a memorable evening at a cinema/theatre/concert
Having a quiet drink with friends (non-alcoholic or alcoholic)

(Adapted from Argyle and Crossland 1987)

Kinds of positive emotions

By combining the different descriptions and analysing what they had in common, Argyle and Crossland found that there seemed to be roughly eight different kinds of positive emotions which were being described. Looking at these can make us realise just how varied our experiences can be. The first emotion on their list (although they were not arranged in any particular order) was the feeling of a sense of one's own **potency** — feeling capable, and able to do whatever is needed. A second one was a **sense of spirituality** or wonder, which might be part of the feeling involved in listening to a particularly beautiful piece of music, or enjoying nature. Feeling **contentment** was also on the list, as was the feeling of being **relaxed**, which is not the same thing at all.

Another positive emotion which people reported was referred to as **self-indulgence** by the researchers. We usually see self-indulgence as a selfish thing, but it is not always. The self-indulgence you experience when having a long hot bath or pampering yourself, for example, is not selfish in the sense of keeping something for yourself and not letting other people have it. But it is a pleasure which is personal, and not to do with sharing. Other kinds of positive emotions, though, are to do with sharing, or with caring for other people, and the researchers referred to these as **altruism**.

Being interested in something, or fascinated by a hobby, is also a kind of emotion which people enjoy experiencing. Argyle and Crossland referred to this as **absorption**. And the eighth positive emotion which they identified is that of **exhilaration** — the sort of emotion we would feel when we were excited about something, or thrilled by an unexpected pleasant experience.

Dimensions of positive emotions

Argyle and Crossland used these eight emotions as the basis for further research, and came to the conclusion that they indicated four basic dimensions which could be used to classify positive emotions. The first of these dimensions is to do with how **involved** we are in what we are doing. When we are having a quiet drink with friends, we tend to be less absorbed than if we are reading a good book or solving an important personal problem. We take things more lightly, and do not plunge into them as deeply.

The second dimension is about how **potent**, or effective, we feel ourselves to be. Some experiences require us to use our abilities fully, in order to achieve success, and those can be very satisfying. But other, equally pleasant experiences do not require the same kind of personal achievement. That type of experience simply is not relevant when we are socialising with friends or going to the cinema or a music concert. So, positive emotions can vary depending on how much they involve a feeling of potency on our part.

The third dimension has to do with whether our attention is focused on social circumstances, as they might be when we are in conversation with friends or meeting new people, or whether they are simply **personal** and self-indulgent experiences, of the type that we looked at before. Some positive experiences seem to direct our attention outwards, to other people, while others direct it inwards, towards our own selves.

The fourth dimension which Argyle and Crossland identified seems to be to do with how **intense** the experience is considered to be. Some experiences are really quite lightweight: having a hot bath or watching a TV thriller are pleasant, but they are not desperately serious activities. Some positive emotions, though, are to do with what people see as more serious things, and in Argyle and Crossland's research, these included solving an important personal problem, getting on with loved ones, and feeling overwhelmed by the beauty of nature.

We can see, then, that there is a much larger range of positive emotions than we sometimes realise. There are other ones, too, which are not on this list. But our tendency only to notice the unpleasant emotions like anger or fear, or to regard them as somehow more important than the positive ones, has meant that this aspect of human experience has often been ignored or neglected in our modern society.

Loving

One positive emotion which is not neglected, though, is love. We hear about love all the time, through the mass of romantic images in the media. But how far does the image actually reflect the reality? What is actually involved in the experience of love, and what is the difference in the love between a couple who have been married for 30 years, and that between two starry-eyed teenagers. Are there different kinds of loving?

Love and 'limerence'

It seems that there are. A number of psychologists have investigated different kinds of love, and have concluded that we often use the same word to describe some very different emotions. One of the most useful distinctions was made by Tennov (1979), who argued that love, as a long-term emotion, was actually very different from the short-term, intensive infatuation which we also call love, or being 'in love'. She suggested that it would be more appropriate if we used the name 'limerence' to describe the intensive experiences, and kept the term love to refer to the attachment involved in longer-term affections and partnerships.

Limerence, according to Tennov (and a vast number of writers, playwrights and musicians), is an intensive, all-consuming passion, which has a very strong element of fantasy in it. The person becomes totally obsessed with their idea of their loved one, and spends a great deal of time thinking about them and day-dreaming. Often, these thoughts are focused around tokens of some kind, such as a letter, a lock of hair or a photograph.

Perhaps the most distinctive feature of this emotion is that it involves a state of intensive longing for the person. Because of this, Tennov argued, it is important that the person should be unreachable in some way if the limerence is to last. When two people experiencing this emotion are together all of the time, the emotion tends to die away, because it is not being fed by longing for one another.

That is not necessarily a bad thing, of course. In many cases, the period of limerence represents an initial blissful period, which is then gradually replaced by a deeper kind of loving, which becomes a basis for a long-term partnership. But some couples find that they have relatively little in common once the period of intensive limerence is over. The problem, of course, is that those experiencing limerence cannot imagine it ever being over, so it is quite possible for them to make serious commitments, like marriage, while they are in this state, and then to regret it later.

The fact that limerence can be perpetuated as long as the couple are prevented from being together as much as they would like explains why parental opposition to love affairs so often has the opposite outcome to the one which they intended. Forbidding the relationship has the effect of increasing the longing which the two people feel for one another, and so can make their attachment stronger. A more sensible course would probably be to make sure that the two people are as much together as possible, to see if they would be likely to form a lasting attachment once the period of limerence is over, or not!

Dimensions of love

Sternberg (1988) accepted Tennov's idea of love and limerence, and went on to look at what seems to be involved in the longer-term loving emotions. He surveyed 80 people between the ages of 17 and 69, asking them about the relationships which they were experiencing at the time and ones which they had experienced in the past. From this, and other data, Sternberg concluded that love seems to consist of three underlying dimensions, with different proportions of these dimensions producing different kinds of love. These dimensions are intimacy, passion and commitment.

The **intimacy** dimension is all to do with how closely the two partners share in one another's lives. But it is much more than simple physical closeness. The intimacy dimension includes aspects of the relationship like how well the two people communicate, how much they understand one another and whether they are able to give each other emotional support. It also involves things like whether the two people really try to help one another, and whether each member of the partnership genuinely tries to promote the welfare of the other person.

The **passion** dimension in loving is not just about physical passion, although of course it does include it. But passion, in Sternberg's terms, involves other kinds of emotions, desires and needs as well. For example, it would include whether the relationship satisfied nurturing and caring needs, or whether the members of the partnership feel able to satisfy their needs for personal fulfilment or self-esteem. Maslow (1954) suggested that for some people (although not for others), loving is a way of compensating for their personal deficiencies. Sternberg would see this as part of the passion dimension in a relationship, too.

The third dimension in a loving relationship is **commitment**. Like the other dimensions, this has more than one side. A short-term commitment to the relationship as it stands is not the same as a long-term commitment to building a lifelong partnership. And the long-term commitment which two people bring to a relationship is vital, because it is only that which will keep them together during difficult times. Most couples who have been together for two or three decades report at least one bad period when they felt like giving up on the relationship altogether, but did not because of their long-term commitment. But because they saw that time through instead of giving up, the relationship was strengthened, and they became able to enjoy one another's company again.

Different combinations of these dimensions produce different kinds of love. For example, the kind of long-term **companionate love** which develops between two people who have been together for many years is often one which is high in intimacy and commitment, but perhaps less so on the passion dimension. **Romantic love**, on the other hand, tends to be high on intimacy and passion, but does not involve as much commitment. Sternberg referred to the kind of love which involves all three dimensions fully as consummate love.

Love over time

Using his sample of 80 people of different ages, Sternberg investigated how loving relationships change over time — and looked in particular at what kinds of things became more or less important as the relationship developed. People in long-term relationships identified five things as important — implying that they mattered more in the long term than in the short term. These were: having similar values, being willing to change in response to the other person, being prepared to put up with the other person's flaws, having matching religious beliefs, and having an equal intellectual level. Interestingly, the last one seemed totally unimportant to those whose relationships had only been going for a few years, but was seen by people in long-lasting relationships as essential.

Some things, though, became less important with time, including how interesting the other person seemed to be, and how attentively each person listened to one another. Some became more important during the first few years of the relationship, but then mattered less as time wore on. These included: physical attractiveness, the ability to make love, the ability to empathise with the partner, and expressing affection towards one another. It is not really possible to tell, though, whether these things really became less important, or whether the couples in the long-term relationships took them so much for granted that they stopped noticing them.

We can see, then, that the positive emotion which we refer to as love actually incorporates many different kinds of experiences. Taking these together with Argyle and Crossland's work, we can see that our positive emotions in general represent a very rich part of human experience, and one which we need to recognise very much more clearly.

Fear and anger

5/22/04

Not all of our emotions are positive, though. In fact, some of them, like anger or extreme fear, can be extremely destructive. Some of the very earliest psychologists were interested in these negative emotions. In particular, they were interested in how the emotion that we feel connects with the physical sensations that we also experience when we are frightened or angry.

Both anger and fear are very active emotions. If you are angry with someone, your muscles tense up, and you become restless: some people will often stand up and pace around the room as a way of helping to control the tension. Similarly, if you are frightened your muscles become tense, and you may make small involuntary movements which express that tension. The two types of tension are not the same, of course, but they do have quite a lot in common. And they are quite different from the quiescent emotions, like depression, which involve listlessness and apathy rather than tension and activity.

In part, the tension which you feel when you are afraid is a survival response, which is shared by all mammals. In the natural world, if an animal is threatened by something, so that it becomes afraid, then there are only two options. It can stay and fight it out, in which case it will need all the strength it can muster, to win. Or it can run away, in which case it will need all the strength it can muster, to escape. In either case, therefore, the animal will need all of its strength. So this survival response is known as the 'fight or flight' reaction.

Most of the time, we only use a small proportion of our potential strength and energy. But during the fight or flight response, the body changes the way that it operates physically, in order to maximise strength and energy. After all, there's no point holding back reserves when you are threatened by something which might kill you — if you die, they will not be much use to you, will they?

The physical changes that happen are all ones which will release more energy to the muscles. Physical energy comes from a chemical reaction between oxygen and forms of glucose, or blood sugars. Both of these are carried in the bloodstream to the muscles which need energy, where, effectively, the sugar is 'burned up' to produce energy. This process takes oxygen, so the muscles that are in action need to have a continuous supply of fresh oxygenated blood if they were to work properly.

So many of these physical changes are concerned with getting oxygen into the bloodstream. We begin to breathe more deeply, and more rapidly, increasing the oxygen supply entering the lungs. Blood pressure increases, carrying blood round the body more quickly. And extra red blood cells (which carry oxygen) are released into the bloodstream.

Some changes are concerned with getting more 'fuel' to the muscles. Stored fats are converted into blood sugars and released into the blood. The digestive system begins to work differently from usual, ignoring those processes which require long-term digestion and increasing digestive processes for rapidly acting foods like sugars. The saliva changes in the same way, so that we can metabolise foods very quickly.

Another set of changes is designed to protect us from injury as much as possible. The amount of vitamin K in the blood increases, making it more ready to clot quickly if there is an injury. And if we are very frightened, blood vessels close to the surface of the skin shrink, making us paler but also likely to lose less blood if we are injured. The blood supply to the internal vital organs of the body, on the other hand, increases. We also have some left-over responses designed to protect us by making us look more fearsome: in many animals, their fur stands on end, making them look bigger and potentially more dangerous. Humans have lost their fur, but the hairs that we have left still try to stand on end, which is what causes goose-pimples.

We can see, then, that the fight or flight response is a very powerful reaction, which serves an important survival function — at least, when we are faced with threats that require physical action. It is not quite as helpful, though, when we are faced with non-physical threats, like anxiety about the mortgage, or fear of failing exams. Because they do not require physical action, we do not have a way of using up that energy, so we can quickly become stressed. We will be looking at this later in this chapter.

There are lesser degrees of the fight or flight response, too. When our attention is caught by something, or when we feel anxious about something, we experience the same kinds of physical changes, but to a much lower degree. The changes are strong enough to be measured, though, using sensitive detectors which will identify changes in pulse rate, heart rate, sweating, blood pressure and the like. A machine which measures several of these changes is known as a **polygraph.** Some people, such as police conducting interrogations, use polygraphs as lie-detectors, because they can detect the slight anxiety which people feel when they tell a lie. Other machines can analyse slight changes in the voice caused by anxiety, which can sometimes be useful for detectives monitoring anonymous telephone calls.

The general name which we give for this kind of physical state is known as **arousal,** because it seems as though lots of physical activities have all been aroused at the same time. The type of arousal which we experience for fear is slightly different from the type we experience when we are angry, but the two conditions have a great deal in common.

In 1953, a psychologist named Ax conducted a study looking at the difference between fear and anger. Ax connected people up to an impressive-looking machine, so that they had wires and connectors all over the body. Then, when they were fully connected up, a technician came rushing into the room saying, 'Hold it! There's a short-circuit in the apparatus.' That was the fear condition. In the anger condition, the person was wired up, and then left alone with a technician who grumbled about the study and insulted them.

Incidentally, it would not be possible for a psychologist to conduct this sort of study nowadays. There are very strict rules about ethical principles which have to be observed while conducting psychological experiments. It is not permitted to cause people who are participating in the research any pain or distress (mental or physical) at all. It also is not permitted to deceive people, except under very special circumstances and with special permission from an ethical committee, and then only as long as they are told the full truth at the earliest possible moment. But when Ax was doing this research, these conditions did not exist.

Anyway, what Ax found was that there were distinct physiological differences between the kind of arousal produced by fear, and that produced by anger. These differences seemed to be produced by the various kinds of hormones and brain chemicals which were involved in the process. A chemical named adrenaline was found in both reactions, but anger also involved a chemical known as noradrenaline.

Adrenaline and noradrenaline are both chemicals which are used by the body to stimulate a special part of the nervous system, known as the **autonomic nervous system**. This consists of a network of nerve fibres, running to all the internal organs of the body. When part of the autonomic nervous system is stimulated — a part known as the **sympathetic division** — the body experiences arousal. But when the other part — known as the **parasympathetic division** — is stimulated, the body becomes quieter, and less active The parasympathetic division seems to be involved in quiet emotions such as depression or sadness.

So if these physical changes happen when we feel emotions, does that mean that our emotions are caused by these physical changes? One of the early psychologists, William James, thought so. He described what happens when you trip going down the stairs and catch hold of the banister to save yourself. During that first second, James pointed out, you simply react, and do what is needed to survive. But a couple of seconds later, your heart begins to beat faster, your hands sweat, and your breathing changes — in other words, the arousal response starts. And it is then, James believed, that we feel the fear.

James went on to suggest that all human emotions actually come from our perceiving the physical condition that we are in. 'We do not weep because we feel sorrow; we feel sorrow because we weep'. He believed that the brain unconsciously monitors the body for changes, and then interprets those changes according to what the situation seems to demand.

Over 60 years later, two psychologists, named Schachter and Singer, conducted an experiment to investigate this idea. Although it was not a very good experiment, because they did not really control it very well, the experiment did seem to give us some useful clues about how physical sensations and our own knowledge of the situation can be connected.

Schachter and Singer's study was really quite complex. They wanted to see what happened when people had the physical symptoms of arousal, and how they would feel in different situations. So some of their research participants were injected with adrenaline, producing the physical symptoms of arousal, while others were just injected with a neutral saline solution, which did not have any effect.

Schachter and Singer then gave some of their research participants an 'explanation' for how they were feeling. Some of them were told accurately what was likely to happen — trembling hands, a pounding heart and feeling flushed. Others were misinformed, by being told that they might experience an itching sensation, a slight headache or numbness. And a third group were not given any information at all, but only told that the injection was mild and harmless and would not have any side-effects.

What happened then was that the research participants were asked to sit in a waiting room for 20 minutes, supposedly to let the injection have its full effect. Each time, there was another person in the room with them, who seemed to be another participant in the study. Really, though, the person was a stooge — an actor who was pretending to be a research participant but was really acting the way the experimenters wanted.

Sometimes, during the twenty minute period, the stooge would act as if he was in a very happy mood: playing 'basketball' with pieces of paper, making paper aeroplanes, and playing with a hula hoop. Each time, he would invite the real research participant to join in, which many of them did. This was known as the 'euphoria' condition, designed to encourage the research participants to feel happy.

Other people, though, experienced a different condition. They were introduced to the stooge, and given a long questionnaire to fill in during the time. The stooge would begin to fill it in, but then become increasingly angry at how personal and insulting some of the questions were. Eventually, he would stamp out of the room in disgust. This was the 'anger' condition, designed to make people feel angry themselves (the questionnaire was really quite intrusive, too).

Schachter and Singer found that, by and large, the mood which people were in after the 20-minute period tended to reflect the mood which the stooge was expressing. In other words, whether they had an adrenaline injection or not, those who were in the 'euphoric' condition tended to be in quite a good mood at the end of the time, while those in the 'anger' condition tended to be irritable. Clearly, our moods can be influenced by social factors — by the other people around us.

But Schachter and Singer also found that the degree of emotion which people experienced depended on the adrenaline, but only if they did not know what effects it would have. People who had been kept ignorant, or who had been misinformed about the effects of the adrenaline, showed quite strong changes in moods. Their aroused state seemed to contribute to the way that they interpreted the situation, so they felt more angry, or happier, than they might have done otherwise. You may have found a similar effect yourself, when you have been running for a bus but have just missed it. Running, and anxiety, both raise the adrenaline levels in the bloodstream, and people often find that they become much more angry at missing the bus than they normally would. It seems to exaggerate the reactions that we feel.

But Schachter and Singer found that this effect only happened when people did not know what to expect from the adrenaline. In both the anger and euphoria conditions, people who were told what effects the adrenaline would have reacted in much the same way as people who hadn't had the adrenaline at all. In other words, they changed their mood a little, just from the social influences, but not a great deal.

The conclusion that they came to, then, was that it is our awareness of the situation which produces the emotion that we actually feel. But it is our physical condition which influences how strongly we actually feel it. As I said before, the study had a number of flaws, in terms of the way that the experimental conditions were controlled; and of course it involved far too much manipulation for anything like that to be permitted today. However, most psychologists still believe that the study gave us some useful insights into emotion and how it works.

There are other angles to the understanding of emotion, though. As we saw in Chapter 1, we need to look at any human activity using a number of different levels. And one useful level is to look at how an emotion is understood by different cultures, and in different languages. In the English language, for example, we tend to use the word 'anger' as a general term to describe a particular emotion. But that can sometimes lead to confusion, because different kinds of anger may actually be quite different, both in their social meanings and in whether we see the angry person as fully responsible for their condition.

Lutz (1991) discussed how the Ifaluk people of Micronesia actually have five different words for anger, and each of these is talking about a different kind of anger. For example, the anger which you might feel with relatives or friends who have not fulfilled their obligations is known as *nguch*. This is regarded as a different emotion from the irritability which people feel when they have been ill, and are convalescing, which is known as *tipmochmoch*.

A third kind of emotion is the anger which we feel when we feel frustrated or helpless, or trapped into doing things that we do not want to do. The Ifaluk know this emotion as *tang*. And this is entirely different from the kind of anger which builds up gradually through lots of irritating little things going wrong, which is known as *lingeringer*. Finally, there is a sort of anger which society actually encourages: the kind of righteous anger or indignation which is to do with morality and justice, and making sure that things which happen are fair and equitable. That kind of anger is known as *song*.

When we look at these different words and their meanings, we can see that each of them reflects a kind of anger which Western people, too, sometimes feel. But the Ifaluk see them as quite different emotions, and so they find it easier to respond to them differently. An Ifaluk person would be much less likely to be disturbed or upset when a convalescent person was being snappy and unreasonable, for example, because, from the outset, they would be aware of where the emotion was coming from. We usually have to learn these things by experience, because our language does not sensitise us to them.

We can learn something about human emotion from non-technological cultures like the Ifaluk, because people in such societies often have a more sophisticated awareness of mental states than people in technological societies. And by distinguishing different types of emotion, like this, we too might be able to interact more effectively with the people around us.

Anxiety and stress

If we have a fright, or if we become angry with someone, the emotion often passes. We calm down, and get over it, and as we do, the physical symptoms of arousal disappear as well. But sometimes we can experience emotional arousal which does not go away. Being anxious about whether there will be enough money to pay the bills, for instance, is a continuous worry, not a passing thing. This means that it is continually producing physiological arousal, which does not go away.

Selye (1956) showed that long-term arousal like this can have a lot of harmful effects, including interfering with our physical health. We call it **stress**, and it is one of the most-studied areas of psychology — mainly because it is such a big problem in modern society. Long-term stress suppresses the action of the body's immune system, making us much more vulnerable to colds, infections and more serious illnesses. In the long term, too, it can make us more liable to contract heart disease. Long-term stress also makes us very jumpy and alert to potential threats — which means that quite often we see something as a threat when it is really quite harmless. Because we over-react to what people say or do, we become more likely to quarrel with the people around us. And it interferes with judgement, so that we are less likely to make sensible decisions or to appraise what is going on realistically.

Clearly, this is not a psychologically healthy condition to be in. But there are ways of coping with long-term stress, so that we do not suffer these effects. Many psychological researchers have investigated **coping mechanisms**: ways of minimising or cancelling out the effects of long-term stress, and making sure that we deal with it in a positive kind of way. Not all stress is bad, and we need to understand how it can be helpful as well as damaging if we are to use it positively. In order to do this, we need to understand how different levels of physiological arousal affect us.

Arousal

As I mentioned earlier, the fight or flight response is an extreme state of physiological arousal. But there are less extreme forms of arousal too. It is best to think of arousal in terms of a continuous scale, which has extreme relaxation at one end, and fight or flight at the other. In between are many different levels of arousal. A disagreement, an unpleasant interview or even just a worrying thought are all things which can make us more aroused. And other influences, like caffeine, exercise (while we are doing it, though not afterwards), or pre-menstrual tension, also raise our level of arousal.

The Yerkes–Dodson Law

That is not necessarily a bad thing, because a small amount of arousal is stimulating. Many people have a cup of coffee in the morning because the additional stimulation helps them to feel more alert. People exercise for the same reason. In fact, up to a point, increased arousal helps us to do things better.

But only up to a point. If we become too aroused — say by becoming very upset, or very angry — then it can actually stop us doing things well. You might find, for instance, that you do better in an argument if you are annoyed by what the other person is saying. Your irritation helps you to find words, and to argue more fluently. But if you become enraged by the other person's comments, so that your arousal level becomes too high, then you might find that you become speechless, and unable to put what you want to say into words. Up to a point, the increased arousal brought on by irritation has improved your performance in the argument; but when the level of arousal went past that point, it interfered with it.

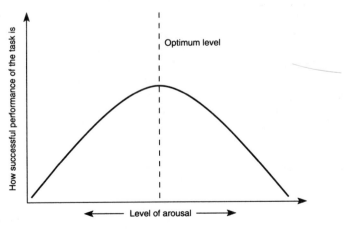

Figure 3.1   The Yerkes–Dodson law of arousal

This principle is known as the Yerkes–Dodson law of arousal (see Fig. 3.1), and it can be applied to almost every task. Being angry or upset might mean that you do the washing-up more quickly and efficiently — but if those feelings were too intense, you might become more careless, and break things or drop them. But with a relatively simple task like washing-up, you can be much more aroused before you actually get to that point. In a complex situation, like an argument or when doing something that you need to concentrate on, the optimal level of arousal for doing the job well is much lower. In other words, you can be put off more easily.

Coping strategies

Athletes, and other people who do highly stressful activities, need to be able to make sure that their levels of arousal will be enough to produce the best possible performance. So they often use **coping strategies**, which allow them to control the amount of arousal that they experience. Some of these strategies are physical ones, using the adrenaline constructively, by exercising. People who do a lot of sport often do better in exams than people of the same intellectual level who do not take regular exercise, and one possible reason for this is that they simply do not experience as much physical stress.

Some coping strategies, though, are **cognitive** — they involve controlling the person's thinking. By doing this, we can make sure that the thoughts which we have are positive ones and not ones which will add to the amount of stress that we feel.

Visualisation

One of the most popular methods which is used in sports psychology is **visualisation**. It is used for training, to help people to learn new techniques, but it is also used for stress management. When it is being used in this way, the person imagines themselves going through the whole activity successfully — winning the race, or passing the exam, or whatever it is. By concentrating only on positive thoughts, the person refuses to entertain doubts and ideas which would add to the level of stress which they are experiencing.

Attributions

In everyday life, people often add to the stress which they feel by thinking in negative ways: worrying about how dreadful things are, or might become. Since even a single worrying thought adds to our level of arousal, thinking in this way adds to the total arousal and stress which that person is feeling. Sometimes, people even develop ways of thinking which are totally self-defeating. Abramson, Seligman and Teasdale (1985) found that chronically depressed people often have what they called a **depressive attributional style**, which makes their depression much worse.

Attributions are the reasons that we give for why things happen. Someone with a depressive attributional style will believe that anything which happens will only turn out for the worse, that it is always going to be that way, and that it cannot be changed. These thoughts keep their depression going, partly by increasing the stress that they are under, and partly by making them feel that there is not any point in trying to do anything anyway. In other words, they feel helpless, and unable to control what happens in their lives.

Locus of control

But people with different attributional styles, who see themselves as able to control events by hard work of effort, and who do not give up, tend to experience stress very differently. They are much less likely to become depressed, and much more likely to be able actually to do something about their situation, because they keep looking for ways to change it. These people have what is known as an internal **locus of control**. They believe that what happens to them is largely controlled by their own efforts. People with a depressive attributional style have an external locus of control, believing that what happens to them is not something that they can influence.

There is a great deal of psychological research which shows that having an internal locus of control is much healthier for a human being — both physically and mentally. Long-term stress can lower the body's resistance to disease, and make us vulnerable to illness. But people with an internal locus of control experience less stress, even though their physical situation may be just as bad. This is because they channel their energies into looking for positive things to do, instead of just worrying. And because they are likely to gain at least a small success through trying so hard, they experience positive emotions like a sense of achievement, which people who are more passive do not feel.

Having an internal locus of control is not something we are born with. We can learn to change our thought-habits and behaviour, so that we shift from an internal to an external locus of control. **Cognitive therapy** is all about teaching the person how to take control of their own lives, and how to avoid the self-defeating beliefs and attributions which have stopped them from doing so in the past. And almost anything which increases someone's self-confidence has the effect of giving them more of an internal locus of control over their own life. So there is a great deal that we can do to cope with stressful problems positively. Problems may be real, and not likely to go away, but we can make their effects worse or better, depending on how we go about it.

We can see, then, that the psychological study of emotions can give us a great many insights into this aspect of our lives. We have many more positive emotions than we sometimes realise, and these may be associated with quite small events as well as quite large ones. Studying fear and anger raises interesting questions about how our experiences relate to the physical states that we are feeling. And the psychological study of anxiety and stress has allowed us to identify positive ways of coping with problems as they arise.

4

── STATES OF MIND ──

In this chapter, we will be looking at the psychology of consciousness. Consciousness is something that we often take for granted: we are aware of being awake, or of being drowsy, but we do not usually think very much about it. But the alertness (or lack of it) that we feel at any given time in the day is the outcome of a great deal of complex activity in the brain. Understanding something of that can tell us quite a lot about why we might be feeling as we are.

─────── Biological rhythms ───────

The state of consciousness that we are in is something which changes continually. We may be in a good mood or a bad mood; we may feel sleepy or alert; we may be relaxed or energetic. Sometimes, we deliberately change our state of consciousness, by using a drug like alcohol or caffeine, and we will be looking at how these work later in this chapter. But often our state of consciousness changes simply because of biological rhythms.

There are many biological rhythms in nature: daily rhythms, lunar rhythms, seasonal rhythms. Plants and animals all respond to these: birds begin courtship rituals when the lengthening days signal that it is spring; some plants open up during the day and close at night, and so on. And human beings, too, respond to natural rhythms.

Seasonal affective disorder

Poets and dramatists have long commented on the way that spring often results in young people thinking of love and romance. I am not aware of any psychological evidence which would either prove or disprove that, but we certainly seem to respond, physically, to increasing day length. Moreover, a number of people experience a form of depression during the long winter months, which clears up completely when spring and summer come.

Seasonal affective disorder, as this kind of depression is called, appears to have a great deal to do with lack of being in natural daylight. After all, for people who work indoors — which is most of us — it is possible to pass several months in the winter only seeing natural daylight at weekends: it is still dark when we go out to work or college, and dark again when we return home. Special lamps which mimic daylight have been quite successful in treating seasonal affective disorder.

So how can day length have such a strong effect? The answer lies in a small gland in the brain, known as the pineal gland. This gland is situated deep in the brain, in a place which is roughly behind the centre of the forehead. The ancient Greeks regarded it as the location of the soul, and in other religions, too, this place often has a mystical significance. As far as psychology is concerned, we have recently become aware that the pineal gland seems to change its activity in response to day length, stimulating the body to produce chemicals which lift our moods and make us feel more energetic.

Circadian rhythms

Human beings have other rhythms, known as circadian rhythms, which are to do with the 24-hour cycle of the day. Through the course of the 24-hour cycle, we experience a regular lowering and raising of a number of physiological systems, including body temperature, blood pressure, pulse rate, blood sugar level, and hormone levels. Our moods, too, vary according to this cycle, and so do our abilities to perform tasks well.

For example, between the hours of 2 and 6 in the morning, our blood sugar levels are low, body temperature is low, and so is blood pressure. Also, if we are awake, we experience quite a subdued mood; and if we are trying to do a demanding task of some kind, we are much more likely to make mistakes. But this is not just from tiredness, because as soon as morning comes we begin to feel better, and more alert, and our performance improves.

Siestas

As we progress through an ordinary day (not one where we have stayed up all night!) we find that there are particular 'low' points, where it is easy to become sleepy and to take a nap. Our biological rhythms are set to bring sleep twice a day: at night, but also in the early afternoon. In hot climates, a siesta is often an accepted cultural practice: everyone dozes or sleeps for a couple of hours, and then wakes up to resume work once the hottest part of the day is over. Even in a colder climate, where a siesta is not the standard practice, many people take a nap after lunch, while others find they are extremely likely to daydream at that time.

There are other changes, too, during the course of the day. For example, many people experience another 'dip' around about 6 pm, and then find that their energy levels gradually rise for the rest of the evening, until they lower again when it is time to go to bed. Fig. 4.1 shows the highs and lows of body temperature rhythms during the 24-hour period. Our psychological alertness often follows the same cycle. In part, the cycles are maintained by what are known as **zeitgebers** — external signals, like daylight and night, which seem to trigger off these rhythms, but in part they are maintained by the body's own internal systems.

Figure 4.1   Body temperature throughout the 24-hour cycle

Shift work and jet lag

Sometimes these body rhythms are disrupted, so that we have to be alert at different times of the day or night. There are two common reasons for this: shift work and international travel. When we are doing shift work, we have to adjust our bodies to a different 24-hour rhythm, sleeping at different times of day, and being awake at times when we would normally be asleep. When we are travelling across time zones, we also have to adjust to a different rhythm very quickly.

Both cases produce the same type of problems, which we call **jet lag** when they are brought about by travel. At its worst, this type of adjustment can produce irritability, poor performance at work, and poor decision-making. But there are ways for it to be minimised, too. For example, it seems to be easier for people to move forwards in time, rather than backwards. So a shift work cycle which progresses through the 24 hour period, with someone going from a night shift to an early one, then from an early shift to a late one, and then to nights again, will be easier for people to adjust to than a shift cycle where someone goes from a late shift to an early one. In international travel, too, shifting the 24-hour system forwards (for example, by staying awake for a longer period than you might do normally) can be helpful in minimising jet lag.

—— Consciousness and the brain ——

Brain cells — in fact all nerve cells — work by generating tiny amounts of electricity, and passing these on to one another. So some psychologists study how the brain works through studying the electrical activity of the brain.

One way of doing this is by using what are known as electro-encephalographs, or EEGs, for short. These are charts of the brain's electrical activity, which is detected using small electrodes which are attached to the scalp. The changes detected by an electrode are recorded by a pen, which rests on a moving sheet of paper and makes small movements whenever the electrical activity varies. Fig. 4.2 shows an EEG chart. The diagram in the top left hand corner shows where each electrode was placed on the person's head, and the lines show the electrical activity which the electrodes detected. There is a different line for each electrode, showing the electrical activity which is going on in different regions of the brain.

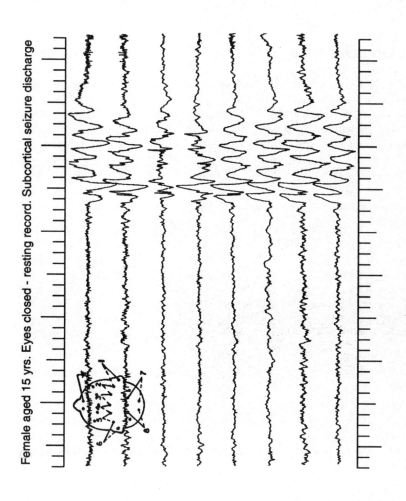

Female aged 15 yrs. Eyes closed - resting record. Subcortical seizure discharge

Figure 4.2 An EEG chart

Of course, all of this is a bit like standing outside a factory and trying to guess what they are making by listening to the noises coming through the window. Studying the brain in this way does not tell us everything, by any means. But it can show us something.

Brain rhythms

One of the things it can show us is the general patterning of brain activity when we are in different states of consciousness. The type of EEG which is produced when we are awake and concentrating on something is very different from the pattern which is produced when we are awake but just lazily relaxed. When we are relaxed, an EEG trace shows quite large waves of electrical activity (large for the brain, that is). These are known as **alpha rhythms**. We produce them just before we drift off to sleep, or when we are daydreaming, or just relaxed and happy.

When we are concentrating hard, though, the EEG trace shows a different kind of activity. There are still detectable rhythms in its pattern, but they are smaller and closer together. These are known as **delta rhythms**. But when we are just generally awake, neither relaxing nor concentrating, the EEG trace does not show any regular rhythms at all. Instead, it shows continuous intensive activity with no particular pattern (see Fig. 4.3). There are different EEG patterns produced when we are asleep, too, and we will be looking at these later in this chapter.

One method that some psychologists have used for investigating brain damage is to give a patient a particular stimulus, like a flashing light or a particular sound, and observe the difference that the stimulus makes to their EEG. These differences are known as **evoked potentials**, and they can be useful, because they will show if a particular area of the brain does not seem to be responding right.

Scanning the brain

Another method of investigating the brain while it is working is to use brain scans. One type of scan, known as a PET scan (short for positron emission tomography), involves looking at how much blood is being used by a particular part of the brain. Each time a nerve cell fires, it uses up some nutrients, and so it needs to replace

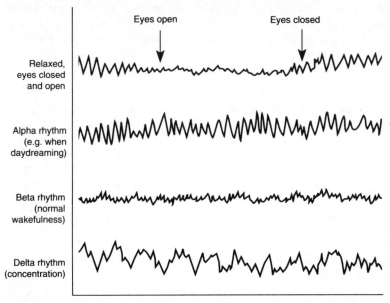

Figure 4.3 EEG traces of consciousness

them from the blood supply. So parts of the brain which are being active need a larger blood supply than those which are not. The PET scan allows a psychologist or doctor to see which parts of the brain are using most blood, because the blood has been 'labelled' using a special radioactive chemical which can be detected by the scanner.

Split-brain studies

The illness epilepsy involves a sudden burst of electrical activity in the brain, when lots of brain cells all fire at once. There are lots of different kinds of epilepsy, and some of them are relatively localised — that is to say, the electrical activity only happens in a relatively small part of the brain. Even so, it can mean that the person becomes disoriented and forgetful, and it can interfere very badly with their ability to concentrate.

Some even more unfortunate people, though, suffer from *grand mal* epilepsy, in which the electrical activity begins on one side of the brain but then spreads across it. This means that it interferes with the parts of the brain that co-ordinate body movement, and the person falls down and has a 'fit', or seizure, as their muscles shake and spasm in response to the random messages being sent to them from the brain. When the seizure is over, they are generally very confused, and can take some time to come back to reality.

In the 1960s, a pioneering operation was developed in an attempt to control epilepsy in a few patients who were experiencing grand mal seizures so often that they could not get on with their lives at all. The surgeons decided to cut through the brain cells which linked the right and left halves of the brain — known as the two cerebral hemispheres. By doing this, they reasoned, the seizure would only affect one side of the brain, because it could not be passed over to the other side. That way, even if the patient had a grand mal seizure, at least they would be able to keep control of one side of the body.

The two halves of the brain

In fact, doing the operation seemed to reduce the fits much more than that. But what was even more interesting was what psychologists found when they came to study these 'split-brain' people. By conducting a whole series of different tests, they found that the two halves of the brain seemed to be able to act quite independently, as if they were each a separate brain in their own right.

One patient, for example, reported how she would sometimes decide to wear a particular dress, and go to her wardrobe to take it out with her right hand, only to find that her left hand would pick out something entirely different for her to wear. Since the right side of the brain controls the left side of the body, and the left side of the brain controls the right side of the body, the action implied that the two halves of the brain had different ideas about what she ought to be wearing that day!

The psychologist, Sperry, also found that the two halves of the brain seemed to act in different ways. It has been known for a long time that our ability to use language comes from a few areas on the left side of the brain. By using a special screen (Fig. 4.4), Sperry showed that split-brain people could easily name an object that was shown to the left eye, because that meant that the image was interpreted by the left side of the brain. But when the right eye was shown something, the person could not say what it was.

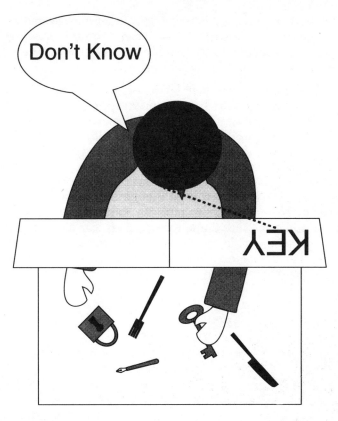

Figure 4.4 A split-brain study

That did not mean, though, that they could not recognise it. They could point to a picture which was the same as it, using the left hand (controlled by the right side of the brain). And they could pick it out by touch from a tray of other objects. They just could not name it, because the image had been passed to the right side of the brain, and the right side of the brain does not have language.

Differences between sides

By doing more tests of this kind, Sperry found that the two sides of the brain seemed to have different abilities. As we have seen, the left side of the brain handles language, and it also seems to be concerned with mathematical problems and arithmetic. The right side of the brain, though, is better at geometric or spatial puzzles, and seems to be particularly good at interpreting drawings. We understand speech with the left side of the brain, but we understand music with the right side.

These findings are interesting, but it is important to realise that we are only talking about how some kinds of information are processed. Some mystics have taken this idea further, and claimed that the right side of the brain contains all of the creative and spiritual side of being, while the left side is purely logical and mechanistic. But there really is not actually any psychological evidence for this. In fact, each side does have the basic rudiments of the other side's abilities, even though they are not very highly developed. The right hemisphere can sometimes cope with very simple language, while the left hemisphere can deal with simple drawings. And if a child under twelve suffers some kind of serious brain damage, the other side usually takes over the damaged side's functions as well as its own.

Alertness and attention

Although I was talking about the brain in the last section, I did not actually mean the whole of the human brain. The whole brain is a highly complex structure, consisting of a lot of different parts. EEGs, scans and split-brain studies have been concerned with the largest part of the human brain, which is the two structures known as the cerebral hemispheres. These are so big that they cover all of the other parts of the brain, and they are the parts of the brain that we think with.

But there are other parts of the brain involved in consciousness too. For example, if something unexpected catches our attention, we often become instantly alert. This involves a set of reactions which are very similar to the arousal which we looked at in the last chapter, although not quite as extreme. For example, the blood pressure goes up slightly and our heart rate increases. We also turn towards the source of the unexpected stimulus, keeping muscle movement to a minimum so that we can catch any slight sounds and keeping our eyes open so that we can see anything there is to see. All this is known as the **orientation response**, and it is partly controlled by a part of the brain known as the reticular formation.

The reticular formation is located above the top of the spine, just above the part of the brain that controls basic, essential activities like breathing or digestion. It seems to act as a general switching mechanism for the cerebral hemispheres, switching them on if we need to be awake, nudging them into greater activity if we need to pay attention to an unexpected stimulus, and damping them down when it is time to sleep.

In a set of studies reported in 1957, French showed how gentle electrical stimulation to a particular part of the reticular formation would rouse a sleeping cat. The cat would wake up in the same way as it did naturally, which suggested that electrical activity in this part of the brain might be the normal way that mammals — including humans — change from sleep to wakefulness. French also found that cats who had the reticular formation removed would sink into a deep coma, from which they could not be woken up. It seems likely that coma in human beings, too, occurs as a result of damage to the reticular formation.

Drugs and consciousness

As human beings, we do not just experience the different states of consciousness involved in waking, concentrating, relaxing and sleeping. We also deliberately change our consciousness by using drugs. Every human society uses some drugs to change people's state of awareness in some way. In our society the main drugs are alcohol, nicotine and caffeine, while in Peru chewing coca leaves (which are used to produce cocaine) is an everyday activity, and in some Middle Eastern countries smoking hashish (marijuana) or opium is legal while alcohol is banned. Drugs which influence our state of consciousness are known as **psychoactive** drugs. But how do they work?

Caffeine

All psychoactive drugs affect the nervous system in some way, but they have different effects by influencing different parts of it. For example, as I mentioned in the last chapter, the drug caffeine, which we take in coffee or cola drinks, acts on the autonomic nervous system to produce a state of arousal in the body. It also acts on the reticular formation of the brain, as a stimulant. So it is not surprising that it helps people to wake up in the morning! It also is not surprising that, while a little caffeine may pep you up, too much of it can make you irritable and edgy.

Alcohol

Alcohol works in almost entirely the opposite way, as a sedative, which calms down the autonomic nervous system and relaxes the muscles. That is why people often slur their words, or even fall asleep, if they are very drunk. In small doses, though, the influence of alcohol can often be quite stimulating, because it relaxes the everyday tension that most of us feel, and allows us to feel more at ease with other people. So we find it easy to talk, and to join in things which are going on. It is not really a stimulant, in a physical sense, but in small doses it can be a sociable drug.

The biggest problems with alcohol, though, come from its other psychological effects. Alcohol can severely interfere with memory, which is why people often drink too much when they have serious problems. Once in a while that does not matter, but people who drink heavily over a period of years can lose their ability to store new memories altogether, which is much more serious. This is known as Korsakoff's syndrome, and it can be very disturbing. Sacks (1985) described a case of a 60-year-old man with Korsakoff's syndrome who could only remember his life up to his mid-twenties. When he looked in a mirror he became extremely upset, because he did not recognise the old man he had become. And since he could not remember anything from day to day, the distress was just as much each time.

The other psychological effect which alcohol has is to impair our ability to make a balanced judgement. People who have been drinking — even quite small amounts — make far more mistakes on physical co-ordination tasks than people who have not. But, perhaps because they feel relaxed by the drug, they usually shrug off these mistakes, or do not even notice them at all. That is why so many people believe that they can drive well even if they have been drinking. It is not that they really can. It is that they do not notice any of their mistakes, so they think they are driving well when really they are quite dangerous.

Nicotine

Many people who smoke believe that the nicotine helps them to relax. But what it really does, is to make their muscles more sluggish, so that they are harder to move. It also damps down the activity of the autonomic nervous system, so that they are less likely to become aroused. In the same way that alcohol can give us the illusion of a stimulant when it is not really, so nicotine gives us the illusion of being relaxed when really we are just feeling more inactive.

To understand how this happens, we need to take a look at how our nerve cells work. When we want to move — say, to lift an arm — the brain sends a small electrical message along our nerve cells (which are very long and stretched out) to the muscles. When the message reaches the end of the nerve cell, it stops. But it causes a special chemical, called a **neurotransmitter**, to spill out of the ends of the nerve cell.

The neurotransmitter spills out just next to a special place on the muscle, known as a receptor site. The molecules of that chemical fit into the receptor site like a key fitting into a lock. When that happens, the muscle receives a message to contract. If it happens with enough receptor sites, then the whole muscle will move, and the arm will be lifted.

What nicotine does is to nip into the receptor site and block out the real neurotransmitter. Nicotine molecules have nearly the same shape as those of the neurotransmitter, so they can be picked up at the receptor site very easily. But they do not pass the message on, as the real chemical would have done, so this means that only about half of the message from the brain actually gets through. The person can still lift their arm, but not as easily — it takes more effort.

This, of course, explains why people often feel fidgety when they are first giving up cigarettes. The brain has become so used to the nicotine that it used to having to send a very strong message to create each movement. But if there is no nicotine in the system, then the whole message gets through, and the muscles respond easily, and that can sometimes feel as if we have too much energy.

Because a similar thing happens in the autonomic nervous system, we also seem to feel our emotions much more freely. People often comment on how they become more irritable when they have stopped smoking, and that is true. But what they often do not notice is that they also become happier, or more easily pleased. In fact, all of our emotions become more intense, not just the negative ones.

It is difficult to be quite so precise about the actions of some of the illegal drugs which people use to change their state of consciousness, mainly because, for obvious reasons, there has been less research into them. But we understand the effects of some of them fairly well. For example, we know that the highly addictive narcotic drugs such as heroin and morphine have their effects because they have a chemical structure which is very similar to naturally occurring painkillers which the body makes by itself.

Morphine and heroin

If you are doing something very demanding, it is possible to ignore injury or hurt while you are actually doing it — indeed, sometimes you might not even notice it at all. In both war and peacetime, there have been many instances of people who have been completely unaware of serious wounds or injuries while they struggled to save someone else's life. In a situation like that, the brain suppresses our own pain until the emergency is over. It does this by releasing special brain chemicals, called endorphins and enkephalins, which act to deaden feeling and sensation in the body.

Morphine and heroin both have chemical structures which are very similar. So they can slip into the receptor sites in the brain which are normally reserved for endorphins and enkephalins, producing similar results. People who take the drug report that it makes them feel euphoric, as though they are not quite in touch with reality, and good because there is no physical discomfort or fatigue at all. But the problem is, of course, that when it wears off, it feels very unpleasant, so it is extremely easy to become both physically and mentally addicted to these drugs.

Endorphins and enkephalins are also released through vigorous exercise, so that is a much better way of getting the same sort of effect. When people talk about 'feeling good' after a strenuous physical work-out, they are talking about much the same effect that taking these illegal drugs produces. But they have managed to get it in a much safer, and more natural, way. And it does not have the unpleasant after-effects when it wears off, either.

Both morphine and heroin are sometimes used medically, because they are such powerful painkillers, so medical researchers have been able to investigate how they work in some detail. However, because of the difficulty of conducting systematic research into illegal drugs, we are much less certain about the effects of marijuana.

Marijuana

We do know that marijuana was widely used as a tranquilliser in the nineteenth century, and for over two thousand years in the Far East. We also know that it acts as a mild depressant, damping down the actions of the autonomic nervous system and producing muscular relaxation. Perhaps because of this, some users report a sense of time passing very slowly, and an increased sensitivity to sensory stimulation such as music or art.

We are a long way yet from understanding exactly how marijuana works, chemically, in the brain. But one important clue happened when researchers in Israel discovered a chemical, anandamide, which seems to be a natural substance that has the same effect in the brain as THC (tetrahydrocannabinol, the active ingredient of marijuana). Not long afterwards, American researchers discovered that there may be specific receptors for anandamide in brain cells, which implies that these would also respond to THC. But these findings are very recent (Mestel 1993). It needs a great deal more research before we can be sure of these processes, but, for social and political reasons it is difficult for scientists to get research funding to investigate this particular drug.

We understand the actions of other psychoactive drugs much better, though. We saw earlier how the brain chemicals known as neurotransmitters are used to pass information from one nerve cell to another, or from one nerve cell to a muscle fibre. There are several different chemicals which act in this way, and some researchers have been able to trace 'pathways' of nerve cells in the brain, which use a particular chemical. Some psychoactive drugs have their effects by acting directly on these pathways.

Ecstasy

One of these is the drug MDMA, which is also known as **ecstasy**. MDMA (which is short for 3,4-methlyenedioxymethamphetamine) is a highly prosocial drug (prosocial is the opposite of antisocial). In other words, it makes people feel social and pleasant towards one another, as opposed to feeling aggressive and irritable. It also enhances awareness of music and colour. MDMA was first discovered in 1914, and used to be used in marriage guidance counselling, to ease the tensions between people so that they could talk over their problems more effectively. In the 1970s, however, it became popular as a recreational drug, and has now been made illegal.

MDMA appears to work by acting directly on a particular neurotransmitter pathway in the brain. This pathway involves nerve cells which use the chemical serotonin. Normally, when the neurotransmitter chemical is spilled out by the nerve cell, it only remains around for a few seconds, because it is then recycled by the cell that it came from. But MDMA prevents this recycling, so the spilled serotonin stays where it is, and continues to work on the next nerve cell. It does this all through the serotonin pathway of the brain, and this seems to be what produces such a strong effect on the person's moods.

Amphetamines

The stimulant drugs known as amphetamines, or 'speed', also sometimes seem to have a prosocial effect, at least in small doses. People find that they can talk to others more easily, and may seem to be in a better mood — although often they may feel slightly edgy or tense. But in large doses, amphetamines can lead to severe mental illness — a disorder which is known as **amphetamine psychosis**. This involves a distortion of reality, with the person often becoming extremely paranoid and disturbed. Since amphetamines are also highly addictive drugs, it is all too easy for people who enjoy the effects which they have in small doses to slip into taking larger and larger ones, often with tragic results.

Where MDMA increases the level of serotonin in the brain, amphetamines work by increasing the level of two other brain chemicals, known as dopamine and noradrenaline. We know that the dopamine pathways in the brain are associated with will-power, or motivation. The illness known as Parkinson's disease comes from a shortage of dopamine in the brain, and it leaves people unable to make deliberate muscle actions. Noradrenaline is associated with active and aroused states of the body, such as anger.

It seems as though it is the combination of these two brain chemicals which produces the psychological effects of amphetamine drugs. In the short term, it increases motivation and arousal, so people may find it easy to be sociable even when they are tired. But in the long term, and in high doses, it makes people more likely to become agitated and suspicious. This is made worse, too, by the fact that amphetamines act as appetite suppressants, so people who take them frequently usually suffer physical debilitation as a result.

LSD

Another well-known psychoactive drug is known as LSD, or sometimes just as 'acid'. LSD (which is short for lysergic acid diethylamide) is a **hallucinogen**, and taking it gives people some very interesting psychological affects. It can produce distortions of reality, so that sounds and colours may become extremely exaggerated. People who take it can also experience hallucinations, seeing things which are not actually present.

Sometimes these experiences can become extremely disturbing, and possibly cause long-term psychological distress. Leary (1965), in research conducted while the drug was still legal, stressed that LSD should not be taken casually, but only when what he called **set** and **setting** were right. Set refers to the person's mental state, since fears or anxieties can produce disturbing effects; while setting refers to the physical situation, which needs to be relaxed and friendly, since being in a strange or threatening place could bring about disturbing experiences.

Like MDMA, LSD involves the serotonin pathways of the brain, but it does not work in the same way. The molecules of LSD are a very similar shape to the molecules of serotonin, so they can fit into serotonin receptor sites. They produce their effects by mimicking the effect of the drug, but in a slightly different way — the chemical is not exactly identical. So where the normal effects of serotonin seem to be to produce a sociable, highly aware mood, the effects of LSD in serotonin receptors seems to be to produce a kind of hyper-awareness, which can easily turn into hallucination.

This discussion of how drugs work may have been a little bit technical, but it shows us how closely consciousness and the chemicals in the brain are linked. We can change the chemical balance in the brain, and we do, each time we have an alcoholic drink or a cup of coffee — or even a glass of milk, which contains mild, naturally occurring morphine-like substances (which is why it can help us to feel calmer). Both natural and synthetic drugs can change our moods, our state of awareness and our perceptions of reality.

Sleep and dreaming

For many years psychologists regarded sleeping as a time when nothing much happened, except for the occasional dream. But in the late 1930s people began to use EEGs to record brain activity. When EEGs were taken of people during the whole of a night's sleep, researchers found that actually the brain is extremely active, even if the body seems to be quiet.

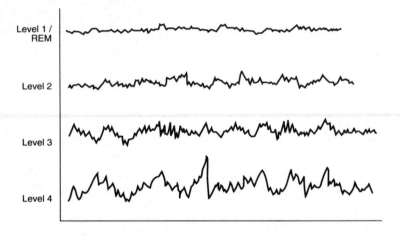

Figure 4.5   EEG traces during sleep

In fact, we seem to have at least four different phases of brain activity which take place while we sleep. These are shown in Fig. 4.5. As we can see from the diagram, level 1 involves very rapid and irregular activity of the brain, with very low voltages. Level 2 sleep still shows rapid and irregular activity, but with greater changes in the voltage becoming apparent from the peaks and troughs on the chart. Also during this level of sleep, patterns, known as spindles, begin to appear, which are very rapid, changeable bursts of activity.

By level 3, the frequency of the electrical activity has become a little slower, and the peaks and troughs on the graphs are higher — meaning that the changes in voltage have become larger than they were in the first and second levels. This trend continues with level 4, which shows very large changes in voltage, and a much slower rate of change.

These patterns of sleep, like so many other aspects of consciousness, happen in regular cycles through the night. We begin sleeping at level 1, and spend maybe ten minutes in it. Then our sleep pattern changes to level 2, and stays there for ten or fifteen minutes before changing again to level 3. During the first part of the night it will shift down to level 4 for about 20 minutes or so, and then come back up to level 3, then to level 2, and then back to level 1 (see Fig. 4.6). A complete cycle, from level 1 to level 4, and back again, usually takes about an hour and a half.

Interestingly, these levels of sleep as shown on an EEG chart also reflect how deeply asleep we are. When researchers wake people up from level 4 sleep, they are very hard to rouse, whereas people in level 2 sleep wake up much more easily. Level 1, though, is a bit special, because that is the part of our sleep when we dream.

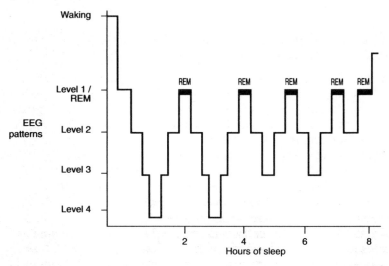

Figure 4.6 Cycles of sleep

When we are in level 1 sleep, our eyes are continually making very quick movements. For this reason, level 1 sleep is often called REM sleep, which is short for rapid eye movements. And if people are woken up from that sort of sleep, they report dreaming. We all dream four or five times during the course of an average night, although some people remember dreaming while others do not. That seems to depend on whether you have woken up from REM sleep (in which case you remember the dream you were just having) or whether you have woken up from level 2 sleep, which feels dreamless.

Although we seem to be 'switched off' while we are asleep and dreaming, we are not totally unaware of our surroundings. Dement and Wolpert (1958) sprinkled people lightly with water while they were in REM sleep. Then, a little later, they woke them up and asked what they had been dreaming about. Some people had dreamt about being under waterfalls, some about swimming, and some about being out in the rain. Most of them had dreamt about water in some way. In other words, they had managed to incorporate the outside stimulation of the water into their dreams.

In fact, we may have far more control over our dreams than we realise. Most of us have occasionally had dreams in which we knew we were dreaming, but the dream carried on anyway. These are known as **lucid dreams**. Recently, psychologists have discovered that it is possible to learn how to make a dream into a lucid dream, and then for the person having the dream to control what happens.

For this to work, people need to know when they have begun to dream. In psychological sleep research laboratories, this is done by giving dreamers a signal, which has been arranged beforehand. The signal will not be enough to wake them up, but just enough for them to become aware that it is happening, like a tiny electrical tickle to the wrist, or a red light flashing on the eyelids. When the person begins REM sleep, they are given the signal, so they become aware that they are dreaming. Once they know this, they can make things happen in the dream.

According to Hearne (1981) the secret of controlling a lucid dream successfully is to make sure that what happens is believable — as far as the dream is concerned. For example, if you wanted to dream about a particular person, you could not just make them appear from nowhere. But you could dream that there was a door nearby, and make the person come in through it. Some people dream about flying, and so they would be able to make themselves fly, in the dream. Other people do not, so it would be impracticable for them to try it in a lucid dream.

But what is dreaming for? In the early days of psychology, the psychoanalysts, led by Sigmund Freud, believed that dreams come from the unconscious mind telling us about our innermost, secret wishes and desires. These are disguised by the brain, using symbols to stand for the real meaning. Popular books of dream interpretation are following this idea.

Some medical researchers believe that dreams come from brain activity, which happens as nerve cells restore and reorganise themselves while we are asleep. The experience of the dream is simply imposed by our minds, as it tries to make sense of random bursts of nerve cell activity — in the same way as we can sometimes 'see' castles or animals in cloud shapes. According to this view, then, dreaming is just an accidental by-product of the physiological activity of the brain, and has no real significance.

Most psychologists, though, do believe that there is a psychological function to dreaming as well as a physiological one. We see dreaming as being an important part of how we organise our psychological experience. Throughout each day, we are bombarded with a massive amount of sensory information and experiences. At some time the mind needs to make sense of it all: to store information in its proper place so that it connects with similar things that we know, to identify patterns in our experiences, and to filter through things that have happened to us to find events which seem to be particularly meaningful. It does this while we are dreaming.

This explains, too, why sleeping on a problem is so often helpful. Before we go to bed, we can be perplexed, upset, or completely at a loss as to how to deal with something. But when we wake up, it somehow all seems clear. That is because we have been working on the problem unconsciously while we sleep. The brain activity which takes place while we dream has allowed us to knit loose ends together, and to put things, mentally, into their proper place. So when we wake up it is much easier to decide what to do.

In this chapter, then, we have looked at a number of aspects of consciousness, and at how consciousness can be changed, influenced or affected in different ways. There are some other aspects of consciousness, too, which we will deal with in other parts of this book. For example, we will be looking at the condition known as hypnotism when we look at social influence. The human state of consciousness is constantly changing, so understanding something about how that happens can help us in our attempt to understand the human being.

5

──────── MOTIVATION ────────

In this chapter, we will be looking at motivation — why we do what we do, and why we bother to do anything at all. If we are to try to understand human beings, we need to look at what makes people 'tick' — what moves us to action. And, as with every other aspect of psychology, there is not a single simple answer to this question. Human motives are complex, ranging from simple physiological ones to complex issues of social respect and identity. And we may do something for more than one reason. Bearing this in mind, though, it is worth looking at the different kinds of reasons that people have for taking action.

─ Physical and behavioural motives ─

Sometimes, what we do is motivated by very basic needs: if you go to the kitchen and fetch a glass of water, it is a fair bet that you did so because you were thirsty. The level of fluid in your body had gone below its ideal level, and this sets off a complex range of physiological mechanisms in the body. Messages about your fluid level are passed from your body to a particular part of the brain, known as the hypothalamus. This sends messages to the cerebral cortex, which is the part of the brain that you think with, so you realise that you feel thirsty and go to get a drink of water.

Homeostasis

Psychologists investigating physiological motives, like this, have found that these mechanisms are all concerned with getting the right balance in the body. As long as everything is at the right kind of level, we do not feel the motivation. But if it becomes unbalanced, so that our blood sugar level gets too low, for instance, or if we do not have a high enough level of body fluid, then we take action to put it right. This is known as **maintaining homeostasis** — maintaining the appropriate balance in the body so that we can function well, physically.

Of course, maintaining homeostasis also means that the brain has to have some model of what the appropriate balance is, so that it can be maintained. Psychologists researching into hunger have found that the body has a kind of **set-weight**, which it seems to try to maintain. In studies with animals, they would eat until they had consumed enough food to reach their set-weight, and then stop eating. Even if they went on a restricted diet for a while, so they lost weight, as soon as the restrictions were off they would eat enough to return to the set-weight.

It seems likely that human beings, too, have this kind of body mechanism, which might explain why so many people have problems with dieting. They are trying to achieve a weight that is lower than the physiological set-weight which their body functioning is based on. So even if they diet, and get their weight down for a short while, they will find it very difficult to maintain that weight.

Physiological motivation, though, does not really have all that much to do with how we act in other ways. Even eating and drinking, in human beings, are affected by other kinds of motives: dieting, for instance, has more to do with social approval than it does with physiological needs, and people often drink even non-alcoholic drinks to be sociable rather than because they are actually thirsty. So we need to look at other levels of explanation as well, if we are really to understand human motivation.

Behavioural motives

Sometimes, what we do comes about as much because of habits as anything else. Habits are behaviours or feelings that are associated with particular settings or situations. We learn ways of acting in certain places, or with certain people, and these come back to us if we find ourselves in that situation again. At such times, we can surprise ourselves with how we react.

It is interesting, for example, how an exam room can affect us, even if we are not actually taking the exam. Exam rooms are something we usually only encounter at school, and under quite tense conditions. People are usually worried and anxious when they go into an exam room to take an exam. And because we do not usually have anything to do with them at other times, those feelings of worry and anxiety come flooding back when we go into an exam room — even years later. So we act nervously, and not like our usual selves at all.

What has happened there is that the behaviours and feelings which are associated with a particular situation have been brought back, simply by being in that situation again. You might habitually buy a certain brand of tights, simply because that is the kind you have bought in the past, in that particular shop. Sometimes, we do things like this even though we meant to try something else, purely because the association of that particular action with that particular situation is so strong.

The same thing can happen, too, with interpersonal relationships. For example, if you meet someone who you have not seen for a while, you can find yourself slipping back into ways of behaving with them that are not like the way that you behave with other people. As a child, I used to argue continually and very vehemently with my cousin, and even now, when I am with my cousin, we tend to do the same thing — though I do not argue in that way with anyone else. Being with that person brings back old habits, and it is sometimes hard to break out of them.

Changing habits

Habits can be broken, though — we are not stuck with them for ever. For instance, teachers who have to invigilate exams as part of their job do not feel anxious when they go into those rooms — at least, not once they have had a couple of years' experience. You can deliberately decide to try a new brand of tights, and remember to choose them when you are in the shop. And even my cousin and I are gradually learning to communicate more reasonably with one another! Breaking a habit involves steadily replacing the actions or feelings which are triggered off by that situation with some other actions or feelings. It is hard at first, but the more often you succeed, the weaker the original habit becomes. We will be looking at this more closely when we look at association learning, in Chapter 7.

——————— Cognitive motives ———————

The way that we think also sometimes motivates us to action. Cognitive motives are motives which come from our thoughts, beliefs and ideas: they are to do with how we understand what is happening to us. And the way that we understand a situation can make all the difference to what we decide to do about it.

Personal constructs

Each of us has had our own personal experiences, and we have learned from those. In particular, we have learned about other people, and about what they are like. We have formed our own personal theories about what other people are like, from the way that people have interacted with us in the past. These theories are called **personal constructs,** and we use them when we meet new people.

Personal constructs take the form of a two-ended kind of classification, such as like 'kind–cruel' or 'hot-tempered–calm'. Table 5.1 gives an interesting exercise which you might like to try, to find out some of your own main constructs. As a general rule, we tend to have about eight or ten main personal constructs, and several extra, less-important ones as well. So when we meet someone new, we weigh them up to see how they seem to fit in our own personal construct system. On that basis, we decide whether we like them or not.

All this is a bit like saying that we judge whether we like new people or not on the basis of whether they remind us of someone else that we once knew. And that is true, to some extent. But the new person does not have to be exactly like the person who we knew before — they may just have one or two qualities in common, which we can recognise as being similar. Using personal constructs, we can identify a particular set of human qualities which different people may have more or less of.

Individual explanations

But since each of us has led a different life, our experiences of other people have varied. So our personal constructs are also

TABLE 5.1   DISCOVERING PERSONAL CONSTRUCTS

This is an exercise which you can do to discover some of your own personal constructs.

Stage 1
Name eight people who are important in your life, and give each one of them a letter, from A to H.

A ....   B ....

C ....   D ....

E ....   F ....

G ....   H ....

Stage 2
Think about these people in groups of three at a time, as suggested in the brackets below. For each group of three, think of a way that two of the people are like each other, and different from the third one. Do this about eight times, using the groups of three suggested below.

(A, B, C) .... and .... are ....,
but .... is ....

(D,E,F) .... and .... are ....,
but .... is ....

(A,F,G) .... and .... are ....,
but .... is ....

(B,D,H) .... and .... are ....,
but .... is ....

(C,E,G) .... and .... are ....,
but .... is ....

(H,B,F) .... and .... are ....,
but .... is ....

(A,E,H) .... and .... are ....,
but .... is ....

(D,G,C) .... and .... are ....,
but .... is ....

(You do not have to use a single word to describe what people are like: a couple of words or a phrase will do. But you do need to be describing what they are like, in your own view.)

Step 3
Take the pairs of descriptions which you have used, and arrange them as two-ended personal constructs, like the ones described in the text. These are some of the personal constructs which you, personally, use to help make sense out of your experience.

different. They represent our own personal way of looking at the world, and that can be quite different from someone else's. Two people could meet a third person for the first time, and even though they were together, and had the same experience of that individual, they could come to very different conclusions. One might judge the new person as being friendly and outgoing, whereas the other saw them as ingratiating and manipulative. Just because we have the same experience, does not mean that we see things the same way.

And that, of course, can motivate our behaviour. If we see someone as manipulative and ingratiating, for example, we would behave very differently towards them than we would if we saw them as friendly and outgoing. If we used the first type of personal constructs, we would be likely to avoid them, and to suspect any approach that they made towards us. If we used the second, we would be likely to be welcoming, and to treat them as a friend.

Social expectations

This type of thing can become circular, of course. As we saw in Chapter 2, the expectations other people have of us can influence our behaviour quite a lot. They can even become **self-fulfilling prophecies**, so that we live up to what people expect of us. So if you had a set of personal constructs which meant that you treated anyone new as if they were not really friendly but had some ulterior motive for pretending to be so, then they would respond to that, and avoid you. So then you would see that as 'proof' that they were not really being friendly, not realising that it was your own behaviour which had produced that effect.

A self-fulfilling set of personal constructs like this can easily mean that someone becomes very isolated from other people, and deeply unhappy. It is good to be cautious, of course, but it is not good to suspect anyone you meet, automatically. Many psychologists use personal construct theory to help people who have become stuck in belief systems like this. They use a number of techniques that will help people to develop a new set of personal constructs, which are helpful to them, rather than giving them more problems in the long run.

Defence mechanisms

There are other ways, too, that our minds can motivate us. Many psychologists are deeply sceptical about the ideas of Sigmund Freud, the psychoanalyst, who developed a theory about the unconscious mind during the last century. But Freud did identify some important mental processes which the mind uses to protect itself against threats. These are called **defence mechanisms**. Other psychologists, too, have found the idea of defence mechanisms to be a useful one, although they do not necessarily share Freud's other views about how the human mind works.

Denial

Defence mechanisms are unconscious, but they can be very powerful. They are all to do with how we protect our own self-image For example, if we are faced with an awkward or uncomfortable fact about ourselves, it can be very challenging, and our first impulse may be simply to deny that it is true. Sometimes, we will be able to get beyond that first impulse, and try to see if perhaps the idea does have some justification. At other times, though, the implications of the idea may be too much for us to cope with. So we stick to our **denial**, even though it may be quite irrational, simply because we are protecting ourselves from having to rethink all our beliefs and ideas. In this situation, denial is acting as a defence mechanism, protecting us from a threat to how we see ourselves.

Repression

There are other kinds of defence mechanisms too. One of them is **repression**. We often repress memories which are personally distressing, or which would seriously challenge our beliefs about ourselves. When a memory is repressed, we forget it — but it is different from normal forgetting, because we become very agitated or upset if something comes close to reminding us of it again. The mind has repressed that particular memory or knowledge because it is too emotionally demanding to cope with.

Reaction-formation

Sometimes, something can be repressed so hard that it turns into its opposite. For example, if someone has a very strong desire or need which they feel is wrong and needs to be suppressed, they may try very hard never to let it come to their awareness (remember that a defence mechanism is unconscious — we do not know we are doing it unless someone else intervenes, and shows us what is happening). So, because they try so hard, they become very hostile to any hint of that particular desire or need in other people, and react aggressively to it. This is known as a **reaction-formation**.

The classic example of a reaction-formation, of course, is **homophobia**. Most people, whether they are homosexual or heterosexual, are unaffected by other people's sexual choices. But some people become very upset and agitated when they encounter any mention of homosexuality. These people can end up reacting quite irrationally — and sometimes very aggressively — towards homosexuals. We refer to these people as homophobic. Their homophobia often comes from their own unconscious homosexual desires, which have been repressed so hard that they have become a reaction-formation.

Self-efficacy and learned helplessness

Another way that our cognitions can motivate us to action is to do with our **self-efficacy beliefs**. These are our beliefs about how effective we are at doing things — how capable, or how skilled, we are. And these are very important, because they affect how hard we try. Bandura (1989) showed how it is generally a good thing if people have high self-efficacy beliefs, because it makes them more self-confident, and more likely to succeed. It is even a good thing to have higher self-efficacy beliefs than the evidence would warrant — in other words, to believe that you are better at things than you really are — because that way, you will take on more challenges, and actually improve your abilities as you deal with them!

The effects of high self-efficacy

In one study which Bandura described, a psychologist looked at how having high or low self-efficacy beliefs affected children's work in school. The children in the study had different abilities: some were good at maths, while others were not very good at all. But they also had different self-efficacy beliefs. Some of the children believed that they would be able to do it, if they made an effort, while others believed that they would not be likely to be successful, no matter how much they tried.

The psychologist found that the children with high self-efficacy beliefs did much better than the other children, regardless of their level of ability. In other words, even if they really were not very good at maths, children with high self-efficacy beliefs did better. They solved more maths problems in the time that they were given, they spotted where they had gone wrong more quickly, and they were more prepared to go over problems which they had done wrong. The children with low self-efficacy beliefs, on the other hand, would make a single try at the problems, and then give up.

It is not hard to see, from this, why having high self-efficacy beliefs helps you to do well. Clearly, if you are prepared to put effort into learning, and to keep trying and learning from your mistakes, then you will eventually get somewhere — even if you are doing something that does not come easily to you. Many psychologists nowadays believe that bringing up children and training adults to believe in their own ability to take effective action is one of the most important things of all.

Learned helplessness

There's another side to this, as well. Some people go through a series of demoralising or unpleasant experiences, which they cannot do anything about, and then they just give up trying altogether. So when they are in a situation which they could actually change, if they made an effort, they do not bother. This is known as **learned helplessness** — they have learned to be passive and helpless, rather than trying to influence what happens to them.

In 1978, Abramson, Seligman and Teasdale argued that learned helplessness has a lot to do with why people suffer from depression. When people are living for a long time in demoralising situations which they cannot do much about, they often slip into a way of thinking things which encourages them to feel helpless and passive. They develop an attributional style, or a way of thinking which suggests that things happen because of global, large-scale reasons which are always likely to be there, and cannot be controlled. So whenever they encounter a new problem, they see it in this way and do not realise that it is actually something they could do something about.

Locus of control and self-efficacy

As we saw in Chapter 3, it is important for people to feel that they have some control over what happens to them. To feel that you are helpless is very stressful, which just makes things worse. So one way that psychologists try to help these people is to set up situations which will help them to raise their self-efficacy beliefs. Maybe they encourage them to tackle an entirely new activity, or to try a different approach in dealing with a problem. By doing this competently, the person comes to realise that they can be effective — that they can actually do something about their situation.

We can see, then, that self-efficacy beliefs are closely linked to the idea of locus of control, which we looked at in Chapter 3. They are all about seeing yourself as someone who can be in control of what happens to you, and who can take effective action when it is necessary. If we are to understand human motivation, we need to understand about these beliefs, because they can make all the difference as to whether we try to influence what is happening to us, or not.

———————— Social motives ————————

What we do is motivated by social influences, as well as cognitive ones. We are surrounded by other people, and how they see us can be a strong influence in whether we do something or not. We are also influenced by shared social understandings, and, as we have already seen, by the expectations which people have of us. So a great deal of our motivation is social in its origins.

Social respect

One of the most important social motives of all is for **respect** from other people. We all feel a deep need to avoid looking foolish in front of other people. Sometimes, if we feel that we have made ourselves look stupid in front of the wrong people, even the memory of it can continue to embarrass us for a long time.

Harré identified the need for social respect as a very fundamental social motive. A great deal of what we do, Harré argued, is aimed to ensure that people will take us seriously, or will at least notice us, and acknowledge us as worthwhile people, and not just dismiss us or — worse still — ignore our existence.

We can see how deeply rooted this need is by looking at children in a playground, when there is an adult present. Most of the children will be clamouring for attention in some way, looking to 'show off' something that they can do. Although this is often dismissed as attention-seeking, it is really a way of looking for social respect. A child who has learned to stand on its hands, or to do a long-jump, wants an adult to acknowledge that skill, and to say 'well done'. Quite rightly, children want to be noticed for their achievements.

Adults need that kind of acknowledgement, too. Most of us work better if our efforts are recognised by other people — especially on those occasions when we have made a special effort. We like to know that we have been noticed. In fact, being ignored is one of the worst thing that can happen to use — we feel it as a deep social insult, and we can go to great lengths to get over it — by proving that those people are less important than we are, or by making sure that they are forced to acknowledge us on a future occasion. This is sometimes the motivation underpinning human ambition and achievement — although not always.

Conflicting personal images

Sometimes, the need for social respect can work in our minds, as well. Because we are always aware of how our behaviour is likely to come across to other people, we need to make sure that our own behaviour appears reasonable, even to ourselves. One consequence of this is that we do not like to seem to be inconsistent. Yet each of us acts differently when we are with different people, so sometimes we can get into difficulties when we are trying to balance the two.

The musical *Grease*, for instance, was based entirely around this problem. A young couple meet during the holidays, as individuals, and fall in love; but when they meet again at school, the boy is in front of his friends, and so he feels he has to appear casual and uncaring, which hurts her. Even though he is still in love with the girl, to show it would be inconsistent with his public image, and might lose him social respect. It is the way that the two resolve this dilemma which forms the plot of the musical.

Cognitive dissonance

Sometimes we resolve dilemmas like this by changing our attitudes or beliefs. In a very famous study conducted in 1956, Festinger, Riecken and Schachter joined in with a religious cult who believed that their city — and the rest of the world — was about to be destroyed by a great flood. On a special day the cult members sold all of their possessions, and spent the night, praying, on a hill outside of the city. Festinger, Riecken and Schachter were there too. They interviewed the cult members, and found that they believed that the flood would happen, and only they would be saved.

The psychologists wanted to know what the cult members would say when the world did not come to an end at the appointed time. So the next day, when no flood had materialised, they interviewed as many cult members as they could. Interestingly, they found that the cult members had adapted their beliefs, so that they did not have to face up to the fact that their actions had been a waste of time. They now believed that it was the fact that they had spent the night praying which had actually saved the world: the flood would have come as scheduled, but God had repented at the last minute, and so everything — thanks to them — was all right.

Festinger, Riecken and Schachter interpreted this in terms of what they called **cognitive dissonance**. We all like to believe that we are consistent, and not irrational. So if things happen which could make us appear irrational, we change our beliefs to make them seem consistent again. Festinger believed that cognitive dissonance is one of the main reasons why people change their beliefs: we do not like to seem foolish to anyone, not even ourselves.

Festinger gave some less dramatic examples of cognitive dissonance, as well. In one study, people were asked to do an extremely boring task for a long time. Then they were asked to go out and tell someone who was waiting that the task was interesting. They were paid either $1 or $20 for doing so. Then the psychologists asked the research participants to say how interesting the task had really been. The psychologists found that the people who had been paid $20 to do the experiment said what they expected — that the task was really boring. But the people who had only been paid $1 said that, actually, they had found it moderately interesting.

Nobody in their right mind could really have found the task interesting. Part of it involved giving each of 48 pegs in a peg-board a quarter-turn, one after the other, for half an hour! But what seemed to have happened was that the research participants needed to justify why they had lied to the person in the waiting room. It was OK for those who had been paid $20, because they could say they did it for the money. But being paid only $1 was not enough, so they needed a better reason for their lying. As a result, they convinced themselves that the task had not really been all that bad.

Cognitive dissonance, then, might be something which goes on in our minds, but it is another aspect of our need for respect. We need to avoid looking silly, even to ourselves. So avoiding cognitive dissonance, and seeming to be consistent in our beliefs and actions, can be an important motive for acting in a particular way.

Aggression and scapegoating

Sometimes, one of the ways that we avoid cognitive dissonance is by blaming other people for what happens to us. This is known as **scapegoating**, and is a significant mechanism which underlies social aggression such as racism. Scapegoating seems to be a mechanism which can bring out the very worst in human nature. As things get difficult, people become frustrated and angry, and they take that anger out on the nearest clearly identifiable target.

Racism and economic recession

It is noticeable, for example, that violent racist incidents increase when the economy is in recession. Recent events in Europe are an example of this, as is the massive increase of racism in Germany and elsewhere during the 1930s depression — an increase which made the concentration camps possible. In the United States, too, Hovland and Sears (1940) showed that the number of lynchings of black people in the southern states was closely linked to the price of cotton. The lower the price, the more lynchings took place.

The key to understanding this side of human nature lies in looking at where all that aggression comes from. For the most part, people tend to live co-operatively with one another. As we will see in

Chapter 8, our first social impulse is to go along with other people, not to confront them aggressively. But sometimes human beings show that they are capable of brutal inhumanity towards one another. How does that happen?

Frustration and aggression

There have been a number of studies which have shown how aggressive behaviour in human beings occurs when we feel frustrated, or helpless, and are unable to get on with our own lives. This idea was first put forward by Dollard *et al.*, in 1939, although at the time they phrased it in a rather limited way. They suggested that people would always react aggressively if they were frustrated in achieving their personal goals. Nowadays, we recognise that people react differently — not everyone becomes aggressive in situations like that. But, for the most part, being prevented from doing something that we feel we should be able to do (even if it is only getting on with our own lives in peace) is something which makes us very tense. And some people express that tension in aggression and violent action.

But why should that tension become displaced on to ethnic minority groups? The reason for this lies in two other important motivators for human behaviour. As we saw earlier, and in Chapter 2, it is very stressful for a human being to feel that they are helpless. Yet an economic recession is something that few of us can do anything about: we all feel helpless as we hear about jobs disappearing and companies collapsing. Many of us, too, are personally threatened by these situations, yet there is little that we can do.

Social representations

One very striking characteristic of people, though, is that we look for explanations for what is happening to us. Some people seek those explanations in ideas like luck, or mystical concepts like astrology; some look for them, as we are doing here, by looking to the human sciences, while others look for them in the general explanations and social beliefs which are shared by the people around them. These general explanations are known as **social representations**, and they are an important key to understanding how economic frustration becomes displaced on to the people who are usually suffering the most from it.

Social representations are shared beliefs, which are held by groups of people in society. Each of us adopts our own set of social representations, by talking with other people, picking ideas up from the mass media, and fitting these into our own personal construct system. They give us ways of explaining what is happening in our everyday experience. In some ways, they are a bit like the personal constructs which we looked at earlier in this chapter, but they are shared by other people too. We will be looking at them again in Chapter 8.

Among racists, a common social representation is the idea that they are somehow in competition with members of ethnic minorities for the benefits of society. So when those benefits become fewer, they blame the members of the ethnic groups because they think they are taking an unfair share of what is available. (In fact it is generally the members of ethnic minority groups who suffer most economic deprivation in situations like this, but racists are not noted for logical thinking.) Where most people will put the blame where it belongs, with the Government or economic forces; racists blame ethnic minority groups, and express their own personal frustration through violent action towards them.

Social identifications

But why should they seize on members of a particular group, rather than on particular individuals? The answer to that one lies in the mechanism of social identification, which we looked at in Chapter 2. As we saw there, it is a very basic tendency for human beings to see the world in terms of 'them' and 'us' groups. We are aware of the social groups and categories that we belong to, and we are also aware of other groups in society.

Stereotyping

Because we tend to know the people in our own groups best, and we only see members of other groups from the outside, we become much more aware of the differences between people in our own group than we are of differences among others. So it is very easy for us to slip into the idea that 'we' are all different, whereas 'they' are all the same. One of the first steps in breaking down any sort of social prejudice is to recognise that any group of people is made up of individuals, with their own different ideas and opinions — that 'they' are not, in fact, all the same.

These are psychological tendencies that all people have to some extent. We all tend to stereotype groups of people if we do not know them that well. The stereotyping is not necessarily about ethnic groups: we also stereotype businessmen, doctors, schoolteachers, Americans, and other groups of people. It is partly a way of making sense of the mass of information that we have to deal with; but it can also be dangerous when it leads us to ignore individual differences.

Social comparison

Another aspect of social identity theory is that we tend to make comparisons with people in groups which are close to us, socially and economically, because that way it helps us to feel good about belonging to our own group. Those racists who engage in violent action tend to be relatively less educated and to undertake unskilled work, when they are employed. So rather than place the blame for their unemployment on those in charge of the economy, who are socially very distant from them, they prefer to blame people who are in a similar economic position, but belong to a different social group.

We can see, then, how looking at why violent racism often rises at times of economic recession reveals a number of motivating mechanisms in human behaviour. One of these is that frustration and discomfort often produce aggressive reactions in people, partly as a way of getting rid of the tension produced by feeling helpless. Another is the tendency to use shared beliefs, or social representations, as a way of explaining what is happening. And a third is to seize on a particular ethnic group because they represent a clearly identifiable target, who are close by, and who are often in a much weaker position, both economically and socially.

Counteracting racism

One thing which has become apparent, though, is that this kind of consequence to economic recession does not seem to be inevitable. In a population which is highly sensitised to issues of racism and multiculturalism, the efforts of racists to stir people up into violent action are much less effective. As people become more aware of individual differences within different ethnic groups, and of how political and economic factors influence recessions, they become less likely to produce such simplistic, and tragic, responses. We may have a long way to go, but understanding the psychological mechanisms which underlie the phenomenon can give us some useful hints as to which direction we should take.

As we know, human beings can act in some astoundingly vicious ways. But it is important to keep this in perspective. For the most part, people tend to co-operate with one another, rather than compete — in fact, some psychologists believe that this is a baseline of human interaction, and that it takes some kind of disruption, like frustration or illness, before people begin to interact in more unpleasant ways. There are individual differences, of course, and there are also questions of social learning, as we model our behaviour on other people around us, including characters on TV and in films. But still, in their everyday lives, most people are not aggressive most of the time. We will be looking at how we go about interacting with one another, socially, in Chapter 8.

Hierarchy of needs and levels of explanation

One of the most famous psychological theories of human motivation was put forward by Maslow, in 1954. Maslow was trying to understand why it is that people never seem to be satisfied with what they've got. We often find that we are dissatisfied with our situation, and want something more; but if we get the thing that we want, then it is not very long before we begin to want something else.

Maslow's hierarchy of needs

Maslow suggested that it is useful to think of human motivation in terms of a hierarchy of needs (Fig. 5.1). We have some needs which are absolutely basic — our physiological survival needs — and if these are not satisfied they will be what motivates our behaviour more than anything else. What we do will be aimed towards getting food, drinks, shelter from the elements, and so on, and we will have little time for anything else. But once those needs are satisfied, a different layer in the hierarchy begins to become

Figure 5.1   Maslow's hierarchy of needs

important. It becomes important to us that we should feel safe and secure, and so that becomes what motivates us. Once that has been achieved, according to Maslow, social needs become paramount, and what we do will be geared towards fulfilling our need to belong with other people and to be accepted.

At the top of the hierarchy, Maslow argued, is self-actualisation — realising our talents and abilities to the full. We have met this idea before, when we looked at Rogers' work, in Chapter 2. But where for Rogers, self-actualisation was a fundamental need which everyone has, Maslow placed it as an ultimate achievement, managed by only a relatively few remarkable people.

Problems with Maslow's theory

The difference between how the two psychologists see self-actualisation also points up one of the weaknesses in Maslow's theory. It may be OK as a description of a general tendency, but there are numerous examples of people acting in ways which are quite different from that which would be predicted by Maslow. What Maslow described as 'higher' needs are important to people, and whether their basic needs have been satisfied sometimes does not come into it.

The classic example, of course, is the dedicated poet or artist, who denies security and sometimes even goes hungry in the quest to fulfil needs for beauty or symmetry. Another example is the person who gives up the safety and security of a salaried job in order to do voluntary work overseas, or to take on something which is less regularly paid, but much more challenging. It may not be what most people do, but such people are less rare than Maslow's theory might predict.

Another great weakness in Maslow's way of looking at motivation is that it is very specific to Western cultures. It assumes that people are motivated by a need for individual achievement, and that things like social needs are somehow optional, at least by comparison with the satisfaction of physical ones. While this may, at least partly, represent how things are in America and other parts of the Western world, it is not by any means a good description of what human beings are like elsewhere.

For example, in many parts of the world, the kind of upward ambition and striving represented by Maslow's approach simply does not apply. To take one èxample: in Balinese culture, people see their identity as firmly located within their village's community, and the idea of accumulating personal wealth is an alien one. If it does happen, the money is usually spent on a particularly elaborate funeral celebration, or something equally transient. While Balinese people would like to be less poor than they are, naturally, the idea of achieving this through personal ambition and saving up personal wealth is not one which comes naturally to members of that particular culture.

There are other ways in which Balinese culture is different from many others. For example, the idea of 'art' as a separate entity does not exist, either. Although Balinese culture is full of what we would call art — in dance, carving, weaving, and many other ways — there is no separate word for art in the Balinese language. It is simply a part of day-to-day living. So to see it as a separate set of motives, which we adopt only once other needs are satiated, simply cannot explain what is going on.

Levels of explanation

This is only one example, but there are many others. It is perhaps more useful, if we are trying to understand human motivation, to take an approach which looks at it in terms of **levels of explanation**, than to try to explain it as a hierarchy of needs. As we saw in Chapter 1, we all operate on different levels at the same time. We may do something because it is approved of by our social group, but also because we want to do it personally, and because we believe it will be good for us.

By looking at the many different kinds of motives which people have for their behaviour, we can identify some of the influences which might be working on any one example of human behaviour at a given time. It is not a simple way of explaining things, like the hierarchical model is, but then human beings are not all that simple, either. It does, though, seem to be more useful in explaining why human beings act as they do than the more simplistic explanations.

6

—————— COGNITION ——————

This chapter is all about cognition — about how we think, how we take in new information, and how we remember. In other words, it is about how the mind works. Although psychology first began as the study of the mind, its emphasis changed during the first half of the twentieth century as many psychologists began to concentrate only on studying behaviour. They thought that studying the mind was impossible since we cannot see it, or analyse it directly. Although some psychologists did continue to study the mind, there were relatively few of them and they only had a limited influence on psychology as a whole, at that time.

But from the 1950s onwards, psychology began to develop ways of studying the mind in a more objective manner. They found that it was possible to do controlled experiments which would show how the mind was working, and by doing this they identified some surprising things about how we think and remember. Most of all, they discovered that the mind is not just a passive recording and analysing machine: it has its own influence on what we perceive and remember, and on how we think.

—————————— Thinking ——————————

When we think, we have to draw on our experience. But that means that the mind has to have that experience available. It has to have information available, like memories, which it can draw on. We cannot just 'think', we need something to think about, and sometimes memories provide the basic material for our thinking. We will be looking at how we remember information later in this chapter.

But we do more than just remember the things which happen to us. Thinking also involves plans, possibilities and ideas. For example, one of the things which makes human beings very special is that we can imagine things which have not happened — and which might actually never happen. And sometimes, as science fiction and other books which train the imagination show, those imaginings can seem almost as real to us as the world that we are actually living in.

Somehow, therefore, the brain needs to contain all of this information, and all of these possibilities, plans and ideas. But it needs to contain them in a way that allows us to use it all, and to draw on it when we need to. In order to do that, the mind has to organise all this material in a way that makes sense, and which means that things can be brought to mind when they become relevant to what we are doing, or thinking.

Concepts

One of the tools which psychologists use to study how the mind is organised is the idea of the **concept**. Concepts are ways of grouping together, or classifying information, so that we can see which kinds of things belong together. For example, we automatically realise that a chair, a table and a bed all have something in common, and are different from, say, a frog. We classify chairs, tables and beds as part of the same concept — as items of furniture. A frog, on the other hand, belongs to a different concept — that of animals, or perhaps amphibian animals.

By grouping things together like this, we are able to make much more sense out of the world that we live in. If we were not able to classify things, and to use concepts, then we would have to treat everything that we came across as if we had never encountered anything like it before, and that would mean that we spent an enormous amount of time trying to work things out from first principles. But if we recognise something as belonging to a particular concept, we can treat it in much the same way as we treat other examples of that concept.

How we store concepts

I mentioned earlier that psychologists began to study the mind again partly because they developed ways of investigating how it works experimentally. One of the famous studies of how we store concepts is a good example of this. Collins and Quillian (1972) asked people to say whether a set of statements was true or not. In order to answer, they had to think about the concept, and the psychologists timed, very exactly, how long it took them to find the answers.

People were asked questions like, 'Is a robin a bird?', 'Does a shark have gills?' or 'Does a goldfish have wings?'. Collins and Quillian found that some questions took longer to answer than others. For example, it took longer to answer the question 'Is a blue jay an animal?', than it did to answer the question 'Is a blue jay a bird?'. By comparing the different times which the answers needed, Collins and Quillian were able to deduce something about how concepts were stored.

Their most important finding was that concepts are stored hierarchically. In other words, we begin with large-scale general concepts, like 'animal' or 'plant', and then we have a number of smaller concepts nested within the larger one. The general concept of 'animal', for example, contains within it lots of smaller categories, such as 'bird', 'fish' or 'mammal'. Each of those has other kinds of concepts within them, like 'shark' or 'goldfish' (see Fig. 6.1).

In the Collins and Quillian study, people could give the answers to the questions quickly if they only involved a single step in the hierarchy. So they could know very rapidly that a blue jay is a bird, because that only involved one step. But when more than one step was involved, they needed to think about it more — to know that a blue jay was an animal involved more than one step, and that meant that they took longer. Even though the time difference was only in fractions of a second, it was possible for the psychologists to use it to tell them something about how the person's mind was working.

Levels of concepts

Another psychologist Rosch (1973) also looked at the different levels of concepts, and how they were stored. Rosch came to the conclusion that there are really three main levels of concepts. There are high level, **superordinate concepts**, which are general classifications about types of things, like 'furniture' or 'animal'. These help us to group together some of the main features of our

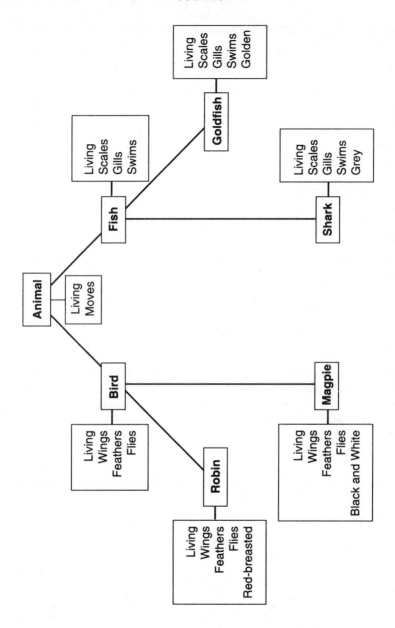

Figure 6.1 Hierarchical organisation of concepts

day-to-day experience, so they are vital in helping us to make sense of the world.

Then there are what Rosch called **basic level concepts**, which are things like 'chairs' or 'horses'. Basic concepts are linked together because of what we actually do with them. There are lots of different types of chairs: some have arms or backs, some have cushions and some do not, and so on. But they all have one thing in common, which is that we sit on them. It is what we do with them which links them together to form the basic concept.

The third type of concept which Rosch identified are **subordinate concepts.** These are more detailed ways of classifying things, which we might use only for specialised purposes. For example, there are many different breeds of horses, and someone who was interested in them could probably tell you a lot about them. For them, the subordinate concepts of the different kinds of horses are ways of organising their more specialised experience. For people who do not have that specialised experience, the subordinate concept is less necessary.

One of the things which becomes apparent from this, then, is that basic level concepts seem to be the main level which we use in day-to-day living. They are the concepts about what we do — which link with our personal actions. And there is some suggestion that these basic level concepts may have a very old history, because researchers have shown that some animals, too, seem to use basic level concepts.

Animal concepts

Seyfarth, Cheyney and Marler (1980) were observing the behaviour of vervet monkeys in Africa, and looking at the ways that wild monkeys responded to threats. They found that the monkeys have three different types of alarm call, which they give when they see one of the three different types of animal which can threaten their lives. When they heard a call, the monkeys would make the appropriate actions to avoid the threat.

One of the calls was given when there was a rock python about, and when other monkeys heard this, they would look around at the ground, to identify the threat. A different call meant that there was a martial eagle around, and these can swoop down and carry off young monkeys. When they heard this, the other monkeys would look up at the sky. The third type of call was given when any monkey sighted a leopard, and when they heard this, the other monkeys would look into the trees.

So the calls which the monkeys gave represented different types of threat. But what was more interesting was the way that the young monkeys learned to give alarm calls themselves. Although they would often get the wrong call, giving the leopard alarm when they saw a warthog, or an eagle alarm when they saw another large bird, they never got the categories wrong. Always, the type of animal which had disturbed them was of the right kind — a bird, a mammal or a snake — even if it was not actually the dangerous variety.

Natural categories

Marler (1982) discussed how this is also similar to the way that some birds use different calls, and suggested that there are **natural categories**, which both animals and human beings are predisposed to learn. These natural categories are based on the idea of different kinds of actions, and Marler suggested that we, and other animals, are particularly ready to learn them, because they help the species to adapt and survive.

Natural categories are all about actions — with things that we do and movements that we make. So in that way they are closely linked with Rosch's idea of basic level concepts. Each species, Marler argued, is particularly ready to learn to organise its experience in some ways rather than others. In human beings, this seems to be what basic level concepts are all about, and may explain why a young child, for instance, learns about 'chairs' and 'doggies' much more easily and quickly than it learns about furniture and animals.

We can see, then, that this way of looking at concepts means that they are much more than just ways of categorising information. They also include ideas about what we do with those things — with the way that we ourselves take action. And this links concepts with another important idea in our attempt to understand how the human mind works: the idea of the schema.

Schemas

A schema, in some ways, is a bit like a concept, but it is much broader than a concept. A schema contains ideas, plans, memories of actions and possibilities of future actions, as well as information. It is what we use to guide and direct our behaviour when we are dealing with the world: a schema is a very active kind of thing, not just a passive way of recording information.

For example, you will probably have a schema to do with using public transport. That will contain memories of buses or train journeys, but it will also contain your knowledge of what to do about paying the fare, and how to signal that you want to get off a bus, and many other aspects of using buses. If you were in a new town and had to get somewhere, you would not be completely uncertain of what to do. Instead, you would begin by using your schema to guide your actions.

Developing schemas

As we learn more about the world, our schemas become more sophisticated, and sometimes even change. The first schema of all is probably the **body-schema**, as a young infant gradually develops the sense that the world consists of some parts which are 'me' and some parts which are 'not-me'. As its experience grows, it learns more about its body and the rest of the world. The schema becomes broader as it assimilates more information. But the schema also adapts and changes, as it accommodates itself to new information.

It may even divide into several entirely different schemas. The infant gradually learns that the part of the world which is 'not-me' actually seems to have two different parts: a part which is other people, who smile and interact with the baby (and which it responds to very easily, as we saw in Chapter 2), and a part which is more static, like the infant's cot or chair. The more we learn, the more our schemas adapt and change — all through life.

Applying schemas

And we use these schemas when we are thinking, or reasoning about problems. In the 1960s and 1970s, a number of psychologists investigated how human beings go about solving problems, and found that often we do not seem to do it particularly logically. This is mainly because we focus on the meaning of the statement, and not on its strict logical form, the way a computer would.

For example: if I were to tell a computer, 'If it is raining on Sunday I shall go to the cinema', then the computer would take that as a logical statement. But if I said that to a human being, they would listen to the meaning of what I had said, which would not necessarily be the same thing. And the two — computer and human being — would draw different conclusions if they found me at the cinema on Sunday. The human being would conclude that I was there because it was raining outside. But a computer would not. As far as the computer is concerned, it could just as well be sunshine outside, because all I actually said was that I would go if it was raining. I did not actually say anything at all about what I would do if it was not raining. The computer works from strict logic, and what I said did not, logically, mean that it was possible to draw that conclusion.

A human being, though, would apply their well-developed schemas about what we usually mean when we say things in conversation. So they would know what I really meant — that I would only go to the pictures if it was raining. They would also see the sense in it — since a cinema is a dry place, and seeing a film is a good thing to do with a wet afternoon. They would see it as a *rational* meaning, even though it might not be a strictly *logical* one. We apply a lot of this type of social knowledge in understanding each other, and it is why human thinking does not fit very easily into computer models.

Mental set

There are other ways that our prior knowledge influences our thinking, too. One of the most important of these is when we have expectations about what we are likely to find, and this affects how we go about doing something. Expectations can mean that we develop what is known as a **mental set**, which is a state of being ready to think in certain ways.

There are lots of examples of mental set, because it is a very strong mental mechanism. One of the most famous demonstrations of this was by Luchins, in 1932, who asked people to solve problems which involved water-jars which would hold different amounts of water, and pouring water from one jar into another in order to get an exact amount (Fig. 6.2). The first few problems could be solved in a particular way, by pouring water from large to small jars in a particular order. As people worked through the problems, they got used to this way of doing things. So when they eventually came across a problem which had a much simpler solution, they did not see the easy answer at all. Instead, they solved the problem a long way round, using the method they had been using before.

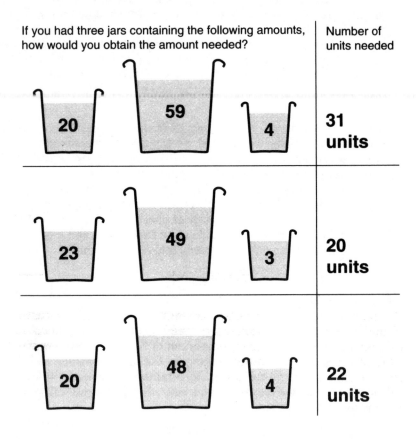

If you had three jars containing the following amounts, how would you obtain the amount needed?

			Number of units needed
20	59	4	31 units
23	49	3	20 units
20	48	4	22 units

Figure 6.2 Luchins' water-jar problem

What had happened was that they had developed a mental set — they were ready to see one particular answer to the problem, but that meant that they could not see the other way of doing it. There are other examples, too, which draw on our existing mental sets rather than creating one specially, as Luchins did. The nine-dot problem (Fig. 6.3) is only hard to do if we assume that the solution

Join the nine dots with four straight lines, without lifting the pen from the paper or going over the same line twice.

Figure 6.3   The nine-dot problem

has to fit within the boundaries of the dots. But that is not in the instructions: nobody has told us to do that. It is our own, previous expectations which have made it difficult.

Perception

Mental sets also make a difference to how we perceive what is around us. We are often particularly ready to notice certain kinds of things rather than others, and this can make a considerable difference to what we think we are looking at. Perception is all about making sense of the information that the mind receives from the outside world. To make sense out of information, we have to interpret it, and consider its meaning. So the psychological study of perception involves looking at how the mind and the senses work to give us our perceptual experience.

Most psychological research into perception has concentrated on visual perception, because vision is our most important sense, as human beings. But there are other kinds of perception too. We also make sense out of the sounds we hear around us, for instance, and some games to do with touching different objects while blindfolded show us how we interpret what we receive through our sense of touch. Smells, too, can often have a powerful influence on our perception — and sometimes a particular smell can bring back a whole flood of memories. And we saw in Chapter 3 how our perceptions of our internal states can influence the emotions that we feel. So perception actually involves all of our senses, not just vision, even though it is vision that we know most about.

Organising perception

One of the first things which we need to explain when we are looking at visual perception is how come we can distinguish things, rather than simply seeing a whole mass of disconnected colours and patches of light and dark. Automatically, it seems, we organise our perception so that we see whole objects and shapes, set against backgrounds. The way that we do that is very interesting.

Principles of perceptual organisation

One of the ways that we do it is that we apply a set of perceptual 'rules' to what we are seeing, which tell us how we should group different bits of information together into whole units. These rules are known as the **Gestalt principles of perception**, after the Gestalt psychologists who discovered them during the first half of the twentieth century. There are four of them altogether, and together they show us how our perceptual system automatically tries to make complete, meaningful units out of the information which it receives.

The first of these is the principle of similarity. In the absence of any other clues, we tend, automatically, to group together items or stimuli which are similar to one another. We have the impression that they 'belong' together as we look at them. The second one, though, can override the first one. It is known as the principle of proximity, and is about how we tend to group together things which are close to one another, even if they are not necessarily similar.

The principle of closure, the third of the Gestalt principles, overrides the other two. If a group of stimuli hint at a closed, or complete figure, the mind automatically groups them together, and fills in the gaps. This tendency is so strong that if people are asked to draw an incomplete figure that they have seen, they will often fill in the gaps automatically, because they did not notice that they were there at all. And the fourth Gestalt principle of perception is that we tend to look for figures which have 'good Gestalt', or whole, complete shapes, rather than figures which seem to be 'bitty' or disconnected. Fig. 6.4 shows how some of these principles work.

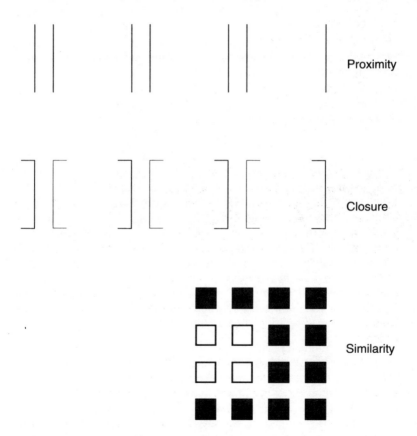

Figure 6.4 Gestalt principles of perception

Brain cells and perception

There is some suggestion, too, that our tendency to see objects and shapes against backgrounds — which is known as figure-ground perception — may be wired into our nervous system. In 1979, Hubel and Wiesel showed that there are special cells in the visual cortex (the part of the brain which interprets visual information) and in the thalamus (the part of the brain which channels information from the eyes to the visual cortex) which help us to identify patterns and shapes.

One type of cell, known as a simple cell, fires when it detects a single type of stimulus — like a line at a particular angle in a particular part of our vision. A second type of cell, known as a complex cell, receives information from lots of simple cells, so that type of cell would fire when it detected a line at that particular angle anywhere in our vision. And a third type of cell, known as a hypercomplex cell, receives information from lots of different complex cells. These cells fire when they detect simple shapes, like a triangle, or a square shape.

Although we are only just beginning to understand how visual cells in the brain combine information, what we do know does suggest that seeing shapes and objects may be something that our cells do automatically, from the way that they are connected up. The psychologists Marr and Nisihara (1982) showed how connecting up information about edges and surfaces, which could be detected by simple and complex cells, and then applying computational rules, including the Gestalt principles of perception, could allow us to identify whole, real objects like people, trees or animals. The process involves several stages, including one where the image which is detected is almost like a stick-figure. But by adding extra information, and applying perceptual principles, we come to be able to see it as a three-dimensional object.

Marr's approach tells us something about how we perceive the physical world, as does work by many other psychologists too. But we do not just spend our time looking at objects and trees. Often, the things we are looking at are more complex than that, and have special meanings. When we are making sense of those, we use our schemas and our existing knowledge, as well as processing the physical image that we receive through our eyes.

Perceptual set

Some psychologists have investigated the way that expectation can influence what we perceive. In the same way that experience can give us mental sets which influence how we think when we are solving problems, so expectation, or mood, or other social influences, can give us perceptual sets which influence what we perceive. In one famous study, Bruner and Minturn (1955) showed people sets of letters or numbers. Each time they saw a letter or a number, they were asked to say what it was out loud. Then they were shown an ambiguous figure, which could be seen as either the figure 13 or the letter B. People who had previously been looking at letters said that it was a B, while people who had previously seen numbers said that it was a 13.

First impressions

First impressions can set up perceptual sets in other ways, as well. Jones *et al.* (1968) asked people to watch as a student tried to solve a set of difficult multiple-choice problems. Each time the student got 15 out of the 30 problems right. But when some people watched, most of the correct ones came near the beginning, so that their first impression was that the student was very good at them, while other people saw the student get more wrong at the beginning, and most correct towards the end.

When they were asked to estimate how many questions the student had got right in the end, the two groups of people made entirely different estimates. Those who had seen more correct answers at first estimated that the student had got around 20 out of the 30 questions right, while those who had seen more wrong answers at first estimated that only about 12 out of 30 answers were right. So our perception can be influenced very strongly by first impressions.

Motivation and perception

Our physical or motivational state, too, can affect what we perceive. Gilchrist and Nesburg (1952) asked people to look at pictures, and rate how brightly coloured they were. If the research participants had gone without food or drink for four hours, they rated pictures of food and drink as being more brightly coloured than pictures of other things. Their motivational state, of hunger, had affected how they perceived the pictures.

We can be influenced by our expectations and mental states, but we can also be surprised by what we see. It is obvious that our expectations do not entirely determine perception, because if they did we could never be surprised. So there must be some kind of link between what we expect to find and what we actually notice around us.

The perceptual cycle

Neisser (1976) described perception as taking place in a continuously active cycle. We begin with the schemas that we are using to make sense of the world: we expect certain things to exist, or to be likely to happen. Those schemas help us to anticipate what we are likely to encounter, so Neisser referred to them as **anticipatory schemas**.

Our schemas direct what sorts of things we take notice of, as we explore the perceptual world. We do not just take in everything around us — that would be far too much to cope with. We could notice everything around us: the shadow of a leaf, the texture of the tarmac on a road, and so on. But if we did, we would become overloaded, and we would never be able to work out when we should do things. Instead, we sample the relevant information: the speed that a car is approaching when we want to cross the road, the width of the road, and so on. Our perceptual exploration tells us which bits of information are the important things that we should sample.

Once we have sampled that information, it in turn leads back to the anticipatory schema, and modifies it. You may have been about to step into the road because your anticipatory schema is to do with being on the other side, but your perceptual exploration led you to focus on approaching cars, and the information available told you that there was one coming up fast. So you modify your anticipatory schema, waiting until it has gone past. The modified schema in turn directs a new set of perceptual exploration (looking further down the road to see how many more cars are coming), and so on.

Figure 6.5 Neisser's perceptual cycle

In Neisser's model, then, perception is a continuous, active cycle, not just a passive snapshot of what is there. What we anticipate, or expect to happen, affects what we perceive; but what is actually there affects what we anticipate. So our expectations are continually changing and adjusting themselves, as we take in new information and revise our schemas accordingly.

Memory

Memory, too, is an active mental process rather than a simple tape-recording of what has happened. In many ways, this is quite hard to grasp, because we always feel as though we are remembering exactly what happened. But it is true, nonetheless. The trouble, though, is that we do not often have a separate, objective record of what actually did happen, so we cannot compare our memories with the real thing.

Active remembering

There are a few occasions when we do have some objective evidence to compare it with, though. Have you ever been to see a film again, that you used to enjoy a great deal several years before? When you do that, you often find that some of your favourite scenes in the film do not happen exactly the way that you remember them. Even though you thought you remembered them word for word, they turn out to be different when you actually watch them again.

It is the same with our other memories, too. Very often we think that we are remembering a conversation word for word, but really we are remembering a slightly different version of it. The great psychologist Ulrich Neisser showed how this can happen in an analysis of some of the evidence given during the Watergate trials in America, which eventually resulted in the impeachment of President Nixon.

John Deane's memory

One of the important witnesses in these trials was John Deane, a man who was considered by many to have an astoundingly accurate memory. During the trials, he related a number of very specific conversations which had taken place between the President and other people in the White House, and was convinced — as were the other people involved — that he had recounted them accurately. However, later on in the trials, a number of tape-recordings of the same conversations were discovered. So in this case it was possible for Neisser to compare the testimony given by John Deane, including word-for-word descriptions of conversations, with an objective record of what had actually been said.

The results were fascinating. In almost every conversation, John Deane's recollection of what had really been said was incorrect. Different words were used, topics were mentioned in a different order, and sometimes particularly memorable phrases had not actually been said at all. And yet, even though the details were all wrong, the social meaning of what had gone on was perfectly correct. Deane did not remember the details accurately, even though he thought he did, but he did remember what had happened. It was the meaning of the events which he actually remembered, and this influenced his recall of the details.

Stories and schemas

This actually reflects a very powerful feature of our memory, which has been known to psychologists for a very long time. Bartlett, in 1932, showed how, when people are asked to remember a story, they first make sense out of the story in their own way. We fit new information into our existing thought structures — into the schemas that we use for understanding the world. And often that means that we adjust the information that we remember so that it will fit.

Bartlett found this out by telling people a story, which was not the sort of story that they were used to hearing. He used an American Indian legend, called 'War of the Ghosts', which was often confusing to European and White American listeners, because it included the involvement of the spirit world. When people wrote down what they remembered of the story, Bartlett found that they made systematic changes to it, as they tried to make sense out of it. The more often the story had to be remembered, the more those changes happened, until eventually the story was nothing like its original.

TABLE 6.1   HOW MEMORIES CHANGE

1. **Changes in importance** – People tend to focus on one part of the story and see that as most important, even if it is not really.

2. **Changes to the emotional impact** – People adjust the story so that it fits with their own reactions and emotions.

3. **Drifting** – The more often the story is told, the more its meaning gradually changes.

4. **Shortening** – The story becomes shorter and less detailed, as things which the person does not understand are left out.

5. **Coherence** – Bits are added to the story, or its sequence is changed around, so that it seems to make sense better.

6. **Conventionality** – Well-known ideas and themes are introduced, so that the story becomes more like other stories which are known in that culture.

7. **Losing names and numbers** – These get lost as the story is repeated, or sometimes change into more familiar forms.

The seven types of change which Bartlett identified are listed in Table 6.1. They happen with other types of information, too, and this can be very important indeed. Much courtroom evidence, for example, is based on the idea that people can remember things very accurately. So it is important to be aware that someone's memory of what happened is likely to be influenced by their own expectations and social assumptions, no matter how accurate they think it is.

Words and memory

Memories can be influenced by all sorts of subtle things, too. In one study, described by Loftus and Loftus (1975), people were shown a film of a traffic accident. Then they were asked a few questions about it. Among the questions there was one about the speed of the cars, and this was phrased very carefully. Half of the people were asked 'How fast were the cars going when they hit one another?', while the other half were asked, 'How fast were the cars going when they smashed into one another?'. All the other questions were the same.

A week later, the same people were asked to remember the film that they had seen. Among other things, they were asked whether there had been any broken glass in the film. There had not been any, and those who had been asked about the cars hitting one another remembered that. But those who had been asked about the cars smashing into one another distinctly remembered broken glass strewn around the road, and were surprised to find that it was not there when they saw the film again. The way that words were used when they were asked about the accident had influenced what they remembered, because the words had suggested that the accident was more serious than it really had been.

This, too, is an important finding, particularly for people who have to ask questions to witnesses for court. People can pick up on the way that we use words, and this can affect what they recall. In some American states, the police are allowed to help witnesses to remember what happened by using hypnosis, because they believe it helps people to recall events. But when people are hypnotised, they can be very easily influenced, and are trying very hard to be co-operative. Because of this, they often adjust their memories without knowing it, to fit what they think the questioner wants to know.

As a result of this, Gibson (1982) argued very strongly that the use of hypnotism on witnesses in police investigations should be regarded as being equivalent to tampering with evidence. Memory does not work like a tape-recording, but can be changed and adjusted even some time after the event — without us even knowing it has happened. And there is no way of telling the difference between a constructed memory, like this, and a 'real' one.

Coding memories

But how, exactly, do we go about storing our memories? Somehow we have to have a way of retaining information in the mind, so that we can bring it back to awareness again when we need it. So a part of the research into the psychology of memory has been concerned with studying **representation** — how information is represented in the brain, as it is stored.

For the most part, the kinds of memories that we are aware of using in everyday life involve four different modes of representation. One of these is one that we have already looked at: when information is stored in complete meaningful units, like concepts and schemas. The other three are also interesting, particularly because we can see how they develop as we grow older.

Enactive representation

When an infant is first born, it has a lot to learn, and a great deal of that learning is something to do with the body. A baby needs to learn how to move its arms, legs, eyes and head when it wants to, and it needs to make sense of the different sensations and feelings it experiences. Since actions and feelings are the central part of the child's interaction with its world, its memories tend to be stored as impressions of actions — as 'muscle memories'. This is known as **enactive representation**.

It is possible to see babies using this enactive representation, as they repeat actions which have given them an effect — like moving a hand as if they were hitting a rattle, even though the rattle is not there. You, too, are likely to have some memories stored using enactive representation. Imagine the feel of a Waltzer, or a roller-coaster, and the chances are you will get an impression of how it felt on the muscles of your body. That is enactive representation. Adults can use it too, but they have other ways of storing information as well.

Iconic representation

One of those other ways is known as **iconic representation**. This involves storing information as images, like pictures, or images of sounds. Iconic representation first develops as the young child's world begins to expand, and they encounter some kinds of information which cannot really be stored using muscle memories. When you are reading a book, for instance, or watching television, the muscle actions which you use are much the same. But the information you are receiving can be quite different. So the brain needs to develop additional ways of storing information.

Children tend to use iconic imagery a great deal. They remember what things looked like, very clearly, and sometimes even photographically. About one child in ten has **eidetic imagery** — visual memory which is so clear that it is almost photographic. But this usually disappears with puberty, and the number of adults with eidetic memory is estimated to be less than one in ten thousand.

One of the reasons why it seems to disappear is because iconic memory is much less flexible and adaptable than other ways of remembering. Bruner and Kenney (1966) showed that children who used iconic imagery could remember a particular pattern of glasses, arranged on a grid in ascending size and order (Fig. 6.6) quite accurately. But when they were asked to describe what they would look like if the order was reversed, they could not do it.

Symbolic representation

Children who used symbolic representation, though, could do it quite easily. Symbolic representation involves remembering things by using symbols to represent the information in the mind. We actually learn this from a very early age: numbers, for instance, are symbols, and we use those to remember many different kinds of information. But as we approach adulthood, symbolic representation becomes more important, because it is much more flexible and adaptable than iconic imagery. It also lets us remember abstract information, which cannot be visualised very easily.

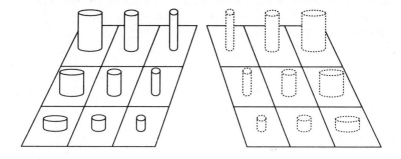

Figure 6.6 Bruner and Kenney's experiment

So by the time we are approaching adulthood, we have a number of ways of remembering which are available to us. We can use enactive representation, iconic representation, symbolic representation, or schemas, as well as some more specific modes which we do not have space to look at here. We draw on each of these as we need to, because each of them works best with remembering different types of information.

What makes a good memory?

There are times, though, when the type of representation which we choose to use makes a great deal of difference to whether we remember things or not. You may have wondered what makes a good memory, and why some people seem to have good memories while others do not. A very large part of that answer is to do with the way that we go about storing the information in the first place.

Whenever we store information, we process it in some way. At the very least, we are changing it from an external stimulus in the outside world to an internal, mental form, and sometimes we change it a great deal more than that. We might, for instance, change something from a verbal form, of words, into a visual form, like a diagram or a picture, and remember it that way. Or we might hear someone say something, and store it in terms of the meaning of what they have said — linking it with other things that we have met which have similar meanings, and so on. All this is mental processing of the information.

Levels of processing

What is particularly interesting is that the **level of processing** that we do affects how well we remember things. People who have bad memories — or who think they have — are people who tend to try to remember things passively, accepting the information but not trying to process it mentally. People who have good memories are people who process the information that they receive. They think about it, work out what it means, and examine how it links with other things that they already know. By the time they've done that, they know it, and can remember it.

In fact, all of us have extremely good memories — for things that we are interested in! Even someone who thinks they have a bad memory has no problem remembering their social life, and what has been happening lately among their friends — because they are interested in it. But usually, they find it difficult to remember schoolwork and other information because they are not all that interested in it, and so they do not process it much.

And that, of course, becomes circular, because schoolwork can only become interesting when you do think about it and link it with other things that you have learned. People who are 'good at school' do this automatically. People who are not generally have not learned the trick of making themselves interested. It can change, though — a lot of people learn how to make themselves interested by following up details and thinking about implications. When they do that, they find that the subject is much more interesting than they thought it was.

Interest and motivation

Being interested in something can make a dramatic difference to how well you remember it. In one classic study, Morris *et al.* (1981) asked people to remember a list of words and numbers — a single number attached to each word — which was read out to them. They had two groups of people participating in their study. One group was not particularly interested in what they were doing, but tried to remember the list anyway. The other group was really, deeply interested in it. When they were tested to see how many items from the list they could remember, the group which was really interested remembered far more then the others.

The reason why they were so interested was because they were very keen football supporters, and this was Saturday afternoon. They had agreed to come along to the researcher's laboratory, and were hearing the results of that day's matches read out on the radio. So, as they listened, they were thinking about each result: about how it fitted into the overall picture, and what difference it would make to that team's league position. In other words, they were processing the information. The others, who were not particularly keen on football, just listened and tried to remember, but they did not process the information as much, which is why they did not remember as many.

The researchers made sure that the two groups were just as good at remembering things by giving them another set of scores to remember, which had been made up. Then, the football supporters were just as bad at remembering as the others. It was because they knew that these were real results that they put the effort into processing the information in the first place.

So, if you want to try to improve your memory, there's the answer. Do not just try to remember things passively: process them. Change the form of the information in some way: use iconic imagery to change it into pictures, or change it into symbolic form. Fit it into your schemas and concepts, by working out what it means and why it matters. You'll be surprised how much you can remember when you do that.

In this chapter, we have taken a brief look at some of cognitive psychology. There is much more which could be said: psychologists have been studying memory for over 100 years now, for instance, and we know a great deal about it. But in a book like this, all we can really do is look at some of the psychological findings which are most helpful in understanding human beings in their everyday lives. In the next chapter, we will go on to look at how people learn things, and at what we mean by the idea of intelligence.

7
—— LEARNING ——

Human beings learn all the time. Indeed, our capacity to learn seems to be one of the main things which distinguishes us from other animals. Not the fact that we can learn at all — other animals can also learn, and those which are closest to us in evolutionary terms can learn a tremendous amount. But human beings seem to have an even greater capacity for learning than any of these other animals. Their ability to learn may be the same type of thing, but we have more of it.

—— Infant learning ——

From its very earliest days, a young infant is learning to handle its world. At first, that learning is largely about being able to control its body movements, and to make sense out of the information which it is receiving through its senses. But as the infant continues to develop, it also continues to learn. What it knows about its world becomes more sophisticated, and its competence in handling it develops throughout childhood. That applies both to social skills and to the physical and co-ordination skills which form the basis of effective human action.

Adaptation

Human infants, then, are born particularly prepared to learn. Moreover, there are some significant features of the ways that they respond to what is around them which encourage this. We have already looked at some of these earlier in this book. One of the most important ones, which we looked at in Chapter 2, is that of **adaptation**. A human infant is able to adapt to a tremendous range of physical environments, child-rearing practices, and, as it grows older, diet. As long as it has a good quality of social interaction, and adequate physical care, an infant is likely to adapt and develop.

Transactions

Part of what enables the infant to adapt so well is its ability to learn. Infants are strongly predisposed to learn, and part of that predisposition involves responding very strongly to certain types of events. One such type of event is to do with **transactions**: exchanges with other people which allow them to take turns and to learn about social interactions. As we saw in Chapter 2, transactions are a very important way that a young infant learns about its social world, and acquires the basis for social interaction in later life.

Contingencies

Another very special mechanism of learning for the infant is learning about **contingencies**. Contingencies are events which are more likely to happen after a particular action has been made: making a car move along a road is contingent on starting the engine; winning a jackpot on a fruit machine is contingent on putting in money and pulling the handle. In the same way that infants are particularly interested in other people, so also they are particularly responsive to things which are contingent on their own actions. If they can make something happen by, say, hitting it, they will do it over and over again.

This is the reason why babies like rattles, and other things which they can do to produce a noise. When the baby discovers that waving its hand around causes the rattle to sound, it explores that effect, and continues to practise it over and over again. In this way, it gradually gains control over the situation. Infants become fascinated when they find that they can do something which makes something else happen — and this interest means that they continue to try to master the skill. In other words, human beings are strongly predisposed to learn from contingencies: it is an important basis for skill learning.

Discrepancy

Another aspect of the young child's learning is that infants also become very interested in moderate amounts of **discrepancy** between what they expect and what actually happens. Part of the infant's learning about its environment involves learning what to expect under different circumstances. As it continues to develop, part of what stimulates further learning is when the results of something are not quite the same as they have been in the past.

Of course, it is only a moderate amount of discrepancy which is helpful to the child's learning. If everything suddenly changes, then all of the child's carefully acquired competence in dealing with its environment has been lost, which does not help it much. But a moderate amount of discrepancy is very good, even for relatively young children. For example, if an infant is staying with a grandparent or other relative, many aspects of its daily routine will be the same, but some will be different. Those differences allow the child to explore new contingencies and transactions, and so help it to broaden its understanding of the world.

Developing competence

All of these mechanisms work together to help the young infant, and later child, to develop **competence** in its dealing with the world. Perhaps the most important principle of child-rearing of all, in psychological terms, is that child development should be a continuous process of developing competence and effectiveness, in dealing with whatever happens. We have already seen how feeling helpless is stressful to human beings. Feeling competent is the opposite: when we feel that we can deal with our world adequately, we thrive, both mentally and physically.

As we saw in Chapter 5, when we feel competent we are more likely to cope with problems, to make efforts to overcome difficulties, and to be successful in the end. So a child who has been brought up to interact competently in its world — who has experienced appropriate kinds of transactions, contingencies and enough discrepancy to keep stimulating its interest in learning more — is a child who is better equipped to deal with problems and disappointments which it may encounter in later life than one who has not had those experiences.

Many of the damaging effects of the experience of refugee children, those who have suffered abuse from adults whom they trusted, and others with traumatic experiences, come from the feelings of helplessness and futility as the child's safe, secure world is torn apart. Not all of it, of course: there are other sources of psychological damage in those situations as well. But enough that it takes a great deal of love, safety and help before the child, or adult, feels secure and competent enough to begin a personal and emotional recovery.

We can see, then, what sort of situations stimulate an infant to learn. But how, exactly, do we go about learning things? As we have seen, human beings are complex, and operate on a number of different levels. Learning, too, can take place on several different levels. As human beings, we have several different kinds of learning available to us, and each kind is appropriate for different aspects of our experience. In the rest of this chapter, we will look at several different aspects of the way that people learn, before going on to look at how modern psychologists see the general abilities and knowledge which we think of as intelligence.

Association learning

One of the most basic forms of learning of all, and one which is shared by other animals too, is known as association learning. Association learning is sometimes called **conditioning**, on the grounds that it is all about producing a particular response under particular conditions. It is not really a 'thinking' type of learning at all. Instead, it is where we have learned to make an automatic response to some outside event or stimulus. That response is even controlled by the lower parts of the brain, and sometimes directly by the spinal cord, rather than by the cerebral cortex, which is part of the brain which is concerned with thinking and decisions.

Classical conditioning

There are two main types of conditioning, known as classical conditioning and operant conditioning. Classical conditioning is the purest form of association learning, and it also seems to be the most primitive kind of learning of all. Even an animal as simple as a flatworm can learn to turn left rather than right at a junction if it is trained using classical conditioning — and a flatworm does not even have a brain, just a kind of grid of nerve cells running through its body.

The most famous examples of classical conditioning were conducted by Pavlov, in 1927. Pavlov observed that the dogs he was studying would begin to produce saliva when they saw the lab assistant bringing their food to them. This interested him, because salivation is a reflex — a response controlled by the lower part of the brain, which occurs automatically in response to an appropriate stimulus. Reflexes are basic survival responses — jerking your hand away from a hot object is also a reflex — but they are nothing to do with thinking or recognition. So the fact that the dogs salivated when they saw the lab assistant was interesting, because it suggested that they had learned to make a connection between the sight of the assistant and dinner.

Pavlov reasoned that the dogs must have learned by association. In which case, they would be able to associate a different stimulus with salivation, too. He experimented by sounding a bell each time food was placed in front of the dogs. After a while, the dogs would produce saliva whenever they heard the bell, even if there was no food nearby. The dogs had become conditioned to salivate when they heard the bell.

Conditioning human beings

Classical conditioning works in human beings, too. One of the best examples of this was a study conducted by Menzies, in 1937. It concerned the reflex which we call **vasoconstriction**. This is something which the body does automatically when it is cold. In order to retain heat, the blood vessels near the surface of the skin shrink, while those in the middle of the body enlarge. That is why your skin will go paler when you are cold. It is an automatic reflex, and one which we cannot control deliberately.

Menzies asked research participants to plunge their arms into a bucket of ice-cold water, and each time they did so, a buzzer sounded. As you might expect, the cold water produced vasoconstriction. What was even more interesting, though, was that after a few trials the vasoconstriction was also produced when the people heard the buzzer. It had become conditioned to the sound of the buzzer.

We can see, then, that classical conditioning can work even on responses which we do not consciously control. Vasoconstriction is an autonomic response — in other words, it is controlled by the **autonomic** nervous system. As we saw in Chapter 3, many of our emotional reactions are also controlled by the autonomic nervous system, and this may be why we sometimes find that emotional reactions can be triggered off suddenly by an unexpected event or situation.

Treating phobias

Certainly, **phobias** — extreme fears which interfere with a person going about their ordinary life — seem to have a lot to do with classical conditioning. They may have been formed by a learned connection between the object and a fear response in the past — many people become frightened of spiders or wasps, for instance, because as small children they see adults responding in a frightened kind of way, and they imitate them.

Phobias are often kept alive and strengthened by the person imagining the feared object, and frightening themselves at the thought. Each time someone does this, they are strengthening the link between fear and the object, through classical conditioning. But classical conditioning can also be used to break a phobia, if it is deliberately used to make new associations with the object.

One method for doing this is called **systematic desensitisation**. In this method, the person gradually learns to relax in the presence of the object. They begin with something very indirect and non-threatening, like, say, a picture of the object, and learn to relax while looking at it. Once they can do this, they move to a slightly closer stimulus, like a realistic photograph of the object, and learn to relax again. Since you cannot relax and feel frightened at the same time, what this method does is to replace the conditioned fear response with a learned relaxation response; and by doing this, the phobia disappears.

Another approach is much more direct. As we saw in Chapter 3, the fear response is all about getting as much energy available as possible. So it is very demanding of the body's resources, and it is hard for us to keep it up for long. After a while, the physiological fear reaction dies away, and we calm down, even if we are still in the presence of the thing that we are frightened of. So another approach to treating phobias, known as **implosion therapy**, is simply for the person to be placed in a room with the thing that they are frightened of until the fear goes. It may sound unpleasant, but it works — and it is much quicker than desensitisation methods are!

One-trial learning

Classical conditioning, as we have seen, is often to do with survival. That applies particularly to a very strong kind of classical conditioning which you have probably experienced at one time or another. If you have ever eaten something which made you sick, the chances are you will not want to eat that thing again — even several years later. This is a particularly powerful kind of classical conditioning, known as **one-trial learning**.

It is actually a very old survival response. After all, if something you eat makes you sick, the odds are that it is poisonous. Being sick is your body's way of trying to get rid of things which are dangerous. So avoiding things which have made you sick would help you to survive, particularly if you were living by foraging in the wild. One-trial learning is not unique to human beings: all mammals seem to have it. It is a survival trait for other animals, too.

Operant conditioning

The other main type of association learning is known as **operant conditioning**. In this type of conditioning we learn something because it is immediately followed by a pleasant effect. That pleasant effect is sometimes a direct reward. For example, a squirrel will learn to climb a pole to reach a bird-feeding tray and gain the food. Sometimes, though, the pleasant effect comes from the removal of something unpleasant. An animal might learn to press a lever in order to avoid receiving an electric shock; or a schoolgirl might do her homework purely in order to avoid getting into trouble the next day.

Reinforcement

These two types of pleasant effect are both known as **reinforcement** — because they reinforce, or strengthen, the behaviour that we have learned. The kind where we receive a reward is called **positive reinforcement,** whereas the kind where we escape from, or avoid, something unpleasant is known as **negative reinforcement.** Both positive and negative reinforcement have to happen immediately after the particular action which is being learned. Conditioning does not work if they happen later — if we do learn from delayed rewards, it is a different type of learning.

Sometimes, people confuse negative reinforcement and punishment. But really the two are quite different. Both positive and negative reinforcement are about training a person or animal to do something — they encourage a particular kind of behaviour. But punishment is about stopping the person or animal from doing something, not about encouraging them to do something else. It is a bit confusing, because the threat of punishment can sometimes act as negative reinforcement, but the punishment itself never does.

The psychologist who became known as the 'father' of operant conditioning, B. F. Skinner, insisted that punishment was a very bad way of training children — or animals, for that matter — because all it did was to try to stop them from doing something, but it did not give them any idea of what they ought to be doing instead. Skinner believed it was better to train children using operant conditioning, because that way they were encouraged to do the right kinds of things.

Training autistic children

Operant conditioning has been used in a number of different ways, including training severely autistic children to talk by rewarding them for making noises and then words using rewards of pieces of fruit. Many of these methods used the principle of **behaviour shaping,** which allows us to use operant conditioning to produce entirely new types of actions. In behaviour shaping, a new action is trained by gradually changing what needs to be done to earn the reward.

For example, at the beginning of training, if an autistic child who is normally silent makes a noise, that would be enough to earn a reward. After a while, the child would come to make noises more often. Once the child was making noises, the psychologist or parent would only reward them when they made noises which sounded a little like words. Once they had learned that, then they would only be rewarded for making proper words. Eventually, the rewards would have 'shaped' the child's behaviour until it was saying proper words, even though at first it had been unable to speak.

Of course, we do not have to produce a reward every time. In fact, learning is generally stronger if the reward only comes now and again. This is known as partial reinforcement. People who play fruit machines are a classic example of how human behaviour can be manipulated by **partial reinforcement**: they will often play for hours (if they can afford it), only receiving a reward now and again. *Gameboy* machines and video games do not give money rewards, but they do give a strong sense of achievement when we get a bit further each time. It is carefully calculated to make sure that we get enough rewards to continue playing with the machine.

Conditioning and society

In 1972, Skinner went on to argue that society as a whole should develop systematic ways of conditioning people into behaving appropriately. People were always conditioned by the reinforcements around them, he argued, but these reinforcements act in a random, haphazard manner. If society were to take control of these reinforcements, it would be better than the random, unplanned approach, because then people would be trained to meet society's needs, and would not act in anti-social ways.

As you might imagine, this caused a considerable amount of debate. The real core of the argument was that Skinner, along with many of the other behaviourists, believed that all human learning and personality came from conditioning. So there was no such thing as 'freedom' or 'dignity' — they were just an illusion. Even language, Skinner argued, was only 'verbal behaviour', and had developed simply through conditioning and association.

Other psychologists, and people from other professions too, disagreed. They argued that people do have free will, and they are able to make real choices. Conditioning, they argued, is only one part of what it is to be human. As we have seen in the other chapters of this book, there are other sources of personality and personal growth. Being human is much more than just being manipulated by reinforcements.

——— Other forms of learning ———

Like almost everything else that human beings do, learning can be understood as having several different levels. Classical conditioning is probably the most basic level of all types of learning, and operant conditioning comes next. But there are other levels too. Some of these are to do with learning ways of behaving, while others are to do with understanding the world around us.

Imitation and modelling

One of the main psychologists exploring alternatives to conditioning was Albert Bandura. Bandura was particularly interested in how we learn by imitating others. **Imitation** is an important form of learning, because it is a kind of short-cut. If we learned everything through operant and classical conditioning, we would have to do everything by trial and error — doing it, and seeing what the consequences are. But life is too short for that. Using imitation, we can learn much more quickly.

Bandura performed a number of studies showing how people learned through imitation, and who they were most likely to imitate. In one well-known study (Bandura and Walters 1963), young children saw someone in a playroom with a lot of toys. The person was acting aggressively towards a bobo doll — a kind of doll which rocks backwards and forwards when it is hit. Some of the children saw the scene in real life, some saw it on film, and some saw a cartoon version. After they had seen this, they were then let into the same playroom, and left to play with the toys.

After a while, the experimenters came in and removed the toys that the children were playing with. This was to make the children feel aggrieved, and frustrated, so that they would be more likely to act aggressively. Then they observed how the children acted. Table 7.1 shows the average number of aggressive actions towards the bobo doll which children made during the next 20 minutes. As you can see, those children who had not seen anyone acting aggressively did not make as many aggressive acts as those who had seen aggression being modelled.

TABLE 7.1	AGGRESSIVE ACTS PERFORMED TOWARDS A BOBO DOLL	
Situation	**Average number of aggressive acts**	
Real-life model	83	
Filmed model	92	
Cartoon model	99	
Model playing unaggressively with toys	54	
(Adapted from Bandura and Walters 1963)		

When the children's actions were analysed more carefully, so that the researchers could tell which were specific copies of what the model had done, Bandura and Walters found that it was the real-life model which was copied most closely. In other studies, Bandura found that children were most likely to imitate models like themselves — other children in preference to adults, people of the same gender, and so on. They also were more likely to imitate people they admired.

Latent learning

But the most important finding of all, at least as far as psychology was concerned, was that what children had learned from the model did not necessarily show up straight away. It remained latent, until it was needed. A child could see someone acting aggressively, and not seem to copy it at all. But later, if it was in a situation where acting aggressively looked as though it would be useful, the child would act out the behaviour it had learned from the model. Children store what they have learned, and only use it when the time seems right.

This is an important finding, for two reasons. The first, of course, is what it suggests to us about the influence of violence on television, and we will be looking at that a bit more closely in Chapter 10. But it is also important in terms of our general understanding of how learning happens. Skinner and the other behaviourists had seen learning as an immediate change in behaviour. But Bandura showed that we can learn things even if we do not change our behaviour straight away. We can store our experience, and use it later.

Cognitive learning

In fact, Bandura was not the only person to have shown how we store our experience and use it later. As early as 1932, Tolman had shown how experimental rats can develop **cognitive maps**, so that they had a mental pattern of what a maze looked like. Tolman gave a set of rats the opportunity to explore a complicated maze. If they were just put in the maze, they would simply wander around. But if they were put in the maze and given a reward for getting out of it quickly, they would make their way straight to the exit point, showing that they could use what they had learned from their explorations.

Human beings use cognitive maps too. Learning our way around somewhere new is often a matter of joining up apparently disconnected places, until we have a mental map which makes sense to us. We organise our cognitive maps in terms of landmarks, such as special buildings that we have particularly noticed. Often, too, we only have a vague idea of the distances between these landmarks. Briggs (1971) found that we under-estimate familiar distances, so they seem shorter. But we over-estimate distances that we do not know very well. That is why, when you go somewhere new, distances often seem very large, but they shrink as you get to know the place.

Insight learning

Imitation and cognitive maps are both cognitive forms of learning, in that they involve remembering and thinking, rather than just linking a stimulus with a response. There are other types of cognitive learning, too. One of these is known as **insight learning**. In this, we learn something new by suddenly understanding its underlying principles. We might solve a maths problem, for instance, by getting a sudden insight into how we should reach the solution — why the problem is like it is.

Animals can show insight learning too. In 1925, Köhler reported a study with a number of different chimpanzees. One of them, Sultan, was particularly good at insight learning. He would be given a problem to solve, such as how to get at a piece of fruit hanging high above his head out of reach. A number of boxes would be scattered about in the cage. In one typical trial, Sultan dragged a box under the fruit and tried to reach it but it was still out of reach. After a few unsuccessful jumps, he would seem to give up. But then, suddenly, he would go to the other boxes and begin to pile them up until they were high enough for him to reach the fruit. He had solved the problem by getting a sudden insight about what he needed to do.

Learning sets

Some researchers argued that the chimpanzees in Köhler's study were not actually thinking at all. Instead, they had simply learned from a lot of experience with trial and error learning. Harlow (1949) showed that monkeys could develop what he called **learning sets** — a readiness to solve a particular type of problem, rather than just learn a single answer. By rewarding a monkey with a raisin or a peanut each time it solved an odd-one-out problem, Harlow showed that monkeys could learn to look for the odd one, instead of just choosing the object which had hidden the reward on the last occasion.

Harlow took this as evidence that simple trial-and-error learning was all that an animal really needed to produce what seemed to be insight. But it can just as well be taken as evidence that animals, too, can develop concepts. It would be very difficult to draw a clear line between a learning set and the type of stored experience which is contained in the concepts and schemas that we looked at in the last chapter.

Schemas

As we saw in Chapter 6, schemas, too, are an important way that human beings learn. We fit new experiences into what we already know, and try to make sense out of them that way. Sometimes we are successful, and the new experience fits into our existing schemas without anything needing to change much. That learning process is known as **assimilation** — where an existing schema is applied to a new situation.

Sometimes, though, the new experience which we have does not fit into our previous schemas very well. When that happens, the schema has to change, as it adjusts itself to the new information. That is known as **accommodation**. Some psychologists and educationists see accommodation as being the basis of all cognitive learning: we develop our understanding by extending and adjusting our existing ideas.

Skill learning

Not all types of learning are to do with absorbing new information. A great deal of the learning that we do is concerned with learning skills — both physical skills and mental ones. And one of the main features of skill learning is that when we are skilled at doing something, we do not think about it.

Whether we think about what we are doing or not is what distinguishes experts from learners. A skilled skater does not think about balancing his body, but someone new to skating thinks about it all the time. A fluent reader does not have to look at each word in a sentence: instead, she usually only looks directly at one or two words in the middle of the sentence, and recognises the others instantly by their shape. Someone who is not very good at reading, though, has to read every single word. A skilled driver does not have to think what to do when changing gears to turn a corner, but a learner tries to remember everything at once, and often gets very flustered as a result.

Automatising actions

All of these skills are different, but they all have one thing in common. That is, that the individual units of the skill have become **automatised**. The person does them automatically, without thinking about it. Because they do not have to think about specific actions, that leaves the person free to concentrate on other aspects of what they are doing — like thinking about their complete performance in a skating display, or the meaning of the story they are reading, or about the best route to follow.

An action which has been automatised is actually controlled by a different part of the brain than an action which we have to think about. The **cerebrum** is the part of the brain which we think with. It also has areas which receive information from our different senses, including the body; and an area which is used for deliberate movement — when we consciously decide to move a particular part of the body. That area is known as the **motor area**, and as you can see from Fig. 7.1, it is the top of the brain, next to the **sensory area**, which receives bodily feelings.

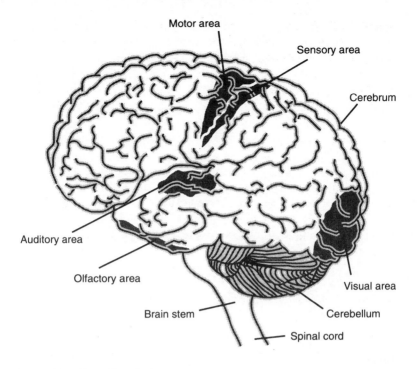

Figure 7.1 Areas of the brain

But the area of the brain which co-ordinates skilled movements is not in the cerebrum at all. Instead, it is an entirely separate part of the brain, known as the **cerebellum**. The cerebellum is still concerned with deliberate movements, but it co-ordinates all the little actions which are involved so that they happen smoothly. If you decide to take a drink from a cup, for example, you do not think about reaching out, closing your fingers around the cup, and so on. All you think, if you think about it at all, is that you'd like a drink. The cerebellum co-ordinates all the actions needed to make that happen.

When a set of actions becomes automatised, control moves from the cerebrum to the cerebellum. A learner driver coming up to a corner has to think about the actions needed for signalling, braking, changing gear, turning the wheel and looking out for other traffic all at the same time, because these actions are all single, conscious ones being controlled by the cerebrum. We become flustered because it is a lot to think of all at once. But as we get more practised, the physical actions gradually weld themselves into a fluent unit, which is controlled by the cerebellum. That leaves the cerebrum free, so it can concentrate on looking out for other traffic, and can be alert for anything unexpected which might happen.

Skills become automatised through practice. The more we do a set of actions, the more likely we are to link those actions into a complete, fluent movement that we do not have to think about. We can automatise mental abilities as well as physical actions: not only reading, but other mental abilities too, like the ability to do arithmetical calculations or to recognise patterns. With enough practice, people can become fluent in many different mental skills. And it is generalised mental skills which we are talking of when we talk about the human quality known as intelligence.

Intelligence

Intelligence is a difficult thing to define. Everyone knows what they mean when they say the word, but it is hard to pin down that meaning exactly. Perhaps the best definition anyone has been able to come up with was from the psychologist Alice Heim, who said: 'Intelligence consists of grasping the essentials in a situation and responding appropriately to them.' It may not be a very specific definition, but it does seem to carry the general meaning which we think of them we think of intelligence.

Psychologists have been studying intelligence throughout this century, although for the first fifty years that research was seriously distorted by political and social influences. These distortions occurred mainly because of some influential psychologists who believed in eugenics: the idea that people who were genetically inferior should not be allowed to reproduce, because they would weaken the species.

It was an old-fashioned idea, stemming partly from a limited view of evolutionary theory, but mainly from the nineteenth-century belief that people inherited their abilities and characters — and also their position in society — and that these could not, and should not, be changed. But it was a vicious idea too. It formed the ideological basis of several political atrocities, including the Nazi concentration camps, restricted immigration for certain groups of people, and compulsory sterilisation laws for those who did not achieve a certain IQ level in some American states.

Temperament and potential

Nowadays, most psychologists take a much more positive view of the human being. We are aware that inheritance provides us with potential — for example, that each infant has a different **temperament**. But we are also aware that the potential is shaped and guided by our subsequent experience. A child which is born with a physically active, fidgety temperament can develop in many different ways, depending on social factors. For example, it will depend whether the family sees its temperament as a positive thing, so that the child is encouraged to explore and develop its skills, or whether they see it as a nuisance, and try to make the child learn to be quiet and restrained.

In other words, the same temperament can develop into very different personality traits depending on how people respond to it. Also, as we have seen, people continue to grow and develop psychologically, throughout life. So to speak of genetic influence as if it were a fixed thing, setting some kind of top limit to our potential, is an idea which has become increasingly implausible as we have discovered more about the mechanisms by which people adapt and develop, throughout adulthood as well as in childhood.

Intelligence tests

Psychologists do, though, use intelligence tests sometimes. Not because they measure the limit of our intelligence (you can get better at intelligence tests, too, if you practise them) but because they can help us to know a bit more about that person. Intelligence tests may not tell us exactly how intelligent someone is, but they do tell us how well-developed certain of their skills are. Some skills — like the ability to comprehend words quickly and accurately — are skills which we often need to do a particular type of job.

There are two kinds of intelligence tests: group tests and individual tests. Group tests are usually pencil and paper tests, which consist of several different problems that the person has to solve as quickly as possible. Because they are done in conditions a bit like an exam, it is possible for several people to be tested at once, and they are often used for selection to courses or some kinds of career opportunities, like the civil service.

Individual tests, though, involve a psychologist seeing just one person, and presenting each part of the test to them individually. They consist of lots of varied tasks, each of which assesses different mental skills, and so they are often useful for helping to understand people who are having specific difficulties, perhaps with learning, or sometimes in coping with their day-to-day lives.

But no psychologist nowadays would see an intelligence test, on its own, as giving enough information to make a decision about whether somebody was suitable for a job or a course. Intelligence tests, like other psychometric tests, have to be used along with interviews and records of achievement: they are not accurate enough to be the basis for decision-making all on their own.

Theories of intelligence

We actually use the word intelligent to mean a lot of different things. Sometimes we are talking about someone who is very quick to grasp things and make decisions. Sometimes, though, we are talking about someone who is a 'deep thinker', and who can see into problems more deeply than the rest of us would. And sometimes we are talking about someone who can be quick-witted and humorous in conversation. Each of these is what we would think of as intelligence, but they are actually very different.

Intelligence as multiple abilities

There are two significant ways of looking at intelligence in modern psychology. One of them is to look at intelligence as consisting of a number of different abilities. Gardner (1986) proposed that there is not a single thing called intelligence, but that what we are actually referring to is a set of seven entirely different intelligences. The seven types of intelligence are listed in Table 7.2.

TABLE 7.2 GARDNER'S SEVEN DIFFERENT INTELLIGENCES
1. **Linguistic intelligence** – to do with language and how we use it.
2. **Musical intelligence** – to do with musical appreciation as well as performing and composing music.
3. **Mathematical-logical intelligence** – to do with calculation and logical reasoning.
4. **Spatial intelligence** – to do with art and design, as well as finding your way around.
5. **Bodily-kinaesthetic intelligence** – to do with physical skills, like sport, dancing, and other aspects of movement.
6. **Interpersonal intelligence** – to do with interacting with people socially and sensitively.
7. **Intrapersonal intelligence** – to do with understanding your own personal self and abilities.

Each of these types, according to Gardner, acts completely separately. Most people that we would call 'intelligent' have a combination of these different abilities, but some are particularly good at only one or two, and not at the others. A musical genius, for example, would have one type of intelligence very highly developed, but might be quite ordinary in other respects. What we call an 'idiot savant' is someone who is well below average intelligence in most respects, but has one outstanding ability — to remember, or to calculate. Gardner's idea of separate intelligences shows how that may be possible.

One problem with Gardner's approach, though, is that it tends to treat these separate intelligences as if they just developed within the person, and have nothing to do with social influences. Although he drew much of his evidence from the biographies of high-achieving people, Gardner ignored the social influences on them. But people who attain outstanding ability in any area have usually had at least one person who believed in them, and encouraged them. Some psychologists believe that this influence may be more important than we realise.

The triarchic theory of intelligence

The other way of looking at intelligence is to see it as nested very firmly within its social and cultural context. Sternberg (1986) developed what became known as the **triarchic theory of intelligence**. He identified three different aspects of intelligence, each of which contributes to how intelligently we interact with other people.

The first facet of intelligence is **contextual intelligence**. Any intelligent act or ability, Sternberg said, takes place within a context. It happens in a society and a culture, and that makes all the difference to how the act or ability is regarded. For instance, imagine someone who is particularly quick at responding to something which is said to them. In one culture, that might be regarded as a sign of intelligence; but in another culture, it might be seen as a sign of impulsiveness and lack of thought. A slower, more thoughtful way of responding would be seen as being more intelligent. So one part of intelligence is to do with how the person responds to the demands and expectations of their culture.

The second facet of intelligence which Sternberg identified is **experiential intelligence**. In the last chapter we saw how experiences and expectations affect the way that we think, perceive and remember. We also learn from our experiences, and all this forms a significant part of our intelligence. Experience can influence intelligence in two ways: first, because of the automatised skills which we have developed, and secondly, because of the way that it helps us to recognise the demands of a particular situation, and what would be the best thing to do.

The third facet of intelligence is the one which is usually assessed by intelligence tests — or at least, by modern intelligence tests. Some of the early ones were very culturally biased, assuming that anyone who was not familiar with the practices of white American of English culture was automatically mentally inferior. But modern tests are much better at assessing what Sternberg called **componential intelligence**. Componential intelligence consists of three parts: first, our ability to learn and acquire knowledge; secondly, how well we actually carry out a task, like problem-solving or calculation; and thirdly, higher mental abilities like our ability to plan and make decisions.

So each part of componential intelligence contributes to how well we think and process information. But how we do it is also influenced strongly by our own personal experience, and by the cultural and social settings in which we find ourselves. Intelligence is not something which just happens in a social vacuum: it is part of social living. And different societies value different intellectual skills, which means that what we consider to be 'intelligent' behaviour also varies.

An adverb, not a noun

Some researchers, such as Rose, Kamin and Lewontin (1984), argue that part of the reason why people find so much difficulty defining what intelligence actually is, is because it is an adverb, not a noun. When we talk of someone being intelligent, what we really mean is that they are able to do something intelligently. They do things in a certain way, which is distinctive. These researchers question whether intelligence as a separate 'thing' actually exists at all. It is more a question of how we go about things, than a separate ability that we actually have. And it is probably more useful if we think of intelligence that way, because that means that we are much more likely to see intelligent actions in their context.

We have seen, then, that human beings can learn in some very different ways. As with all of the other aspects of psychology in this book, we have only been able to skim over some of the main areas — there are other forms of learning, too, and much more psychological research into these areas than we have been able to look at here. What is important, though, is to remember that as human beings we do not just use one way of learning. We can learn in a number of different ways, and sometimes even on several levels at once.

8

UNDERSTANDING OTHER PEOPLE

Social psychology is all about how people interact with and understand one another. In this chapter we will be looking at some of the most fundamental aspects of human social psychology. We will look at how we communicate with other people, why we sometimes help others and sometimes do not, and when we are likely to co-operate or obey. But we have already looked at several other aspects of social psychology in other chapters. For example, in Chapter 2 we looked at social identity theory and at how prejudice works, in Chapter 3 we looked at some of the social influences involved in our experience of emotion, and in Chapter 5 we looked at social motivation.

Co-operation and compliance

People are basically social animals, so other people are very important to us. Often we regulate what we do by imagining what other people would think if they knew about it. This form of social influence is very strong, even if we are alone, and nobody else would know. It becomes internalised, as a part of the way that our minds work. We do not actually have to see someone react to what we are doing: we use what we know about people to predict, or imagine, how they will respond.

The predictions we make are not always accurate, either. For example, people often avoid openly disagreeing with someone else, because they imagine that doing so will have more dramatic consequences than it really would. They think they might become upset or angry. In fact, we seem to spend a lot of time avoiding other people's imaginary anger, although if we do actually confront someone and disagree with them, it is not nearly as difficult as all that.

Conforming to the majority

Asch (1952) showed just how much we try not to disagree openly with other people. He set up a situation in which several people were asked to sit in the same room and to judge whether various lines they were shown were longer or shorter than a test line. Most of the people were actors, who had been told to give an answer which was obviously wrong. Only one unsuspecting person was the real research participant on each occasion. They could see what the right answer was, but they also heard all of the other people giving the same wrong answer. So they were forced into a situation where they either had to disagree with the others, or lie.

Even though they knew it was wrong, the research participants gave the same answer as the others about a third of the time. Also, Asch reported, whether they disagreed with the others or not, it was clear that even the thought of disagreeing was clearly very difficult. People became extremely nervous and tense just before it was their turn, and said later that they had only given the correct answer because they knew it was an experiment and they felt it was their duty to report it accurately.

A later study of the same thing, conducted by Perrin and Spencer (1980), found that fewer people actually lied, but that they all became just as anxious. Perrin and Spencer suggested that perhaps fewer people actually lied because modern people are less likely to conform. Other researchers, though, disputed this idea, on the grounds that they had found the 'Asch effect' to be as strong as ever when they too had repeated the study.

The debates about how much people actually conform and how much they do not continue. But all researchers have found that openly disagreeing with other people is something which is deeply stressful, and something which their research participants did as much because they believed it was important to tell the truth for the experiment as for any other reason. It is not at all easy for us to disagree openly with other people.

Minority influence

Sometimes, though, it is important to disagree. All of the great social reforms which took place in the eighteenth century, for instance, began as the dedicated campaigns of a handful of people who saw something as wrong, and did not let it rest. Slavery was widely accepted in Europe in the eighteenth century, for example, but as a result of consistent campaigning the slave trade was made illegal near the beginning of the nineteenth century, and the owning of slaves became illegal a few years later.

So it is clear that sometimes a minority can have quite a lot of influence. Moscovici and Nemeth (1974) showed that if just a few people stick to a particular view, which they are convinced is right, then they can have a great deal of influence on a larger group. The important thing, though, is that people who are in a minority and trying to influence the majority should be seen by the others to be consistent, and to be resisting social pressure. If we see people acting like that, we tend to become curious about why they are doing it, and so will tend to think more seriously about what they are saying than we might have done otherwise.

—— Understanding other people ——

All of this adds up to the idea that we spend quite a lot of time thinking about what other people are going to think. In other words, we are aware that other people have minds of their own, and we use our social experience to guess how they will use those minds. We develop what is known as a **theory of mind** — an awareness of other people as thinking, feeling individuals — which we use to interact effectively with other people.

The child's theory of mind

But how does that theory of mind develop? As most mothers know, a 2-year-old has little idea that other people have minds or needs of their own. Bringing up children at that age can often become a battle of wills, as the infant insists that the world must conform to its own demands, while the parent insists that the child must learn to act in socially acceptable ways. It can be an exhausting time, particularly because the child has no idea about how the other person might be feeling.

Yet by the age of 5, children are very well acquainted with the idea that other people may think differently from them, may have good and bad moods, and may be upset or made happy by the child's actions. It is obvious that something happens during this time which allows the child to become much more socially sensitive. Between the age of 3 and 4, the child develops its own theory of mind. It becomes aware that other people think and see the world differently, and that the child's own experience is not necessarily shared by everyone else.

Perner, Leekam and Wimmer (1987) looked at how 3-year-olds understand what other people believe. The 3-year-old would be in a room, aware that a friend was waiting outside. Then the child was shown a Smarties tube and asked what was in it. The child, naturally, would answer 'Smarties'. The tube was opened, and they saw that it actually contained a pencil and not chocolates. Then it was closed again, and the children were asked what their friend would think was in the box, if they came into the room now.

There was a difference in children's answers, depending on how old they were. Those who were just 3 gave one type of answer, whereas those who were nearly 4 gave a different one. The older children could predict what their friend would think, and said that the friend would believe that the box contained Smarties. But the younger children said that the friend would think that the box contained a pencil. Because they had not yet developed a theory of mind, they could not imagine that the friend would think differently.

Having a theory of mind — being able to put ourselves in someone else's place, mentally — is the basis for almost all social interaction. Harris (1989) discussed how this seems to be the problem with autistic children. They can often talk, and do everything that is needed for social interaction, and yet they do not interact socially. But they also fail on tests like the Smarties experiment. Harris suggested that autistic children simply do not have a theory of mind, which is why they cannot really communicate, or make contact, with anyone else.

Communication

The experience of autistic children shows us how one of the most important aspects of interaction is the way that we communicate with other people. Deliberate communication depends on being able to guess what the other person will think, so that we can make our message clear. If we do not know that the other person is thinking independently at all, we cannot engage in the give-and-take which conversation needs.

Non-verbal communication

Communication is not always deliberate, though. We pass information to one another in all sorts of ways, and sometimes we may not even realise that we have sent or received information. We influence other people by what we say, of course, but also by how we say it, and the context that we say it in. This is known as **non-verbal communication** — communication without words.

As a general rule, we use these aspects of communication automatically, without particularly thinking about them. For example: imagine that you were working in an office, and that one day you came into work and were told to go to the general manager's office. When you arrived there, you would be trying hard to understand what it is that the manager was trying to communicate to you. The first thing you would want to know, of course, is whether there was trouble coming. You might also be curious about the whole action, if it was unusual for the general manager to summon people like that.

There are several features of that situation which we would use as communication. In fact, the actual words that the manager said would be only a small part of what was being communicated. You would listen to them, of course, but you would also be taking notice of all of the other messages. We are all experts at non-verbal communication, even if we do not always realise it.

You would, for instance, be getting messages — consciously or unconsciously — from the body language which the manager was showing. You would notice whether she seemed angry, or tense, or worried, and you would pick upon that without any words being necessary. If she smiled at you as soon as you came through the door, you would be reassured, because that would be a message to tell you that you personally were not in trouble.

You would also be taking notice of the particular tone of voice which she used, because that is another important signal. Facial expressions, posture and gestures, and tones of voice are all important indicators of our feelings and attitudes. If you had been summoned to the general manager's office, it would be important for you to pick up on those feelings and attitudes, if only so that you could get some idea as to how you should be responding.

Signs and symbols

There are other messages in that situation too. Human life is full of signs and symbols which convey different meanings to us. For example, the fact that you were summoned to the general manager's office is in itself a message. There is communication in who says and does what, and to whom — usually a communication about power. If the general manager had come to see you, at your workplace, that would be an entirely different message, and it would be a signal that, on this occasion, the manager wanted issues of power to be left out of the discussion, or minimised. In the normal run of things, it would be the kind of message that someone might use if they wanted to consult with you, or gain your opinion.

Being summoned to the office is quite different. It is a message about who is in control of the interaction: who has the power. The same message is also communicated by the layout of the office, and where people sit in it. Typically, a general manager sits behind a large desk — a symbolic barrier, as well as a symbol of power — and has access to devices which will control the situation: telephones, secretarial intercoms and the like. The person who they want to talk to, however, has nothing like that to hand.

This example is only the tip of the iceberg. Non-verbal communication has been studied extensively by psychologists, because there are so many ways that we communicate messages to one another, and so many messages contained within any episode of human interaction.

Believing non-verbal signals

One of the most interesting findings has been that people tend to believe non-verbal communication far more easily than they believe the words that we actually say. In one study, Argyle, Alkema and Gilmour asked actors to communicate different messages to people. Then the people concerned were asked to tell someone else what they had been told. The actual words of the messages could have one of three meanings: friendly, hostile, or neutral. The non-verbal manner in which the actors delivered the messages could also be friendly, hostile or neutral.

Clearly, when the actor's manner and their words carried the same implications, there was little misunderstanding. But it was different when the actor's non-verbal communication contradicted what they actually said. When that happened, the researchers found that people were four times more likely to take notice of the non-verbal communication than of the actual words which were used!

Discourse analysis

It is apparent, then, that we are very ready to take in information of this kind, and that we consider it to be extremely important. But we do listen to what people say, as well. In fact, people often convey information in the way that they choose and use words, as well as non-verbally. Looking at the ways that people say things has become a major source of interest in psychology. It is known as **discourse analysis**, because the researchers who are doing it are analysing the pattern of discourse, or conversation, which is going on.

For example, Beattie and Speakman (1983) showed how people who are discussing something like politics or society often settle on a single type of metaphor, which helps them to picture the problems that they are discussing. The metaphor might involve something like describing the country's economy as if it were a sick person, by using phrases like 'an ailing economy' or the need for an 'injection' of capital, as if capital is a kind of medicine, which will help to 'cure' the problem.

The sickness metaphor is not the only one people can use. A different group of people might refer to the economy as if it were, say, a garden, and talk about 'cultivating growth', or 'pruning surplus expenditure'. That particular **metaphorical frame** for a conversation would lead to different conclusions from a metaphorical frame which was based on illness, because a garden is something which has to be consistently cared for and looked after, while an illness simply has to be cured and then it will look after itself. The metaphors actually contain different theories about what a 'normal' economy is like. So, by listening to the pattern of words which people use we can see more clearly how they understand the problem that they are discussing.

Attributions and explanations

Another part of discourse analysis involves looking directly at the reasons and explanations which people give for why things happen. This is part of understanding how we make sense out of our social experience. We do not just accept what happens to us passively — we try to work out why it has happened, and whether we could have done anything about it.

Finding a reason why something has happened often involves making decisions about intentions: did so-and-so do that deliberately, or was it just an accident? We also draw on our knowledge of other people, and on more general social explanations and assumptions, in forming these explanations. The process of ascribing reasons for why things happened and why people acted in certain ways is known as **attribution**.

In Chapter 3 we saw how the different kinds of attributions which people make can influence how they behave. People who are chronically depressed often have a depressive attributional style, which means that the explanations they give for why things happen are always the kind of explanations which will make them feel helpless and out of control. Other people tend to accept different kinds of explanations, which allow them to see themselves as able to act positively and to be in control of things.

One of the interesting things about how we use attributions is that we tend to judge other people's actions differently from the way we judge our own. When we are giving reasons for what we do, we make what are known as **situational attributions** — in other words, we give reasons which are to do with the situation. For example, Nisbett *et al.*, in 1973, asked college students to write a paragraph explaining why they had chosen to study their particular course at college. The students all gave situational reasons, such as saying that doing the course would help them to get a better job.

But when we are judging someone else's actions, we generally use **dispositional attributions** — we conclude that the reason why they are doing something is because of their personality or character. When the same students were asked to explain why their best friend had chosen to study that particular course, they gave dispositional reasons, such as, 'he's good at maths', or 'he likes studying rocks'.

Our tendency to make dispositional attributions about other people is very strong. It is known as the **fundamental attribution error**, and we do it even when we know that the situation is really the most important thing. Ross, Amabile and Steinmetz (1977) asked people to observe a quiz game. They also observed how the people playing the game were chosen: it was entirely random whether someone acted as a contestant or as the quizmaster. The quizmasters had free choice of subject, so they could choose topics that they knew about. But even though they knew that, the observers always judged the person asking the questions to have higher general knowledge than the contestant. They knew about the situational factors, but still believed that the person's disposition was more important.

Social representations

The types of reasons that we use to explain why things happen are not always entirely personal. Often, we will adopt explanations which are shared by other people as well, or which are held to be true by society in general. These shared explanations are known as **social representations**, and they can be a very powerful influence in society. A social representation is a kind of theory about why things happen, but it is shared by a lot of people, rather than just one individual.

The social representations that we share influence how we act. For example, in a study of medical social representations, Herzlich showed that some doctors tended to see all problems which were brought to them as having physical causes, while other doctors saw many problems as having psychological causes. The doctors recommended entirely different forms of treatment for the same kinds of problem, depending on which social representations they held.

Cultural differences in social representations

Social representations are also influential in determining social policy. For example, in Britain, the prevailing social representation is that people become criminals because of something inside themselves — because they are in some way inherently bad. This means that we tend to ignore, or discount, serious attempts to rehabilitate criminals, because we think it will not work. And even when we try a rehabilitation scheme, we do not usually give it enough time or resources for a long-term effect.

But other societies have different social representations. Unlike Britain, for instance, American society has a general social representation that people can change — that they do not stay the same all their lives. (That does not mean that everyone in America believes that, of course, but it means that most people do, or at least enough to influence social policy.) So in America, rehabilitation units attempt to develop serious re-education programmes, which will get criminals to change their ways.

I remember once being at a conference on child abuse, and watching an argument between an English woman and an American woman. The American woman ran a rehabilitation centre for young men who were sexual abusers of children. The centre had a very intensive treatment programme, which took several months if not years to complete. The programme was carefully worked out, and was very arduous to go through, but it also had a very high success rate.

The argument between the English woman and the American, though, was not about exchanging information. Essentially, it was a clash of social representations. The English woman simply did not believe that child sexual abusers could change their ways, and the American woman knew, from her own experience, that they could. So she became very frustrated with the discussion, and ended up almost jumping up and down (though not quite — it was a professional conference, after all) because she could not understand why she was unable to get her point across!

People who share different social representations often end up talking past one another, like this. Di Giacomo (1980) looked at the social representations which were held by student political leaders in a Belgian University in the 1970s, and compared them with the social representations which were shared by most of the ordinary students. Di Giacomo found that the two groups had very different social representations, and so they entirely failed to understand one another.

It was almost as if the student leaders were talking a different language from the ordinary students. They would use phrases like 'student–worker solidarity', but the majority of the ordinary students could not see what students and workers had in common at all. So, to them, the idea of solidarity between students and workers did not make much sense. As a result, when the student leaders tried to mobilise the students in a protest movement, they failed to get enough support for the movement to be successful.

Helping other people

How we explain things to ourselves also has quite an influence on how we interact with other people. For example, if we come across someone who is asking for help, whether we actually step in and help them or not depends on how we define the situation. If we conclude that the situation is not really serious, then we are much less likely to help the person than if we define it differently.

Darley and Latané conducted a study in which an actor went up to people passing by on the street, and asked them to give him ten cents. People responded differently, depending on what the actor said about why it was necessary. As you can see from Table 8.1, the more 'worthy' the person's cause seemed to be, the more likely people were to give him the money.

TABLE 8.1 REASONS FOR HELPING	
Reason	**% of people asked who gave money**
No reason given	34%
Money needed for a phone call	64%
Wallet stolen	70%
(Adapted from Darley and Latané 1970)	

The way that other people act influences whether we are likely to help others, as well. The same psychologists set up a situation in which people who were sitting in a waiting room heard a crash from the next room, and a woman's voice crying out for help. When someone was waiting alone, they were very likely to go into the next room to see if they could help — in fact, 70 per cent of the people in that situation did so. But if there were three other people in the waiting room as well, then they were much less likely to go and help. Only 40 per cent of the research participants would offer help under those conditions.

When they were interviewed afterwards, the people participating in the study said that they had taken their cues from the other people around. Because they seemed to be reasonably calm, the person had come to the conclusion that the situation was not really serious, and so had not bothered to do anything. They had redefined the situation to themselves, so that it seemed as though help was not really needed after all. Also, they felt that the responsibility for acting was somehow shared with the other people, so it was less important that they offered their personal help than it was when they were alone.

We can see, then, that whether we actually exert ourselves to go and help someone depends on how we explain what is going on to ourselves. Having an unclear situation, or having other people around, can make a difference. But, nonetheless, if we are sure that someone really does need help, we do tend to help them. In a study on the New York subway, Piliavin *et al.* found that commuters would usually help someone who collapsed on the train. If the person seemed to be ill, he was helped 95 per cent of the time, and even if he seemed to be drunk, people helped out on half of the occasions that he 'collapsed'.

Obedience

As we have seen earlier in this chapter, co-operating with other people is something which people tend to do almost automatically — at least when those other people are present. When we are away from other people, or after we have had time to think about it, whether we co-operate or not may be quite another matter. But the tendency is strong, and some studies show that even if other people are not present, we may still be likely to conform to what we think other people are saying.

In 1954, Crutchfield reported a study which was conducted during a management training session, with a number of military officers. It was a replication of the study by Asch, which we looked at earlier, in that people were asked to give the answers to a set of very easy problems, while believing that other people also taking part were all giving the same wrong answer.

In Crutchfield's study, though, the other people were not physically present. The research participants worked in booths, with a display of lights in front of them which supposedly told them the solution that the other people had chosen. (The lights were rigged, of course, so that they implied that the others had got the answer wrong.) But even though the other people doing the study were not actually there — so there was no need to confront them face to face — the research participants still conformed to the majority view half of the time.

Of course, it is always possible that this is a higher figure than we might normally get in those circumstances, because of the research participants all being military personnel. It is possible that, because of their training, they value conformity more than other people would. But, at the same time, they also value accurate perception, and knew that the answers they were giving were wrong. So it does seem as though our tendency to conform to other people is more than simply avoiding face-to-face interpersonal conflict.

Obeying authority

But what happens when that type of situation could mean that we end up doing something which is morally wrong? We usually obey authority figures, sometimes even if we disagree personally with what they are asking us to do. But will we obey them if they are asking us to, say, give someone a lethal electric shock? The social psychologist Milgram asked that question to a wide sample of psychologists, psychiatrists and other people, in the early 1960s. All of them were positive that only a very small minority of people — less than 3 per cent — would be prepared to kill or seriously harm another person in obedience to the demands of a psychological experiment.

So Milgram decided to set up the situation — at least so that people would believe their actions had been harmful, even though nobody would actually be hurt. He advertised for volunteers, and when they arrived they were told that it was an experiment about punishment and learning. The volunteers were to act as 'experimenters', and to give increasing electric shocks to a 'subject' in the next room by pressing switches each time the 'subject' got an answer wrong.

The switches were clearly labelled as being of increasing severity, and went up to 450 volts, and the 'subject' (who was really an actor) said at the beginning of the study that he had a weak heart. Both the labels of the switches and the sounds which came from the other room implied that the person was in serious pain as the voltage increased, before finally falling ominously silent. Even then, the 'experimenter' was instructed to keep giving the shocks by a grey-coated supervisor who oversaw the whole operation and insisted that they should continue with what they were doing.

Milgram found that nearly two-thirds of the people that he tested would carry on obeying the supervisor even to the very end of the experiment. That did not mean that they liked doing it: they would argue, point out that he needed help, and try to refuse to do any more. They almost always became very distressed indeed. But the supervisor would insist that they continue, and in the end they would obey.

People who disobey

A third of the people in the study, though, refused to obey once things reached the point where they felt that the 'subject' was in danger. They would simply, and calmly, refuse. When they were interviewed afterwards, these people generally turned out to have had some previous experience with unthinking obedience and what it could do. One of them had been brought up in Nazi Germany, for instance. These people made disobeying, and acting in accordance with their own conscience, seem a very ordinary thing to do. They simply made up their minds that to go any further would be wrong, and ignored all of the pressure which was put on them to continue.

It is apparent, then, that we are able to act as independent people in accord with our own conscience, or we can simply do what we are told. But in many ways we are trained to do what we are told far more than we are encouraged to act independently. Throughout school we are trained to obey authority, and in later life, too, there are still some people who we are expected to obey without question, like police officers. When this goes together with our natural tendency to conform to other people, we can see why most people would obey in a situation like that, even if they did not want to.

There were a lot of things about the situation which encouraged obedience, such as the way that each electric shock was only a little bit stronger than the one before. That made it very hard for someone to draw a line and say, 'I won't go any further', because what they were being asked to do next was not very different from what they had already done. The people who were aware of the dangers of unquestioning obedience, though, stopped anyway when they felt they had gone far enough. They knew, in their own minds, that to go further would be wrong, and that was enough. They did not feel any need to justify or rationalise what they were doing, apart from that.

Obedience in everyday life

Unthinking obedience can happen in real life, too. Hofling *et al.* (1966) set up a study in a hospital, in which nurses working on night shift were telephoned by a doctor, who they did not know, and asked to administer medication to a patient. They were told to go to the drugs cabinet and find a medication, which was labelled 'Astroten'. On the label it said very clearly that the maximum daily dose was 10 mg, but the doctor asked the nurse to administer 20 mg.

Even though it violated several hospital rules — doctors were not supposed to give orders by telephone, for instance — 95 per cent of the nurses in the study were prepared to administer the medication. They were stopped at the last minute by a staff psychiatrist who had been observing what was going on in secret. The problem was that in real life the hospital doctors were accustomed to breaking these types of rules, and that because of the hierarchy of power, and their training, it was very difficult for a nurse to disobey a doctor.

Rebellion

But we do disobey sometimes. Gamson, Fireman and Rytina set up a study in which people were asked to take part in a marketing research exercise. This involved filming a group discussion about a case of a manager of a petrol station who was in dispute with the franchise company. The research participants were told that company said they wanted to revoke his franchise because he was living with someone and not married to them; but the manager said it was because he had publicly criticised their pricing policies.

As the people in the study discussed the case, they were frequently asked to argue a particular case in front of the video camera. For instance, at one point, three members of the group were asked to argue as if they were personally insulted by the manager's behaviour. It became very apparent that the group was actually being asked to provide videotaped evidence which could be used by the company to discredit the manager. At the end, they were asked to sign an affidavit giving the company the right to use the videotapes as evidence.

It was obvious to the groups that they were being manipulated, and most people, at that point, refused to co-operate and sign the affidavit. In 16 of the 33 groups, all of the group members refused to sign, and in eight more groups a majority refused. Even in the other groups, there was a strong minority who refused to co-operate any further. So it is apparent that we will refuse to obey other people, if we are clear enough about what is going on and why they are trying to make us act that way.

When do we stand up for ourselves?

So why is it, then, that people will sometimes stand up for their own beliefs, and at other times simply go along with what they are told? One of the answers is to do with **social expectations**. In Chapter 2 we looked at how powerful expectations can be, and how simply expecting something to happen can sometimes become a self-fulfilling prophecy, which comes true simply because we expect it to, and we act as if it already is. That is one factor which is at work here.

Another factor, as I've already discussed, is the power of our previous training. We learn to obey people who are in charge, and to do what we are told. This can be a powerful form of **social conditioning**: many people become very distressed at the thought of disobeying someone who is in authority, even when they know it is the right thing to do. Our early learning has taught us that, and it remains a powerful influence throughout our adult life.

It is reinforced, too, by the way people communicate. As we have seen, the way that people use words, and the actual words that they use, convey messages about possible options. They encourage us to see possibilities in certain ways. And the non-verbal dimensions of communication, too, reinforce those messages. It was no accident that the supervisor in Milgram's study wore a grey lab coat and acted in a distant, official manner. It made his authority seem even stronger.

Social scripts

Then there are the **social scripts** which are present in most situations. As we grow up, much of what we learn is about acting in the ways that society expects. We learn about social roles, and how to behave in a way that fits with the part that we are playing. We also learn to conform to social scripts, which give the pattern of how people ought to behave. If we go to a restaurant, for instance, there is a definite script which tells us when we should do certain things, and when we can expect things to happen. We would be deeply disconcerted if the waiter brought coffee before the main course, for instance, and we would wonder what was going on.

Other social situations, too, have their own scripts, and sometimes these can cause us to act in unusual ways. Orne (1972) showed how, normally, if you ask people to add up a set of numbers on a piece of paper and then tear the paper up and throw it in the bin, they will refuse. They might do it once or twice, but no more. But if you tell them that it is part of a psychology experiment, they will do it over and over again. In Orne's study, one research participant even had to be stopped after six hours because the experimenter wanted to go home!

So it is apparent that we weigh up the situation that we are in, and match what we do to what we think that situation requires. The attributions and explanations that we make influence how we understand what is required, and from there our social schemas guide our choice of actions. We interpret and analyse the situation that we are in, and that also influences how we behave.

We can see, then, that our social behaviour, too, is complex, and draws from many levels of explanation. We are influenced by our early conditioning, by non-verbal and verbal communication, by our social roles and social scripts, and by our personal attributions and social representations. Each of them works together, and by looking at these different factors in human interaction, we can gain some ideas as to why it is like it is.

9

PSYCHOLOGY IN WORK

Up until now, we have been looking at a small sample of the type of knowledge about human beings which is available in psychology. There's much more, of course, but it gives a general idea. More importantly, it gives us a basis for understanding people. In the next few chapters, we will be using that base, along with other information, to see how psychology can help us to understand people in everyday situations. We will begin, in this chapter, by looking at how psychology can help us to understand people at work.

Unemployment and retirement

For a human being, work is a deeply important part of life. Although we might daydream about a life of leisure, the reality is that most of us are psychologically, and physically, healthier if we are working. If we are prevented from working, by unemployment or redundancy, we are very likely to become depressed. If that unemployment continues for a long time, we are also liable to fall into a kind of learned helplessness (see Chapter 3), which can sometimes make it very difficult for us to find work again, or to make the sustained effort that is necessary if an opportunity does come along.

Unemployment has other negative effects, as well. Warr (1987) found that between 20 per cent and 30 per cent of unemployed people in a survey showed a deterioration in their physical health. And Binns and Mars (1984) found that unemployment often leads to difficulties in personal relationships as well, often because of the additional strain brought on by continuing financial difficulties.

And, of course, the longer we are unemployed, the more these problems are likely to become exaggerated.

Latent functions of working

Jahoda (1982) suggested that the reason why long-term unemployment is so damaging is because working is more than it appears. It does not just serve the obvious functions for us, like earning money to live on, it also has other functions, which are not so apparent. Jahoda identified five latent functions of working, which are listed in Table 9.1. We do not really notice these functions while we are working, but they are actually extremely important in helping to keep our emotional and psychological life balanced.

TABLE 9.1 LATENT FUNCTIONS OF WORKING
1. Employment imposes a time structure on the waking day
2. Employment brings about regularly shared experiences and contacts with people outside the family
3. A job links the individual with goals and purposes beyond one's own
4. A job defines aspects of presonal status and identity
5. Paid employment enforces its own activity

Thinking of work in this way can be useful, too, because it can give us some hints as to how unemployment can be survived. For example, people who are unemployed but keep themselves busy by doing voluntary work do not usually suffer from the depression and learned helplessness that so many other unemployed people experience. That seems to be partly because they gain the latent functions of working from their voluntary commitment. It can sometimes be like that for people who are committed to a particular hobby, as well.

Disengagement

The importance of these latent functions in working becomes particularly obvious when people retire. The first psychological theories about retirement tended to take a rather negative position. Cummings and Henry (1961) saw retirement as a gradual process of **disengagement** from society. Old people might be numerous, but they were less visible than younger people, and less involved in social activities. Cummings and Henry saw this as part of a biological mechanism, like a weakened animal withdrawing from its herd to die.

Social exchange

But that type of explanation ignores the social factors which are involved in retirement. Dowd (1975) suggested that it is more useful to see retirement as a kind of **social exchange**, in which people make an unspoken contract with society. They receive an 'honourable discharge' from society's expectations about work, and in return they feel that society expects them to be less active and involved.

Activity theory

More recently, however, people are showing signs of being less prepared to accept this type of social contract. After all, we live much longer now than they did when retirement was first introduced, and we keep our health for longer, too. Among business and professional people, it is not at all uncommon for retirement to signal the beginning of a second career, and a much more independent one which allows them to use their experience, such as working as a consultant.

In other groups of society, too, people are beginning to see retirement as an opportunity to do new things. Organisations like the University of the Third Age encourage retired people to develop new hobbies and pursue new interests, and are becoming more popular and successful all the time. Many psychologists now take the view that successful retirement is all about making sure that you acquire new social roles, to replace the ones that you have lost through work, and activities of this sort are exactly the way that people do that.

Some people who reach retiring age, though, still hold to the old negative ideas about retirement. They often do see it as a fair type of social exchange for most old people, although that does not mean that they think it is the right thing for them personally. On a personal level, such people often feel that society has simply thrown them away, even though they are as fit as ever. But feeling socially useless is a major source of stress and helplessness. Unless such people manage to find another source of self-esteem, such as through a hobby or voluntary work, they can become extremely depressed, and appear to give up on active living.

Retirement and responsibility

People who take this view of retirement are actually much more likely to die in the first few years afterwards than people who take a more positive view. It seems that they find it much harder to find anything worth living for, because they feel so useless. This also helps to explain why women live longer than men (although there are other factors too, naturally). Women who are past retiring age grew up in a culture in which the home was considered to be their primary responsibility. Even after they have retired, that responsibility still remains, so they still have something in their lives to be involved with.

But men of the same age were usually brought up to believe that their primary responsibility was to work and be the breadwinner for the family. That responsibility vanishes with compulsory retirement, and this can be emotionally devastating. Even people who have looked forward to retirement can find, after the first few months, that feeling socially useless is more than they can cope with, and they can become very depressed, even, sometimes, to the point where they give up trying to live.

That is why it is so important for retired people to make sure that they have some other interest in their lives, and more than just one if at all possible. Many retired people take up another responsibility, where they can still feel needed. Some do voluntary work in charity shops or other places. Gardening is particularly popular, because a garden needs to be looked after — it cannot be neglected or it will quickly turn wild. So someone who looks after a garden knows that their efforts are necessary and worthwhile. Some people, too, develop hobbies, like travelling, or learn a new sport, such as golf or bowls. All these are ways for people to develop other sources of self-esteem, to make up for the consequences of being without paid employment.

Why do people work?

Looking at what happens when people do not work can tell us a great deal about what working actually does for us. But what of people at work? What motivates them to continue working? One of the first psychological theories of working was the very straightforward one which has probably occurred to you already, as you read this chapter: people work for money.

Scientific management

F. W. Taylor, in 1911, adopted this explanation for work motivation. From there, he reasoned that, if this is the case, then a system of working which allows people to earn more by being more efficient will be useful, both to employees and to employers. Taylor developed an approach to work which became known as 'scientific management', and this was entirely based on the idea of work being as efficient as possible.

Time and motion

Taylor began with a labourer loading pig-iron on to railway trucks. From observing the labourers working, he became convinced that it could be done much more efficiently. He got one man to agree to do exactly as Taylor suggested: lifting when he was told, resting when he was told, and so on. By the end of that working day, the labourer had loaded $47^1/_2$ tons of pig iron, instead of the usual $12^1/_2$.

Taylor went on from there to develop the principle of **time and motion studies**, in which production and labouring jobs were carefully observed and timed, in order to identify the most efficient ways of working. The 'scientific management' approach became very popular before the 1930s, and seemed to represent a new and better way of organising work.

Like many ideas of that time, though, it was simply too mechanistic for human beings. At that time, it was common for people to be seen as much like machines — we have already seen something of this, in the behaviourist approach to learning which we looked at in Chapter 7. The problem, though, is that people are not machines, and when they are treated as if they were, they tend to rebel.

Sometimes that rebellion is unconscious. The rates of industrial accidents, for example, increased with the introduction of scientific management. Although some early industrial researchers (e.g. Greenwood and Woods, 1919) came to the conclusion that some people were simply 'accident prone', later researchers saw it as a simple consequence of expecting human beings to act in exactly the same way, day after day, hour after hour. Sickness and absenteeism rates also increased, as did rates of staff turnover — the number of staff who simply left.

Social aspects of working

In the 1930s, a group of psychologists showed that there were important social dimensions to working, as well. In a series of studies at the Hawthorne Electric Plant in Chicago, Elton Mayo and his colleagues Roethlisberger and Dickson began by trying to find the best lighting levels in a particular workshop. However, they found that, almost no matter what they did, the employees in that area worked harder as a result. The fact that the researchers were taking an interest in what the employees were doing was enough to increase their motivation.

Group standards

In another part of the company, the researchers investigated a department called the bank-wiring room. This consisted of a group of people who were usually left to work without much supervision. They had developed their own way of working, which produced a regular, steady rate of production. They did not increase it much, even when paid extra, but then they did not slow down either. Mayo and the others found that this group had developed a clear code of practice, which was about how each person should do their share, and not do anything which might get the rest of the group into trouble. As a result, it was one of the most reliable and dependable parts of the organisation.

Informal leadership

In some later studies, Mayo and his colleagues explored the idea of group leadership. They were investigating an aircraft factory in southern California, which had grave problems with staff turnover -

people were leaving, and new people being taken on, at a rate which made it very difficult for the factory to operate properly. In one department, though, there was very little staff turnover indeed.

When they investigated, they found that this department had an informal leader, who took charge and sorted out disagreements between people when they arose. The leader also welcomed new people when they joined the department, and took care that they should meet everyone, and get to know what each person was doing. Then, they were also taken on a tour of the whole factory, so that the person could see how their own job contributed to the production of the whole aircraft.

Each of these different studies, and several others, pointed to different aspects of work motivation, and showed that there is much more involved for people than simply earning money. The first study, on lighting, had shown that people respond to management or others taking an interest in what they do. The bank-wiring room showed that doing the right thing by one's colleagues is more important than simply trying to get extra pay. The aircraft factory study showed the value of effective leadership, and also the value of people being able to see their own job in an overall context.

Expectations and management

As a result of the Hawthorne studies, the attention of work psychologists shifted away from looking at physical aspects of working conditions, and into investigating the social dimensions of working. What became apparent almost immediately was the way that people tend to respond to the **expectations** which other people have of them. If managers distrust their staff, and show that by close supervision and not allowing them to make even minor decisions for themselves, people will often respond by trying to 'get one over' on the management. But if a manager trusts their staff, and shows it by listening to their ideas and giving them enough autonomy to get on with doing their work properly, people tend to respond by acting responsibly.

Theory X and Theory Y

McGregor (1960) drew these and many other findings together, and argued that people actually like to work. We like to feel valued, and appreciated, and if we are given the opportunity, we will work hard. But some managers, McGregor argued, actually create irresponsibility among their employees by showing, through their everyday practices, that they do not trust their staff, and that they think they are naturally lazy.

McGregor argued that there are two different underlying theories about human nature, which managers apply to their employees. The first one, which he called Theory X, is the old-fashioned idea that people are really shiftless and lazy, and will not work unless they are made to. That type of theory, according to McGregor, led to these self-defeating approaches to management and supervision.

The second theory, which McGregor called Theory Y, is the idea that people really like to work, and that the job of the manager is to provide a working context which will allow them to show what they can do. Managers who hold Theory Y, McGregor argued, set up working conditions in which staff feel valued and trusted. As a result, their staff really do work hard, because they know that their efforts are appreciated.

—— Human resource management ——

These early theories of what motivates people at work form an important background to what is known as **human resource management**. That, as its name suggests, is the branch of management which is particularly concerned with people, and with ensuring that the people in an organisation or company work well, and can adapt to change when it is needed. A great many organisational psychologists are involved in human resource management.

Team building

Another aspect of human resource management is to do with working teams, and making sure that people can work together as effectively as possible. Psychologists in organisations have developed various kinds of team-building exercises, which can be used to give people who are going to be working together a chance to get to know one another, and to learn each other's strengths and weaknesses.

Sensitivity training

In the 1960s and 1970s, team-building exercises often focused on **sensitivity training**, in which people learned to become more sensitive to one another. They would learn, for example, about non-verbal communication (see Chapter 8), and how to offer support when people were doing something which was particularly challenging. In other words, they learned to respond to the interpersonal messages and feelings which other members of the group were showing

Roles and tasks

More recently, approaches to team-building have tended to emphasise the roles and tasks which people in the group are concerned with. Adair (1968) argued that any given team has to take account of three sets of needs: the **task needs**, which are the practical things which have to be done in order to do the job at hand; **group needs**, which are to do with overcoming interpersonal quarrels or disputes, and making sure that people can act effectively together; and **individual needs**, which are to do with what the individual members of the team want to get out of it.

The job of the team leader, in this model, is to pay attention to all three types of needs, and to make sure that they are all at least partly satisfied. It is not enough just to concentrate on the demands of the job at hand and to ignore the group needs, because that could mean that tensions between members of the group become so strong that afterwards those people could not work together again. And it is not really very good only to concentrate on task and group needs and ignore individual ones. It might get the job done, but in the long term people work much better when they benefit personally from being involved, too.

Social identification at work

The personal benefits of belonging to a team, though, do not need to be visible ones. In Chapter 2 we looked at the process of social identification, and the way that people like to be able to feel proud of belonging to a particular group. Being part of a successful, achieving group, and being recognised as contributing to it, is often enough to satisfy individual needs. Alternatively, teamwork may be seen as a way of accumulating experience which will stand them in good stead for later promotion.

The important thing, really, is the attitude of management. Imai (1988) showed how Japanese management systems involve all of the workers, at any level in the company, in a continuous drive for improvement. People are encouraged to feel proud of, and committed to, their company, and are treated as intelligent and responsible people, no matter what job they are doing. So if they are asked to join a specific team to solve a problem, they are often pleased to be involved, and to be recognised as someone who has something worthwhile to contribute.

In too many organisations in the Western world, however, contributions like this are still ignored or unrecognised by management, so they are seen as just an additional chore for the individual. Although a skilled team leader will be able to get round this, by ensuring that their team, at least, pays attention to people's individual needs, their job can be made a great deal harder or a great deal easier by the organisation's general policies towards its staff.

Leadership

Organisational psychologists have also been involved in studying leadership. Much of the early research into leadership tended to look for particular people who had leadership 'qualities' — who automatically acted like leaders and took on leadership responsibilities when that sort of situation arose. Later, though, largely as a result of a particularly interesting study conducted in the 1930s, psychologists became more and more interested in the idea that effective leadership was actually a style of interacting with people, rather than a specific inherited personality trait.

Leadership styles

The study was conducted by Lewin, Lippitt and White (1939), and was actually done in a boys' after-school model-making club. The

TABLE 9.2   LEADERSHIP STYLES AND THEIR EFFECTS

	Style	Effect
Authoritarian	Leader makes arbitrary decisions, doesn't consult group, gives orders, supervises closely	Group worked hard when leader present, stopped work when absent. Competitive and attention seeking.
Democratic	Leader makes decisions on basis of group discussions, delegates responsibility, gives requests rather than orders, expects co-operation	Group workedsteadily whether supervised or not. Helpful with one another, solved problems jointly
Laissez-faire	Leader leaves group alone to get on with work; does not intervene or attempt to influence them	Group disorganised, did very little work. Easily demoralised by small problems

boys were divided into three groups, and each group was given a leader who acted in a different way. Later, the leaders were changed round, to make sure that it was really their influence and not just differences between the groups of boys. The styles and their results are described in Table 9.2. As you can see, they support McGregor's idea that leaders bring out particular behaviour in their subordinates — and in fact this study and the other research which it stimulated was an important part of McGregor's evidence.

Task- and process-oriented leaders

Following this work, approaches to leadership became concerned with just how organisational leaders or managers influence the people in their working groups. Some theories have seen effective leaders as having preferred styles, which concentrate on either the job at hand, or on the people they are dealing with. Task-oriented leaders are people who focus on the job which has to be done, whereas process-oriented leaders are more concerned with making sure that everything in the group runs smoothly, and that people get along well together.

Interestingly, and contrary to what we might expect, the evidence suggests that process-oriented leaders actually get more done in the end. Although the task-oriented leaders are only concerned with what needs to be done, they are less efficient overall because they allow tensions and resentments to build up in their teams, and in the end this means that people work less productively. Process-oriented leaders, on the other hand, concentrate on making sure that people are reasonably happy with one another, and with what is going on, so that they are free to give their best efforts to the job.

Transactional leadership

This led to a focus on leadership as being all about the **transactions** which take place between manager and employee. Transactions are interpersonal exchanges between two people. Often these take the form of **strokes**: ritual greetings or enquiries which signal that the two people have recognised one another. A habitual 'good morning' exchanged between two people at a bus stop or train station is a good example of a stroke. The words of the exchange are relatively unimportant, but the greeting signals that the two have acknowledged one another. As we have already seen, being recognised by other people matters to us, so the everyday strokes that we get from other people can be very important. We may not notice them much when they happen, but we certainly miss them if they do not.

The idea of transactional leadership is that effective leadership is essentially a joint thing, depending on both the manager and the employee. How effective a leader is depends on how both the leader and the employees interact. It does not just depend on the leader alone. After all, people will not co-operate with someone who does not seem to come up to scratch, so a leader who comes across as being ineffectual or incompetent is not going to be able to influence other people very much.

What this means is that a manager, consciously or unconsciously, negotiates their position with the employees. It is an interpersonal relationship, and their influence depends on being respected or valued. That is where the transactions come in. Strokes, for instance, can be either positive or negative: they can help us to feel good, or they can make us feel unhappy. Positive leaders look for ways of encouraging their staff to feel good — by recognising their achievements and helping them to get around difficulties. Negative leaders criticise their staff, and only notice mistakes rather than positive achievements. As decades of organisational psychology have taught us, it is not a method that gets the best out of people, but they do it anyway.

Transformational leadership

An even more recent way of looking at leadership is to do with the way that large organisations can often become very unwieldy. This makes them slow to respond to changes in society, which means that they are not able to compete properly with other companies in the same line of work. A great many organisational psychologists are involved in **organisational change**, and one of the outcomes of this has been to make it clearer what influence some kinds of leadership can have.

Some leaders seem to be particularly good at getting their staff to deal positively with change, and to approach their jobs in new ways. They are known as **transformational leaders**, because they have the knack of being able to encourage an organisation to transform itself — to adapt a different style of working. In recent years, with so many organisations having to adjust to an entirely different economic context, this has become an important feature of leadership.

Getting people to deal positively with change is not as easy as it sounds. People will often resist changes to the way that they work. But that is not because they are simply being obstructive. As we saw in Chapters 5 and 6, we actively make sense of our worlds, and we act in ways that fit with what we understand is going on. So sometimes people will object to changes in how they work because they cannot see how it will improve things.

A transformational leader is generally someone who realises how important it is that people should understand what is happening, and who makes an effort to show them why, and how, it will be worth while to make the efforts. Transformational leaders help people to come to terms with organisational change by showing how the new approach can be linked with what people are already doing. Smith and Peterson (1988) showed how these leaders often use metaphors and stories to help to make these links clear.

Another feature of transformational leadership is that such leaders also encourage members of the organisation to be involved in the changes. They listen to what they have to say, and take their ideas into account. In the end, of course, this means that the employees are much more likely to work effectively and to make the changes successful, because they, too, are aware that there are good reasons for them.

That does not mean, though, that all organisational change is always a good thing, or that it is always successful. Sometimes, attempts to change how organisations work are resisted by the people working in them because they really are impractical — they have been badly thought out, and nobody has consulted the people who are really doing the work. Sometimes, too, people have simply had more change than they can cope with, and need a period to consolidate the new ways and let the new ideas sink in.

Organisational cultures

Transformational leaders are people who are trying to change the general culture of the organisation that they are working in. Organisational culture is all about the general assumptions, beliefs and practices in an organisation — its distinctive style of working. Sometimes, you can find two organisations, in exactly the same line of work, but which go about doing that work in entirely different ways. The people working in those organisations have quite different approaches to what they are doing; they deal with problems differently, and they expect different attitudes from management. It was observations like this that led to the idea of organisational cultures.

Levels of culture

Although some organisational researchers have spent their time trying to classify different types of organisational cultures, organisational psychologists tend to be more interested in how cultures work, and why they influence the people working in them the way that they do. Lundberg (1990) observed that organisational cultures seem to have three different levels, which are listed in Table 9.3. Psychologists have studied culture at each of these levels, of course, but we tend to be particularly interested in the deepest level, of shared assumptions and beliefs.

TABLE 9.3   LEVELS OF ORGANISATIONAL CULTURE

(i)	**The manifest level**	Symbols, language, stories, rituals, etc
(ii)	**The strategic level**	Beliefs about the company's direction, planning and expectations, internal management strategies
(iii)	**The core level**	Ideologies, values and assumptions about human nature and what people and the world are like

(Lundberg 1990)

Groups in organisations

Other researchers, such as Van Maanen and Barley (1985), showed how organisational cultures are not really just single things, with everyone in the organisation thinking the same way. Instead, different groups within the organisation have their own ways of thinking. In an organisation with a strong culture, these different groups overlap, so they all have something in common. But in other types of organisation, different groups may have entirely different assumptions and beliefs.

Any organisation contains a whole host of in-groups and out-groups: there are friendship groups, departmental groups, working teams, and many others. People often feel more loyalty to some of these groups than to others. Some organisational change does not happen, for instance, because it is resisted by 'canteen cultures' which keep certain beliefs and ideas going among the workforce even when management are trying to change it.

Canteen cultures

The classic example of how a canteen culture can work against organisational change is in equal opportunities. An organisation may adopt an official equal opportunities policy, but sometiomes groups of employees still perpetuate racist beliefs. So anyone from an ethnic minority background has a very hard time indeed. Officially, for example, the police force is trying to be non-racist. It has maintained an equal opportunities policy for many years now, and has attempted to develop better community relations with ethnic minority groups.

But several studies have shown how canteen cultures in the police perpetuate a high level of racism, which is not really affected by official policy. And it is the canteen culture, of course, which the new recruit encounters when they are learning practical policing. As we have seen, we develop our schemas and our understanding of the world from our experience, and we use them as a guide for action. So first experiences like that are important in shaping future working practices.

Social psychology and organisational culture

Hayes (1991) showed how an understanding of the kind of **social identity** processes which we looked at in Chapter 2 could help us to understand how canteen cultures work, and why they are so influential. Knowing about **social representations** (see Chapter 8), too, can help us to understand how these shared beliefs develop. People tend to take more notice of people who they think are like themselves, or who belong to the same in-group. So it is particularly easy for a group in an organisation to come to develop shared beliefs about their work, and about life in general. Applying these two social psychology theories, therefore, can help us to understand how to tackle this sort of problem.

This is only a brief glimpse of organisational psychology, and, of course, there is much more that work psychologists do. For example, ergonomic psychologists are involved in studying the human–machine interface — in other words, they design machines which people can operate easily, and which will reduce the likelihood of mistakes. **Ergonomics** is a very large branch of work psychology, which has had a powerful presence in industry for many decades. But there is not really enough room to write about it here.

—— Choosing people for jobs ——

There is another way, too, that psychologists have been involved in work, and this also is one which has been around for many decades. **Occupational psychology** is concerned with selecting the right people for particular jobs, and with training and retraining systems to help people to learn new skills.

Psychometric testing

One of the main areas of occupational psychology is in the field of **psychometric testing**. Psychometric tests are tests which are designed to assess some aspect of a person's psychology. Sometimes they aim to assess how much someone knows, or what skills they have; sometimes they are concerned with personality, or intelligence, or some other character quality; and sometimes they are assessing what a person's potential might be — what particular aptitudes they have, and what sort of skills they might find easy to learn.

One thing which all psychologists agree on, though, is that no psychometric test is enough in itself. We should not base any decisions on the outcomes of psychometric tests alone, because they are not that definite. They can be useful, but they are not the whole answer — and if they are taken as absolute truth, then they can do more harm than good. What they actually do is to give us an indication of what the person is like, but that always has to be backed up by other information — their previous experience, other people's opinions, and what they themselves have to say.

Uses of psychometric tests

Psychometric tests are used by occupational psychologists in a number of ways. One of these is in **vocational guidance**. People who are contemplating a change of job, or a new career, often find it helpful to do a psychometric test which will help to identify what kinds of work they might do best. Of course, they still have to decide which out of several possibilities they actually want to do (if any), and then they have to acquire the relevant skills and experience to get the job; but a vocational guidance test can be a useful first step in making a career decision.

Psychometric tests are also used for **job selection** — choosing the right person for the job. Again, they cannot be used on their own: as Shackleton (1989) showed, a psychometric test is only one part of a range of information that needs to be taken into account in choosing the right person for a particular job. Sometimes, too, psychometric tests are used to help to select managers or technical staff for promotion. Those making the decision want to know whether someone will be able to cope with the demands of a new job, and use information from psychometric tests along with work records and managers' opinions to make the decision.

Types of occupational test

It is apparent, then, that psychometric tests are used by occupational psychologists in quite a few different ways, and they have a great many different tests to use in the process. There are three types of tests which they tend to use. The first of these are tests of general ability, which are usually **intelligence tests** of one form or another. These are really just to make sure that someone has a reasonable capacity for grasping what is expected of them.

The second major type of test is the **personality test**. These tests are designed to identify personality characteristics which can influence how people interact with others at work, and how they approach the job. They might show, for instance, whether someone is mainly of a sociable disposition, or whether they tend to be quiet and introverted, keeping themselves to themselves. They might also show whether someone has a personal need always to keep control over what is happening, or whether they are happy to allow other people to make the running.

The third major type of psychometric test which occupational psychologists use are **ability and aptitude tests**. Ability tests assess how skilled someone is at a particular type of task. For example, someone thinking of employing a secretary would usually ask them to type out a letter, so that they could see how capable they were at typing. Psychometric ability tests work on the same principle, but everything has been carefully standardised, so that we can compare people with different abilities effectively.

Aptitude tests do not assess existing skills. Instead, they assess how well someone would learn to do something. If a computer firm is taking on a trainee, for instance, it would not make sense to ask them to program something, because they intend to train the person. Instead, they would give the person an aptitude test, which assessed whether that person could think in the way that is needed for good computer programing. Someone who could not think that way, clearly, would not be any good as a trainee. But just because someone could, does not mean they would be the right person. There are other angles, too, like motivation and character, which would need to be evaluated at an interview and from the person's background. The test would be helpful, but not enough in itself.

We can see, then, that psychology has been involved in a great many different sides of working life. Organisational psychologists are involved in issues to do with human resource management, in understanding what motivates people at work, and in helping organisations to change their ways of working. Occupational psychologists are also involved in developing training systems and in the different aspects of personnel selection. There are other ways that psychologists are involved in work, too, but to cover all of them would need a book in its own right!

10
__PSYCHOLOGY AND__
LEISURE

In this chapter we will look at some of the psychology which underlies leisure activities. People have varied interests and hobbies, and, as we saw in Chapter 2, it is possible to see them as an expression of our basic need for self-actualisation. We enjoy developing our skills and interests. But we also, sometimes, spend our leisure time in more passive activities, like watching television, and this too is something that has been studied by psychologists.

Watching television

In Western society, watching television is a large part of what people do when they are relaxing. Over 97 per cent of homes in Britain have a television set, and over half have more than one: television watching is a significant cultural activity. We hear a great deal about the effects of television watching, and psychologists have been studying its effects for some considerable time.

The effects of television viewing

One of the most popular debates, of course, is whether or not television increases aggressive behaviour. Most psychologists firmly believe that it does, although it is hard to obtain definitive evidence, since there are so many other things which also influence people's lives. The earliest psychological studies of television's influence on aggressive behaviour were direct laboratory experiments, which were designed to assess an immediate change in behaviour as a result of people being exposed to aggressive images on television. They did show some of these effects, although not as definitely as some people expected them to.

Problems with studying television effects

But these laboratory studies were really very artificial situations. Whether people are influenced by violence on television or not, it is unlikely that it would show straight away, in the next half-hour. Rather, as Bandura showed in his studies of imitative learning, we would be unlikely to show aggressive behaviour until it was somehow worth while for us to do so. So the reason why laboratory studies of television violence often have contradictory results is largely because of the methods which they adopt.

Another problem with these studies is that they look for group influences. They will study a large number of people to see whether, on the whole, their behaviour seems to be influenced by the type of programmes that they watch. By studying people as a whole, they aim to cancel out individual differences and just look at general trends. But when it comes to something as important as this, it is individuals who matter. Even if only one, extremely disturbed, person out of six million imitates a television murderer, that is one too many to be acceptable.

Social scripts and social understanding

It is difficult, then, to obtain absolute proof that television violence directly affects people. But that does not mean there is no evidence at all. As we saw in the early part of this book, the human being is particularly ready to acquire social scripts and awareness of social value, and learns from any kind of social contact. Television has a capacity to define a form of reality for people which can make a great deal of difference to how we live our lives. It acts as a window into the wider world, and tells people what that world is like. Studies which look at the amount of television that people actually watch can tell us quite a lot.

What we do know, for instance, is that watching a great deal of television can distort how we see the world. Gerbner and Gross (1976) compared heavy television watchers with people who do not watch very much television. They found that heavy viewers had a very unrealistic perception of the outside world, seeing it as an extremely dangerous place. Sometimes these people believed that they were likely to get mugged as soon as they stepped outside their own doors, even though the towns they lived in made such an event extremely unlikely indeed.

The way that television tends to concentrate on violent action, both in reporting news and in its drama, means that heavy television viewers see the world as a much more dangerous place than it really is. People who watch less television, on the other hand, generally have a much more realistic perception of the risks of everyday living. They are aware that dangers exist, of course, but they do not exaggerate their extent the way that the heavy viewers often do. They can weigh up, realistically, the odds against something untoward happening, and so carry on with their lives in a positive way.

The problem is not really the fact that violence occurs on television. It is more to do with the proportion of violence which is shown on television by comparison with the amount of other types of human activity which are shown. Most people will go their whole lives without ever coming across a murder in real life, for instance, yet an average television-watching child has seen something over 600 television murders by the time it reaches 10 years old. Such an unrealistic proportion cannot help but distort any child's picture of what the world is like.

Positive television

Not all television is bad, of course. Some kinds of television, such as nature or science documentaries or historical programmes, can be educational — broadening out our awareness of the world that we live in. For people living in modern industrial societies, television has replaced books as the main way that we come to know our world. It has become a major agent of socialisation, showing both children and adults how the world works.

Television also contains positive messages in terms of humour and fun. Entertainment programmes such as quiz shows may appear trivial to those who look for high-culture entertainment, but actually show a friendly and positive approach in their dealings with people. Sports and music programmes, too, serve positive psychological functions rather than any other, stimulating people's interest and enthusiasm.

Teaching prosocial behaviour

There have been a great many studies of the influence of children's programmes in teaching children prosocial behaviour. For example, Rubinstein *et al.*, in 1976, found that 5- and 6-year-olds who saw an episode of *Lassie* in which a boy helped a dog were more likely to help puppies in distress than children who had not seen the programme.

There is also some evidence that soap operas, or at least the British and Australian ones, have prosocial effects on children — and possibly adults too. The Australian soap *Neighbours*, for instance, has many very clearly positive messages in its content. It contains ideas like: if you see your friend is in trouble, try to help them out, or if someone has upset you, try to work out the problem with them so that you can be friends again. Soap operas portray people belonging to a community, in which people will help one another out. That is a very different message from the competitive aggression of so much television drama. Maybe that is why they are so popular!

Television and reading

There is quite a lot of concern as to the influence which television has on children's reading. Gunter (1982) showed how heavy television viewing can seriously impair a child's learning to read, particularly during the earliest years of the child's education. The reasons for this are all tied up with the child's own perceptions of what reading is for, and why it should make the effort to learn to read in the first place.

As we saw in Chapter 7, the experience of an expert is quite different from the experience of a novice, and that applies in reading too. Expert readers see reading as a doorway into another world of information; but children who are only just learning to read have quite a different experience. One reason why some children find it hard to learn to read is because they have not actually realised that it will be much easier once they are good at doing it. A novice reader is often so concerned with the mechanics of reading that they hardly notice the story. To them, reading is very hard, and they sometimes cannot see any point in doing it.

This is made even more extreme by television, because the child sees television as like reading, but much easier. Reading needs a lot of practice: it takes time and effort before you recognise words at a glance, and so can concentrate on the meaning of what you are reading. Television, on the other hand, gives you instant access to information. Moreover, it tells you stories, and lets you know about the outside world. So some children simply cannot see the point in learning to read, and unless someone takes the time and trouble to show them what the point is, they will never put in the effort needed to become fluent readers.

But television is not really a substitute for reading. It is an entirely different type of cognitive experience. For one thing, reading trains the child's imagination, because the child needs to create their own mental pictures of what they are reading about. Reading also introduces the child to abstract ideas, that cannot really be portrayed in a concrete form — and that forms an important basis for later understanding and analytical thinking. Television, as we have seen, can have some positive effects on the child's development — it is not all negative. But reading is a different skill, which trains different mental abilities. So it is important that the young child sees it as such, not as equivalent to television.

Consumer psychology

One of the most popular leisure activities in Western consumer society, so we are often told, is shopping. Large shopping malls provide a focus for a range of businesses, and also often provide the shopper with additional sources of entertainment. The aim is to encourage the idea that a visit to a large shopping complex is a 'day out', and much more than just a visit to the shops.

The shopping mall is one extreme, but not all shopping, of course, is done in shopping malls. Town High Streets on a Saturday afternoon, for instance, are full of people strolling into and out of shops, wandering through markets, and inspecting items on street stalls. Many people also buy some regular items from small corner shops, and frequent supermarkets for regular food and household purchasing.

We also do a lot of our shopping at home — or at least, we do a lot of the decision-making part of it. We might see an advertisement for a new food product, and decide to try it out. Next time we go shopping and see the product, we remember that decision and buy it — if we have decided that we can afford it. Or we might be contemplating redecorating a room, or making a major purchase like a car. In such cases, we often look through catalogues and advertising leaflets at home. Being interested in the area, also, gives us a **perceptual set**, which means that we pay particular attention to advertisements which seem relevant to what we are about to do.

Psychologists have been involved in just about all aspects of this process. From the early part of the century, psychologists were involved in the newly forming advertising industry: the founder of behaviourism, J. B. Watson, left academic life and went to work in an advertising firm, and that was in the 1920s. But consumer psychology as a formal discipline did not really develop until the

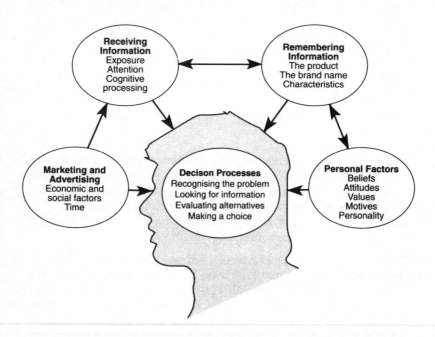

Figure 10.1   The consumer process

consumer boom of the 1960s. Consumer psychology, ultimately, is concerned with how people spend their money. It is often described as having five major areas: consumer inputs, attention, memory, personal factors, and decisions (see Fig. 10.1). Consumer psychologists investigate how all of these different factors affect what we buy.

Consumer inputs

Consumer inputs can take many different forms. The most obvious, of course, are the deliberate influences which advertisers expose us to — things like television, radio and magazine advertisements, promotions, packaging, information from salespeople, and so on. But we are also influenced by the physical situation that we are in: our surroundings. The design of shops and malls, shelf layouts, and where particular products are to be found by shoppers are all aspects of consumerism which have attracted the attention of consumer psychologists.

Social influences

Then there are the social influences on our buying behaviour. Sometimes they will take the form of a direct opinion from a member of the family, or from a friend. But sometimes they are more indirect. We might choose an item of clothing because we want to project a particular image among our friends, for example, or buy a particular CD because all our friends like it too. As we have already seen, social influences are powerful for human beings, and they apply to our consumer behaviour as well.

We are also strongly influenced by why we are shopping in the first place. We make different decisions if we are buying food for the weekend, buying a dress for a special party, or buying a present for a friend — and we go about making those decisions in a quite different way. Shopping for a present is an entirely different experience from going round a supermarket to buy groceries for the next week. It might not matter if we try out a brand of washing-up liquid that we do not really like in the end, but it would matter if we bought a car in the same way. Buying a car is a major decision, and one that we usually spend a lot of time thinking about, because we will be stuck with the results of that single purchase for a very long time.

Attention

Some consumer psychologists have concentrated on attention: what catches our attention, and what does not? Does it matter whether we particularly notice advertisements, or are we influenced by them anyway? If your attention is suddenly attracted by a particularly vivid display, or label, does that mean that you are more likely to buy the product? And what types of labels would be likely to have this effect?

Keeping our interest

As you can see from the advertisements around you, a great many of them are designed to keep you interested and paying attention to what they have to say. They use some very different strategies to do this, too. Some television advertisements have become an art form in themselves, with some adverts humorously imitating others, and some developing as episodes of stories over time. As ways of keeping our attention, they are very successful, and often enjoyable.

The main thing such adverts are trying to prevent, of course, is **habituation**. If we are exposed to the same stimulus, over and over again, after a while we will ignore it. So keeping our attention means giving us new things to attract us. Since we see so many adverts all of the time, that really means stimulating our curiosity, or appealing to our existing knowledge, or simply making the advert interesting in its own right.

Subliminal perception

But sometimes we can be influenced by things even when we are not paying conscious attention to them. In the 1960s, psychologists investigating attention discovered that we sometimes use information that we are not aware of. One interesting study came about as a result of cognitive psychologists having shown that we are often slower to recognise words which are disturbing or obscene, than words which are just ordinary. A debate sprang up about whether people really did not recognise these words as easily — in other words, whether their perceptual system defended them against a disturbing experience — or whether they seemed slower simply because they did not want to say these words out loud in front of the experimenter.

Worthington (1969) performed a study which showed that **perceptual defence** really does seem to happen, at least sometimes (although **response bias** happens too, of course). People were shown round discs of light on a screen, and they were able to adjust the brightness of these discs by turning a knob. They were asked to adjust the discs of light until they were the same degree of brightness.

Unknown to the people taking part in the study, each of the discs had a word embedded in it, too faint to be detected consciously. When the discs had been adjusted to the participant's satisfaction, the researchers found that if they had obscene or disturbing words hidden in them, they seemed fainter to the participants than if they had ordinary words in them. Even though the research participants had not even known that the words were there, their presence had influenced how their surrounding was perceived.

In other words, we can receive information even if we are not consciously aware of it. This is known as **subliminal perception**, and, understandably, it attracted a great deal of attention from the advertising industry. There were even one or two experiments in which advertisements containing subliminal images were tried out, but these were eventually banned as being unethical and excessively manipulative.

Colour and music

The discovery, though, that information does not have to be consciously processed to affect us had wider effects. For example, the use of colour and music in advertisements is not generally something that we notice much, but it can make a great deal of difference to how we perceive the product. For example, milk cartons tend to include a lot of blues, because manufacturers are trying to encourage us to see the product as fresh, and blue is a colour associated with freshness.

Different types of music, too, have an affect on how people purchase things. Milliman (1982) caused fast or slow background music to be played in supermarkets while people shopped. Shoppers, Milliman found, tended to move in time with the music. When the supermarkets were playing fast background music, people shopped quite quickly, but when the music was slow, they lingered. In fact, the supermarkets made something like a third more sales when the slow music was playing, because people spent so much longer in the store.

Milliman's study was conducted in the relatively quiet shopping period between New Year and Easter. At busy times, it is often more advantageous to a shop if people do their purchasing relatively quickly. In the weeks coming up to Christmas, for instance, music tends to be faster. This is not the only way that music can influence us, either. Other studies have shown that people are more likely to buy things if they like the music which is playing at the time they are looking at the object on the shelf. So we can see that unconscious influences can be quite strong. Music is not particularly hidden, but most of the time we just do not notice it.

Memory

Studies of memory in consumer psychology are usually about how people remember brand names, and what marketing people refer to as 'brand identity'. An advertisement can be as entertaining as a television programme, but ultimately it has a different purpose — and that purpose is to make sure that you remember the name of the product which it is advertising. Sometimes that product name is apparent in the advertisement; at other times, it is hidden, and we have to do a little bit of mental 'work' to realise what it is.

Levels of processing

On the surface, it might seem as though an advertisement which does not tell you what the product is would be pretty pointless. But as we saw in Chapter 6, human memory is very affected by how much mental 'work' we do to remember something. The **levels of processing** theory shows us that having to think about something — to work out what it means, or to change the way that we perceive it — means that we are much more likely to remember that thing. So in fact not providing the brand name is a very good strategy for advertisers — as long as they give us enough clues to work it out. By filling in the information ourselves, we have had to think about what the advert is advertising, and that makes us more likely to remember it than if we were told the name directly.

Jingles and imagery

There are other ways of getting people to remember product names, of course. One powerful advertising strategy is the development of the 'jingle' — a little tune which reminds us of the product name. This was used very successfully in early television advertisements, such as for Pepsodent toothpaste — and was so successful that many older people still remember that product name even though the toothpaste itself seems to have gone off the market.

The use of visual imagery, too, is a potent aid to remembering. Distinctive logos can remind us of a brand name, even if we are too far away to read the name itself. Think of Coca-Cola, for instance, and you will almost certainly have a mental image of the Coca-Cola logo — and perhaps even of the Coca-Cola bottle. Both of these are indelibly associated with the product name in people's minds, and remind us of the name each time we see them.

We can see, then, that almost all of the aspects of memory which we looked at earlier in this book have been used by advertisers to strengthen our recall of particular products. Different modes of remembering, such as visual or auditory impressions, as well as different levels of processing, are systematically applied in consumer psychology.

Personal influences and decision-making

But we are not just robots, responding automatically to these stimuli — even if it may sometimes seem as though advertisers expect us to be. People in consumer societies have become very sophisticated in their attitude to marketing, and will pick and choose their own way among different products. Personal factors, too, are very important.

Personal constructs

Some of those personal factors are ones which we have looked at earlier in this book. In Chapter 5 we saw how we each have our own system of **personal constructs**, which we use to make sense of our worlds. We apply this system to the advertisements and products which are around us too, and it makes a great deal of difference to whether we are affected by the advertisements. We may even enjoy a television advertisement relating to a particular product, but have no intention whatsoever of ever buying it. It is all a question of how we make sense of what we are looking at.

When advertisers study personal factors they often try to classify people into different types of consumer. That way they are able to make general statements about what kinds of products people are likely to buy. For example, Sadalla and Burroughs (1981) looked at how eating preferences relate to people's personal lifestyles. The researchers found quite a lot of agreement between how these people rated themselves, and how they were seen by other people.

Among other things, Sadalla and Burroughs found that people who liked highly processed food, such as instant meal drinks or processed cheese snacks, tended to be conservative in their politics, logical in argument, and also quite religious (it was an American study, which may possibly be relevant to their findings). Vegetarians were seen as being non-competitive, sexual, and as liking crafts and folk dancing, whereas people who liked gourmet food were seen as living alone, using drugs, and as having tolerant and progressive political beliefs.

Problems with classifying people

Classifying people into types, like this, is a popular exercise in consumer psychology, although some psychologists are unsure about how useful it really is. The classifications are mainly used to decide on the kind of advertising strategy which is going to be used for that particular product — what kind of lifestyle will be represented, and how the product will be made to look appealing. But one reason why marketing people are often surprised by the way that the public does not fit their predictions may be because they rely too much on this kind of stereotype.

The problem is, of course, that people do not really fit very neatly into types. All of us are different: we can identify general trends, but general trends are not really enough to understand an individual human being. When it comes to the final decisions about whether or not to buy something, then our personal experience, our own awareness of options, and our own preferences matter a great deal. So to understand how consumers actually make decisions, we have to look at those processes as well.

That often means applying our knowledge of underlying psychological mechanisms. For example, Stratton and Siviter (1993) showed how understanding **attributions** — the reasons people give for why things are like they are — can give us a great deal of insight into how people perceive different brands, and why some of them are seen as having a particular 'image'. That still does not tell us everything we need to know about people's individual decision-making, but it does help us to understand a little more about the whole process. Really, it is only by looking at the whole human being, with its many complex levels, that we will become able to understand why we make the decisions that we do.

Sport psychology

Sport is another important way that people use their leisure time. Many of us are involved in sport in one way or another, whether we do it ourselves, or whether we just watch other people do it. Sporting activities range from everyday exercises like walking or jogging to team sports like playing football, rugby or hockey, to performance sports like skating, athletics or cycling. In many ways, it is difficult to draw a hard and fast line between exercise and sport, but when the full range is taken into account most of us do something vaguely sport-like, even if it is only to go swimming now and again.

Some people, though, engage in sport much more seriously. They decide, from a relatively early age, that they are going to compete seriously in their particular sporting activity, and from that point on they devote tremendous amounts of time to improving their skills, learning new techniques, and ensuring that their physical and mental condition is as perfect as they can get it. Some people do this as amateurs, aiming to participate in sports as a serious hobby, but not intending to make a living from it. Others aim to take sport up as a profession, by achieving international standards of performance — or, possibly, by training others. But whatever their ultimate aim, these people devote a considerable amount of their lives to perfecting their sporting performance.

Music and dance

Sport is not the only area of human activity which is like this, of course. Exactly the same things could be said about both dance and music. To become a professional dancer or musician does not just require a personal talent. It also requires devoting a large part of one's daily life to learning and perfecting performance techniques.

That is particularly true if someone aims to take music or dance up as a profession, but it is also true if they want to acquit themselves competently as an amateur. Many of the findings of sports psychologists also have some application to the psychology of music and dance.

Sport psychology is all about using psychology to help people to learn skills, keep motivated, and perform as well as possible. It draws from psychological knowledge and experience of sporting practice to try to understand how different factors can influence sportspeople in their performance, and what the best methods of training might be. One of the central aspects of sport psychology, therefore, is how we learn physical skills.

Learning physical skills

Learning to perform a physical action precisely is really quite a complicated thing. It involves hundreds, or even thousands, of different muscle groups, each contracting and relaxing at precisely the right moments. Each muscle contracts in response to a message from the brain, so the different messages which are sent from the brain to the muscles need to be highly co-ordinated if the movement is to be exactly right.

In Chapter 7 we saw how this involves **automatising** the actions, so that they can be carried out without any conscious thinking, apart from the decision to perform them. This happens as the sequence of actions becomes controlled by the part of the brain that co-ordinates action, the cerebellum, instead of being controlled by the cerebrum, which is the part of the brain that we think with. And, as we saw in Chapter 4, drugs like nicotine interfere with the messages from the brain to the muscles, which is one reason why high-performance sportspeople do not smoke. The other reason, of course, is that it also interferes with how efficiently we breathe, and with the amount of oxygen that the blood can carry.

The learning curve

When we are learning something new, we generally take quite a long time to do it successfully, at first. But the more we do it, the easier it becomes. Someone learning to perform a new tennis stroke may fail entirely the first time they attempt it. As they practise, though, they are likely to succeed more and more often, until eventually they can do the stroke successfully all the time — at least, while they are practising!

It is the same with any physical skill. Someone who is learning to type will be very slow at first, but will become faster as they become more familiar with the positions of the letters on the keyboard. If we were to plot their speed of typing on a chart, measuring it against the amount of practice they had had, we would find that it made a curve, which picked up very steeply at first, and then rounded off more gently. And if we were to do the same with the practising of the tennis stroke, we would find that it, too, made the same curve (Fig. 10.2). This is known as the **learning curve**, and it shows how we go about learning any new skill.

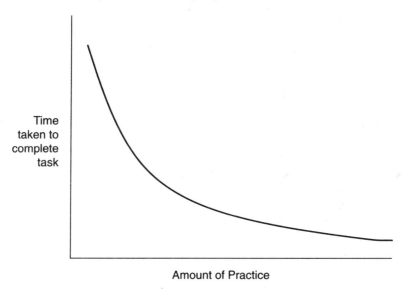

Time taken to complete task

Amount of Practice

Figure 10.2 A learning curve

Actually, though, the basic learning curve is only the beginning. In a complex sport, or skill, we often experience several different curves, with a levelling out between them (Fig 10.3). We are likely improve with practice a great deal at first, but then we hit what is known as a plateau, where we do not seem to get any better for a while. But if we keep on working at it, then eventually we begin to improve again. Most complex skills involve **plateau learning**,

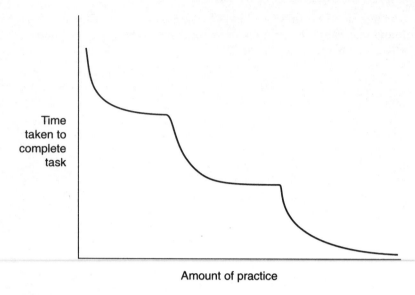

Amount of practice

Figure 10.3   Plateau learning

because they actually consist of many skills combined together, and it takes time to master each one. It is also possible that the time spent apparently not getting any better is useful because we consolidate those skills we do have, and make sure that they are fully under control.

The use of feedback

Another very important part of skill learning is **feedback**. Feedback is all about knowing what we have done — knowledge of results. If we did not get any feedback about the outcomes of our actions, we would not be able to learn anything. You could not get better at darts if you were blindfolded, so that you could not see where the darts had landed on the board! Instead, when playing darts, we use the outcome of our first action — throwing the first dart — to help us to get the second one even more precise.

One of the most important tasks of a sports coach is to provide feedback. But it matters what kind of feedback we get. De Brinker *et al.*, in 1986, investigated how important feedback is when learning to ski. They used a ski simulator, and asked people to learn how to make slalom-type movements while on the machine.

The researchers varied the kind of feedback people received, and found that the most useful type was when they were given feedback about the amplitude of their body movements — how much they swayed with the actions. They learned much faster from this than they did when they were given feedback about how often they moved, or how smooth their movements were.

Mental training

Another aspect of complex skill learning which sports psychologists have become very experienced with, is that of mental training. Mental training involves using the imagination, in a carefully controlled way, to improve performance. For example, Ainscoe and Hardy (1987) developed a training programme with gymnasts in which they were asked to practise their performance not just physically, but also mentally — visualising themselves going through each action successfully and smoothly. They found that using this method produced a noticeable improvement in how well the gymnasts learned.

Ainscoe and Hardy were not the only psychologists to have discovered this. In 1983, Feltz and Landers reviewed 60 different studies into the mental training of physical skills. They came to the conclusion that this method was a useful way of improving performance. Many athletes and other sportspeople use **visualisation** as a regular part of their practice, and find that it does not just help their physical learning, but it also helps their concentration.

Practice

Any new skill requires practice — it will not become a skill until enough time and effort has been put into perfecting it for it to have become virtually automatic. Some sports psychologists have investigated whether it is better to have long, concentrated sessions of practice, or whether it is better to break them up into smaller chunks. The answer seems to be somewhere between the two. Practice sessions need to be long enough for the person to get some physical control of the skill that they are working on, but it is also important to have breaks. They do not just give the person a chance to rest: they also seem to help us to consolidate the learning, so that it comes more easily the next time we try it.

Gruson (1988) looked at how skilled pianists practised, and compared it with people who were still working through the lower grades. She found that the experts went about their practising in a different way from the novices. The experts, for instance, would spend much more time practising whole units. They would never repeat single notes — if they made a mistake, they would repeat the whole section. Novices, on the other hand, would repeat single notes if they made a mistake — and this did not really help them to learn the whole piece of music at all.

The implication, then, is that practising whole units is important for the development of fluent skills. If we wish to produce a performance which is polished and continuous, we need to practise what we are doing in a way that is also continuous. It is obvious really, when you think about it, but it is surprising how many people do not do it!

Keeping motivated

Another important aspect of sport psychology is in studying how it is that successful athletes manage to maintain the motivation which keeps them continually training and striving to improve their performance. Becoming a competent sportsperson involves giving up a great deal of free time, and putting oneself through a considerable amount of physical effort. For many people such efforts would be too much. So what is it that distinguishes someone who is prepared to do this from the rest of us?

Internal and external motivation

One of the most important distinctions which sports psychologists make is between internal and external sources of motivation. An internal source of motivation is one which comes from inside ourselves — which derives from our own intentions, ambitions, and personal goals. An external source of motivation, as its name suggests, comes from outside. External motivators include rewards — such as money — avoiding punishment, and living up to other people's expectations.

Interestingly, there is quite a lot of evidence which shows that giving people external rewards, like money, for achieving success in sport, music or exams can actually be counter-productive. It can reduce someone's motivation, not increase it. For example, Orlick and Mosher (1978) asked children to carry out a balancing task on a bar, for ten minutes. Before and after the test, the children could spend as much time as they liked practising. The amount of time that they practised was taken as showing their level of intrinsic motivation.

Orlick and Mosher found that all the children spent much the same amount of time practising before the test. When they did the test, they gave one group of children a special award, saying that it was because they had done such a good job. Another group of children did not get any reward at all, even though they were just as good. The children did not know about the other group, so they did not feel disappointed. But after the test the children who had received the award actually spent much less time practising than the children who had not been given anything. Receiving the award had actually decreased their level of intrinsic motivation.

Of course, that does not mean that all awards are a bad thing. Sometimes they can help motivation, because they encourage people to feel competent, and that they are getting somewhere. When Orlick and Mosher told children beforehand that they could earn an award by doing the balancing task, those children did not lose motivation at all. So things which tell us that our skills are improving as a result of our efforts help us to feel competent, and do not actually reduce our motivation. But rewards which are not relevant to our efforts, such as money or unexpected awards, do seem to reduce intrinsic motivation.

The reason for this seems to be that we tend to focus on just one explanation for why we are doing things. Even though, as we have seen, human beings often do things for more than one reason, we still prefer to identify just one reason at a time. So if someone receives an external reward for doing well, then they are likely to see themselves as being motivated by the reward, instead of by their own interest and commitment. So if the rewards do not continue, or do not seem to be important, the person loses motivation. Someone who knows that they are doing something for their own personal pleasure and ambition, though, is not likely to lose that motivation unless their whole ambitions change.

Competency

That does not mean, though, that we could carry on putting lots of effort into mastering a sporting or musical skill if we did not feel that we were getting anywhere. It is very important that we should be able to feel **competent** in our learning — that we should feel that our skills are improving, and that our own personal abilities to do things are getting better. Having good feedback is a part of that, because that shows us when we are improving.

But another important part of that is the way that we set our own personal goals. We need to have something to aim at, and that something must be something that we think we could manage. It needs to give us a challenge to rise to, but not be so far ahead that we feel we could never get there. **Setting manageable goals** is an important part of retaining motivation, because the feeling that we have achieved something more helps us to keep going.

Achieving peak performance

Sport psychology is also concerned with making sure that people can perform to the absolute limit of their ability, at the times when it matters. Training and motivation are part of that, but there are other factors, too, which are the concern of sport psychology. On the training field, for instance, many athletes reach top performance. But when it comes to actual competitive events, some people consistently win, while others just do not seem to be able to manage that last, final edge which means success.

Positive thinking

Positive thinking is a crucial factor in distinguishing between people who are likely to be successful and those who are not. Highly successful sportspeople do not allow themselves to think about failure. They do not just block it off — instead, they think positively about success. Not about winning the gold medal, but about actually doing the activities successfully.

That sort of approach requires a high level of mental discipline on the part of the athlete or performer. There are various techniques for doing this. One of them is learning how to concentrate your mental focus, so that you are only aware of the part of your surroundings which matter. The champion tennis player Billie Jean King described how her mental focus would change from a wide range, encompassing the whole court, while the ball was over the other side of the net, to a tight, narrow focus the minute the ball was hit by her opponent. The gold medal-winning athlete Linford Christie keeps his mental focus on the track in front of him during the few minutes before the race begins.

Another way that successful athletes use positive thinking is in visualising success and achievement. The hurdler David Hemery described how one year he tried to prepare himself for disappointment, by imagining realistically how he would deal with failure. He lost. The next year, throughout his training, he only allowed himself to think about success, and did not entertain the thought that he might not win. That was the year that he won his Olympic gold medal.

As with using visualisation for training, Hemery's mental images were not particularly about standing on the podium. He would practise, mentally, completing the track without a single mistake, and in the best possible time. By creating a positive mental image of what he was capable of achieving, Hemery was able to build up his feelings of competence and confidence, and to make sure that his performance on the day was the very best that he could do.

Managing performance anxiety

Another aspect of making sure that you do the best you can, whether in a sporting competition or in an exam, is making sure that your anxiety levels do not get out of hand. We saw in Chapter 3 how being anxious or upset can interfere with how well we do things, so it is important for an athlete not to allow themselves to get too worried. Using positive thinking is also a good way of doing this. By filling the mind up with positive mental images, there is not much room for thoughts about failure or mistakes.

Athletes also manage performance anxiety by making sure that their bodies are not physically stressed in the wrong way. Anxiety can be increased by eating the wrong things, or by eating at too infrequent intervals. If we have not eaten for several hours, for instance, we automatically become more anxious and aroused, because that is an old biological mechanism for encouraging us to go out and look for food. Many athletes drink milk, because it contains naturally calming substances which work in the brain to reduce anxiety without interfering with our physical abilities. And, of course, they regard it as very important that they are properly rested and have a good night's sleep before a key competition.

Exactly the same principles apply to any sort of demanding human contest. It is just as important when you are doing an exam, or entering a sporting competition or taking a graded test, to eat properly and to be rested. But it is astounding how many people ignore the physical demands of their bodies, and make their anxiety much worse by not eating properly, or by staying up the night before to 'study'. There is a physical aspect to managing any kind of performance anxiety, even exam performance.

Using setbacks constructively

Another feature which seems to distinguish between the top performers and those who do not do as well, is the way that they handle failure when it actually happens. Many people respond to failing a test, or an exam, or losing a competition, by feeling upset and disappointed. But the top sportspeople do not do that. Instead, they react by being angry with themselves. They know that they can do better than that, and so they resolve to make sure that it will not happen again.

This has everything to do with the process of attribution that we looked at in Chapter 8. Attribution, you may remember, is about the reasons that we give for why things happen. And that makes all the difference to how we respond to failure. If someone attributes their failure to lack of talent or ability, for instance, then they are unlikely to try very hard to overcome it, because they will not think there's any point. If they think it was just a 'bad day', or something temporary, then they will continue with their normal training, and not be too bothered about it. But if they think it is because they were doing something badly, which they could do better, then they will work very hard to make sure that they do not make the same mistake again.

Sport psychology, then, like so many other aspects of psychology, brings together many different levels of human functioning. We have to perfect our physical skills, and ensure that they are fully co-ordinated. We learn by practice, accustoming ourselves to repetition and association. But we are also affected by our thoughts, beliefs and imagination — and these can make all the difference to how we learn, and how we perform, skilled actions.

11

PSYCHOLOGY IN — EDUCATION AND — HEALTH

In one way or another, psychologists have been involved with both education and health care since psychology first began. But the ideas which have developed in psychology during that time have changed considerably, as our understanding of the human being has developed. And as these ideas have developed, so, too, have many of the social practices which emerged from them.

For example, in the middle of the twentieth century, a number of politically influential psychologists, particularly Sir Cyril Burt, believed that intelligence was a fixed, inherited quality. Since Burt was directly involved in giving advice to the Ministry of Education, this led to the introduction of a school system in which children were sent to different schools, offering different types of education, depending on their performance in an examination and intelligence test which they took at the age of 11.

Nowadays, we do not see intelligence in quite the same way. We see it as much more of an interaction between a person's own personal temperament, and their experiences and environment. The experiences of mature students, who were unsuccessful at school but who take exams, degrees and even higher degrees later in their adult lives shows that intelligence — in practical terms — can change dramatically with experience. And research evidence also suggests that as long as we use it, our intelligence increases as we get older, not decreases. So the old idea that a person has a fixed intelligence, which does not change through their lifespan, is pretty well discredited.

In the health field, too, psychological ideas and knowledge have developed considerably. During the first part of the twentieth century, this area of psychology was strongly influenced by the idea of the psychoanalyst, Sigmund Freud, who believed that people were largely acting out the demands of unconscious parts of their personality. Freud believed that unconscious infantile conflicts could lead to both mental and physical disturbance, even in adults.

More recently, psychoanalysis has become pretty well separated from psychology. Although some of its ideas have been very useful to clinical psychologists — in particular the idea of defence mechanisms, which we looked at in Chapter 5 — psychoanalysis, as a way of studying the world, adopts a different style of reasoning from modern psychology and takes a different view of scientific evidence. For the most part, modern clinical psychologists draw on a different set of psychological insights and theories in their work. In this chapter, we will look briefly at some of the main ideas which psychologists working in education and health tend to use. Some of them will probably seem familiar, because often we will be looking at how the concepts which we looked at in the early part of this book are being applied in real life.

The psychology of teaching and learning

The idea of a rigidly fixed intelligence may have been largely discredited, but, nonetheless, some of us are faster to understand things than others. People still differ. We each have our own aptitudes, our own interests, and our own talents. But even if we have an aptitude for something, if we are not interested in it, then we are unlikely to put any effort into mastering it.

Student motivation

As we have already seen, being interested in something can make all the difference to whether we remember it or not. And, as we have also seen, becoming skilled at anything, whether it is an intellectual skill like reading or a physical skill like skating, takes practice. So a vital part of the psychology of teaching and learning consists of understanding how students come to be interested in what they are learning, so that they will have the motivation needed to keep working.

The learning environment

In Chapter 5 we saw how human motivation can operate on several different levels. Our behaviour is sometimes energised and directed by how we think about things, sometimes by the situation itself, and sometimes by social and cultural factors. All of these are relevant to education too. For example, if we take one of the more basic levels of explanation, we are all influenced by the environment around us. A formal classroom layout produces different behaviour from people in it than an informal setting.

Partly, this stems from our social understanding of what a formal layout is intended to convey: it is a kind of **non-verbal communication**. But partly, also, it is a learned association between stimulus and response. Our past experiences have formed that link, and so we act in the same way when we find ourselves in the same situation.

This might seem trivial, but it is one of the things that we need to take into account when we are considering the psychology of teaching and learning. For instance, many people who take qualifications in further education colleges are returning to study as mature students. Although they do want to study, often their first experience of being in a classroom again brings back unpleasant associations of school and feelings of inadequacy and failure.

A teacher who is aware of this process is in a position to make sure that these feelings are quickly replaced by ones which will help the student to learn, and not hinder them, by providing more positive, learning experiences in that setting. But someone who was unaware of what was going on could easily dismiss these people as not having the necessary motivation to learn.

Programmed learning

Stimulus – reponse learning can be important in other ways, too. The behaviourist B. F. Skinner developed a system known as programmed learning, which used the principle of **positive reinforcement** for learned behaviour. Skinner, as we have seen, believed that it is better to reward appropriate behaviour, than to punish inappropriate acts. So the learning system which he developed was based on the idea that the more people could get right, the more they would learn.

In the programmed learning system, information which needs to be learned is divided into very small chunks, each of which leads on to the next. By dividing it up like this, it is relatively easy for a student to get each answer right. If they do not, they go back and re-learn the section until they do. Skinner believed that maximising the chances of right answers like this would provide sufficient motivation for learning — unlike conventional educational programmes of the time, which tended to emphasise failure and wrong answers rather than rewarding right ones.

Personal dimensions of teaching and learning

Skinner's ideas have been incorporated, often in a modified form, into many educational systems. But not all of them. Skinner, as a behaviourist, believed that the stimulus – response level of explanation was enough to explain all human behaviour. So he believed that just the association between the information and the right answer would be enough for people to learn — and that could be provided just as well by teaching machines as by anything else (Skinner 1966).

But that ignores other aspects of how human beings function. Our social knowledge and the expectations of other people are equally important in how we learn, if not more so. We have already seen how important expectations can be in educational performance, through Rosenthal and Jacobsen's work, which we looked at in Chapter 2. And there are many other aspects of teaching and learning in which interpersonal relationships and social interactions are extremely important.

Achievement motivation

For example, as any teacher will tell you, some children seem to have a much stronger **need for achievement** than others. These children often learn well, because success is important to them and so they put a great deal of effort into studying. They are not the only children who learn well, of course: some do it purely because they are interested in what they are learning. But it is helpful for a child to have a reasonably high level of achievement motivation, because that will see it through temporary difficulties and setbacks as it comes to terms with new things.

Rosen and D'Andrade (1959) showed that achievement motivation seems to have a great deal to do with the way that parents interact with their children. In one of their studies they gave a child a difficult task to do, while its parents were watching. The child was blindfolded and asked to build a tower, as high as possible, out of building bricks. The researchers took note of how hard the child tried to do this — how much effort it would put into getting the tower as high as possible — on the grounds that this would give them some idea of the child's general level of achievement motivation.

Rosen and D'Andrade also observed the parents closely while the child was trying to complete the task. They found that those children with the highest level of achievement motivation had parents who consistently gave them praise and encouragement. These parents also had quite high expectations — they anticipated that their child would do quite well in the task, and the children often lived up to those expectations. Parents of children who had low achievement motivation, though, did not expect their children to achieve very much, and did not particularly encourage them either.

Self-efficacy

Psychologists of that time tended to think of achievement motivation as a general trait, which would be roughly the same for anything the child encountered. Nowadays, many psychologists see achievement motivation as being linked with **self-efficacy beliefs** — our personal beliefs about how effective we can be (see Chapter 5). Since our self-efficacy beliefs vary, depending on which type of activity they are concerned with, this means that achievement motivation, too, can be variable.

For example, someone might have very high self-efficacy beliefs when it comes to maths — they know they can learn it, and so they try hard in maths lessons and are successful in exams. But the same person might have much lower self-efficacy beliefs when it comes to learning history. If they have low self-efficacy beliefs for history, then they are less likely to put in the effort that is needed to master the subject and pass the exams.

But self-efficacy beliefs are not fixed. They can be changed by experience. As we saw in Chapter 2, experiencing repeated failure often leads to **learned helplessness**, and giving up, but if we have the experience of learning effectively, and realise that we are able to do so competently, our self-efficacy beliefs rise, and we are more likely to work harder. So, a successful teacher, in this respect, is one who makes sure that her students experience success from time to time, and also see that success as the result of their own efforts. This raises their self-efficacy beliefs, and provides them with the motivation to work at the subject, achieving things competently.

Personal constructs

Personal constructs, too, are also important in the classroom. Personal constructs are the individual theories and ideas about the world that we develop from our personal experiences, and apply to new situations. Driver (1983) showed how these can be extremely important when people are trying to understand information at school. If our own personal understanding of the world does not fit with what we are supposed to learn, then we will only absorb part of what we are learning. We will adjust the information so it fits with our own personal construct system.

This, Driver argued, is the source of most of the common factual errors which schoolchildren — and adults — make. She looked at children's everyday understanding of scientific ideas, like heat or falling (gravity), and showed that if we develop knowledge of these things purely from our own experience, then the conclusions we come to are not the same as those developed by physicists. By the time the child learns about these things in school, it has had plenty of time to develop its own theories and ideas about how the world works. As the child tries to understand what it is learning, these theories get in the way.

Driver showed how understanding how students develop and apply their own personal construct systems to what they are learning can help teachers to teach more effectively. Mistakes do not come from stupidity, or being unwilling to learn, but from applying the wrong kind of theories to what they are supposed to be learning.

Understanding this helps teachers to know what kind of explanations will be needed and why some students are having difficulty.

Levels of processing in remembering

In Chapter 6, we saw how we remember things far better if we have processed the information deeply. Being interested in something means that we do process the information, because we think about what it means, and what effects it might have. So we do not usually have any trouble remembering things that we are interested in. But knowing about **levels of processing** in memory can also help us with other aspects of educational experiences.

For example, taking examinations generally means learning a great deal of information, not all of which is scintillatingly interesting. But it is possible to use the idea of levels of processing to ensure that we can remember the information, even though we may not be totally thrilled by it. By changing the form of the information — drawing up charts, or diagrams, or making summaries — we force our minds to process the information and think about what it actually means. And once we are aware of what it means, it is much harder to forget it.

In fact, books about how to revise are full of advice about working with the material. Drawing on their own, good experience with students, the authors recommend various different methods for revising, all of which actually add up to processing the information more deeply. The problem, though, is that they do not usually explain why we should do it. Unless we can see a good reason for doing something, we do not usually do it. So, understanding the psychological processes of memory and why drawing up a table or a chart helps us to learn are important.

Positive emotions

Another aspect of psychological knowledge which is important in understanding teaching and learning is how emotional states affect learning. In Chapter 2 we saw how people need a positive interpersonal climate if they are to be open to learning new things and developing their ideas. Nobody learns well in a climate of hostility or sarcasm, but if they feel approved of and safe, people often surprise us with what they can actually achieve.

So one of the things which a skilled teacher learns is how to create an atmosphere of interpersonal warmth in the classroom, which will encourage their students to become confident and to learn positively. Although many non-psychologists, including, unfortunately, some teachers, believe that we can learn when we are tense or anxious, there is not any psychological evidence for that at all — not when it comes to education, anyway. About all we learn in those situations is how to avoid pain, which is a basic and primitive form of learning. But there is plenty of psychological evidence for the opposite — that in education as well as in everyday hobbies and interests, people learn best when they feel confident and approved of.

Social dimensions to teaching and learning

There are also social dimensions to the psychology of teaching and learning. As we have already seen in this chapter, we cannot really separate the personal and social aspects of learning, because we are all personally influenced by social factors. But there are other issues too. For example, in Chapter 2 we saw how **social identification**, or belonging to groups, is an important part of how we see ourselves. The attitudes which our friends and family take to education will affect us, as well as whether the teacher encourages the class to feel special, and a social group in their own right.

Social identification

A knowledge of social identification is useful for a teacher, because it shows us how intergroup conflicts can develop. If students feel that their group identity is being disparaged or threatened, they may respond by reacting against classwork, or even against being in school at all.

But people can have many different social identifications, and these do not have to be in conflict. Someone may be a member of a teenage gang yet still work hard when they are in the classroom — as long as that working hard is not seen as a threat to their gang identity. Many extremely effective teachers have worked success-fully with people who, on the surface, appear to be directly opposed to what they are trying to do. They have been able to do this because they have made it clear that there is no conflict between them.

A vital part of this involves knowing how important social identity is to our self-esteem. This helps a teacher to see why the student's social group is so important, and why it matters that the student should see how working for the future — which is what school or college work really is — is not a threat to social identity in the present. But, without such an understanding of social identity processes, many teachers are either dismissive of their students' social groups, or see them as inevitably in conflict with educational values. And these students, on their part, often feel misjudged and unfairly stereotyped.

We can see, then, that the psychology of teaching and learning spans a number of different **levels of explanation**. It ranges from the personal and emotional aspects of human psychology, to the cognitive, social, and even cultural levels of explanation. As with so many other aspects of human behaviour, we can gain insights from each of these levels of explanation; but if we are to get a more rounded picture of how human beings are, we need to take them all into account.

Educational disadvantage

Psychologists are also involved in helping children and adults who are experiencing some kind of educational disadvantage. Such psychologists are known as educational psychologists in Britain, although they are called school psychologists in the United States, where educational psychologists are more concerned with the applied psychology of teaching and learning. In Britain, educational psychologists are responsible for assessing children who are thought to need a special type of education, and recommending what sort of education that should be.

Specific learning difficulties

There are several different kinds of educational disadvantage. Sometimes children have **specific learning difficulties**, so that they find certain kinds of information very hard to learn. If they experience a special school environment, in which the teacher pays particular attention to training them to handle the things which they find difficult, they can often learn a great deal more than they would do in an ordinary school.

Other children who have specific learning difficulties, though, might benefit more from being in an ordinary school and mixing with the children there. The educational psychologist's judgement as to which type of schooling will be best for that particular child will take into account as many different facets of the child's experience as possible.

For example: we have already seen how much social expectations can influence us. They can affect our self-image, our interactions with other people, and how well we learn. If a child attends a special school, it is possible that people will not expect as much from them as they would do if they went to an ordinary school. So in some cases, if a child's problem is not very extreme, it may be better for them to go to an ordinary school and perhaps have some additional tuition to help them overcome their difficulties than to go to a special school. The decision about whether to send a child to a special school depends very much on the child itself, and on how severe his or her problems are.

Educational psychologists undergo rigorous training in diagnosing learning difficulties. Some problems have a physical source: certain kinds of brain damage, for example, can produce very specific effects on how a child learns. Sometimes it is possible to overcome these effects with the right kind of training. Most children recover very well from accidental brain injury, for instance, and if they have the right kind of therapy, the effects can often disappear completely.

Sometimes, though, the problem is not the kind you can get over. In that case, the psychologist would decide that **amelioration** was the best approach, and the child would be taught how to cope with, and get round, its problem. By developing training which is relevant to the kinds of situations that the child is likely to meet, it can learn how to live a relatively normal life, even though it may have some difficulties.

Dyslexia

One of the specific learning difficulties which educational psychologists often need to diagnose is the problem known as **dyslexia**. Dyslexia used to be known as word-blindness, and people who experience dyslexia often have difficulty in identifying letters, or recognising how they should be written. For example, a dyslexic person might write a letter like y or r back to front, but not realise that they had done it. They seem to be 'blind' to the image of the letter. Other dyslexics have different problems recognising words.

Sometimes dyslexia comes about as a result of some kind of accident which causes an injury to the person's brain. This is known as **acquired dyslexia**. Shallice and Warrington (1980) described two kinds of acquired dyslexia. One of them, which is known as surface dyslexia, is when someone has problems with the forms of words, like difficulties recognising letters, as above, or problems with spelling — like writing 'lurn' instead of 'learn'.

The second kind of dyslexia is not about the forms of words, but about understanding them. People with this type of dyslexia have difficulty with words which are hard to visualise: they can understand words like 'tree' easily enough, but have more problems with words like 'and'. Shallice and Warrington called this **deep dyslexia**, because it relates to a deeper understanding of words.

Acquired dyslexia is not particularly controversial in psychology. It is a recognised outcome of some forms of brain damage, and there is a great deal of evidence for how people who previously had these abilities intact experience problems with them after their accident. But there is a second type of dyslexia — the kind that an educational psychologist would often encounter — which is much more controversial. This is known as **developmental dyslexia**.

Developmental dyslexia is a problem which becomes apparent as a child develops and goes through school. A few children seem to be virtually unable to identify words and letters properly, and so they have problems with spelling. Some psychologists believe that this problem occurs because of an inherent deficit in the brain, and some have even gone as far as to suggest that it is a genetic disorder, although as yet the evidence for this is a little sketchy.

So far, so good. There certainly do seem to be cases in which children have difficulties of this kind, which really do seem to result from some kind of inherent problem. The controversy comes, though, in whether all children who are called dyslexic really have these problems. Many psychologists (e.g. Whittaker 1982) see the word 'dyslexic' as a convenient label which is used in many entirely inappropriate cases. Whittaker *et al.* believe that children are often labelled dyslexic when all they really have are problems with spelling.

The problem is compounded by the fact that the concept of dyslexia became popular in Britain soon after a nation-wide experiment on reading, which tried to teach reading using a special phonetic alphabet, known as i.t.a., or initial teaching alphabet. This was based on the principle that children learned to read by 'hearing' the words — a principle which we now know is not how it works. But as a result of the use of i.t.a. a great many children became confused about the need to spell accurately, and many schools gave up on teaching spelling formally.

In view of this social context, and the fact that spelling is something which does not come naturally to anyone — it always has to be learned by heart, and that takes effort — there is a great deal of anxiety that too many children have been labelled as dyslexic when really they could overcome their problem with a different kind of teaching. This is also exaggerated by a tendency to see a diagnosis of 'dyslexic' as a message that there is no point trying to teach this child words or spelling. As with many other educational disorders, special training programmes which recognise the difficulty and address it directly can often overcome the problem, at least if it is in a mild form.

So there are two aspects to the controversy about dyslexia. It is not really about whether dyslexia exists. The first part is about whether all the children who have been labelled dyslexic really are, or whether the label has been given to them simply because they are finding words or spelling hard. The second part is about whether an accurate diagnosis of dyslexia means that the problem is permanent or fixed. Special training programmes suggest that it is not, and that it can be overcome, but many people seem to see such a diagnosis as if it were a life sentence.

Childhood autism

Sometimes the problems which educational psychologists encounter are broader than straightforward learning disorders. For example, the problem known as **childhood autism** seems to be a broadly based emotional and personal disorder, which results in such children being unable to relate effectively to the people in their lives.

Autism was first identified as a general syndrome by Kanner (1943), who identified four characteristics which autistic children possess. The first, and probably the most important, is that they are unable to form relationships with other people. Although they may interact, they seem to be aware only of the way that another body impinges on them, not of the person as a human being.

The second characteristic which Kanner identified was that autistic children rarely play spontaneously — and, particularly, that they do not engage in play which is about pretending. Ordinary children, though, begin pretend play from quite an early age, and do not need to be taught it at all.

Autistic children also show differences in the way that they learn to speak. Some of them never actually learn to talk at all. Others, though, will talk quite a lot, but when they do, they do not speak in the same way as do ordinary children. For instance, they never quite get the hang of reversing pronouns, so that when they are talking to someone they say 'you' but the person they are talking to will say 'I'. Although ordinary children learn this quite easily, autistic children say what they have heard other people saying, so they tend to refer to themselves as 'you'.

The fourth distinctive characteristic of childhood autism which Kanner identified is that the child has an almost obsessive insistence on certain routines or repeated activities. These children seem to enjoy repetition and routine, and can become very upset if their routines are interrupted for some reason.

Harris (1988) discussed how a range of psychological evidence all points to the idea that autistic children do not have a **theory of mind**. In other words, they are not aware that other people have minds of their own, and may see things differently. Baron-Cohen (1992) described an autistic girl, Jane, who had no problem remembering people or information, but who had absolutely no awareness of the fact that other people were independent, thinking and feeling human beings. Her inability to empathise, or to understand someone else's point of view, resulted in a great many of her autistic symptoms.

——— Counselling and therapy ———

A different area of activity for psychologists is in health care. Psychologists are involved both in mental and physical health care, in one way or another. Clinical psychologists have been concerned with helping people who are suffering from emotional disorders or mental illness since the early part of the twentieth century. More recently, health psychologists have become increasingly concerned with aspects of our physical health care, as it has become more apparent that so many aspects of our physical health depend on psychological, rather than medical, factors.

Clinical psychology

Clinical psychology, for the most part, has been concerned with people who are suffering from some kind of mental or behavioural abnormality — people who we might call mentally ill, although often thinking of them as 'ill' is not the best way to understand what is going on. Clinical psychologists often work alongside psychiatrists (doctors who specialise in mental illness) in psychiatric hospitals or clinics, but their approach to dealing with the patients is very different. Where a psychiatrist draws on a knowledge of physiology, which means adopting treatments like chemotherapy (drugs) or physical treatments like electro-convulsive therapy, clinical psychologists use their knowledge of human psychology to tackle the problem.

Behaviour therapy

For example, some of the types of problems which clinical psychologists might deal with are what we know as **neuroses** — fears or anxieties which have become so extreme that the person has difficulty living a normal life. In the 1950s, psychologists who were interested in conditioning approaches to learning took the view that many of these problems could be understood entirely as problems of behaviour. These people, they argued, had learned inappropriate ways of dealing with their environments, and this inappropriate learning was causing them problems. So the way to tackle those problems was for them to learn appropriate ways of dealing with their environments instead.

This led to the development of a number of different, behavioural, methods for dealing with neurotic problems. As we saw in Chapter 7, psychologists began to use conditioning techniques for dealing with the irrational fears known as phobias. By treating the feared object as the stimulus, and substituting new, learned associations such as relaxation for the fear reaction, people could learn to deal with their phobias, and overcome them.

Other psychologists used approaches which derived from operant conditioning, or from social learning. Bandura (1977) showed how **modelling** could also be useful in teaching people to overcome everyday fears. Seeing someone handling a snake harmlessly often gave those who were frightened of snakes a role model to imitate, and they found that their own level of fear became much less as a result.

Behaviour shaping

Many psychologists used the idea of **behaviour shaping** which had come from operant conditioning theory. A person becomes able to carry out an entirely new type of behaviour by learning it a little at a time. This principle was very successful in helping people with agoraphobia — a fear of open spaces. Rather than force them into dealing with the whole problem all at once, a psychologist would gradually help the person to build up their abilities, a little at a time. They might begin, for instance, by getting used to going just a short distance away from their own home. Once they could do that easily, then a little more would be added until eventually they could manage to deal with the outside world more easily.

Another way that behaviour shaping was used was in **token economy** systems, introduced to help long-stay psychiatric patients to take more responsibility for their own lives. In the 1960s and 1970s, some patients had been in psychiatric hospitals for decades, and they had become thoroughly institutionalised — dependent, and unable to look after themselves. Psychologists developed training systems which would allow them gradually to learn how to do basic things, like sweeping a floor or taking care of their own clothes.

Since it is important for operant conditioning that the reward, or reinforcement, should be given immediately after the person performs the behaviour which is to be rewarded, the patient would be given a token when they did something right. In very severe cases, this might at first be as little as holding a broom and making vague sweeping movements. Once they had learned that, they would only be rewarded for sweeping a bit more thoroughly. At the end of the day or week, they could exchange their tokens for privileges of one kind or another. In this way, long-stay patients were gradually taught the kinds of behaviours which they would need if they were ever to leave the institution and live in a hostel.

Cognitive therapy

In the late 1970s and early 1980s, as psychology changed its emphasis, clinical psychologists began to develop new approaches which drew on other psychological knowledge. A new form of therapy, known as cognitive therapy, emerged. Psychologists began to work on the self-defeating beliefs of many of their clients, showing them how to recognise negative attributional styles and how to develop realistic and positive self-efficacy beliefs. Research into stress management showed how important it is for people to have a sense of control over their own lives, and many clinical psychologists adopted these principles in their work.

Counselling psychology

Another form of clinical psychology had first emerged in the 1950s, with the work of the psychologist Carl Rogers. As we saw in Chapter 2, Rogers believed that human beings had two basic needs: the need for positive regard from others, and the need for self-actualisation. From his experience with his own patients, he came to the conclusion that providing an environment in which people would experience unconditional positive regard would allow them the security to be able to explore their own potential and to make their own choices.

Client-centred therapy

Rogers' work became the foundation of what was later to become counselling psychology. He developed an approach which he called **client-centred therapy,** to emphasise that it was the client who held the responsibility and made the decisions, rather than the professional who was supposed to be helping them. In client-centred therapy the therapist provides a supportive, warm environment in which the person explores their own options and makes their own decisions.

Following on from this, Rogers concluded that it was equally possible for other people to provide a supportive and warm environment. He developed the idea of **encounter groups** — groups in which people would share their problems, and encounter one another openly, as individual human beings. It was this which provided the basic principle of the self-help groups which have become such an important part of Western societies.

Rogers' ideas became extremely influential in many areas, and were taken up by many people, both psychologists and otherwise. Counselling as a profession was developed on the basis of Rogerian principles, although since then it has developed other approaches as well. Although many counsellors are not psychologists, there are also counselling psychologists — qualified psychologists who apply their professional skills and training in counselling work.

Health psychology

Psychologists are also involved in working to enhance physical health. Health psychology is a very broad area, because it is concerned with the different psychological aspects of our physical health, and there are a lot of them. Maintaining physical health is not just about avoiding illness: it is also about making sure that we stay well, so lifestyles and beliefs are very important in health psychology.

Doctor – patient communication

Some health psychologists are interested in doctor — patient communication. For example, people often do not give their doctor all of the information which the doctor needs to make an accurate diagnosis because they feel intimidated by the doctor's manner, and by the formal setting of the surgery. Health psychologists use their knowledge of non-verbal communication and social appraisal to help doctors to communicate more effectively, so that they can overcome these problems.

Another aspect of doctor — patient communication is the question of following medical instructions. Surveys show that as many as 60 per cent of people do not actually use medical treatments in the ways that they have been told — and this is important, because that can make all the difference to whether the treatment is effective or not. A drug which has to be taken with food will not do its job properly if it is taken on an empty stomach, because it interacts with the chemicals involved in digestion to have its effect.

So health psychologists look at the various reasons why people do or do not follow medical instructions. They explore issues like lifestyle — given the person's everyday life, is it actually difficult for them to do what they have been told to do? They also look at people's beliefs about medicines and how they work, and at how instructions can be misunderstood. Research of this kind has produced a number of recommendations for medical personnel which improve how accurately people use their treatments.

Behavioural treatments

Another aspect of health psychology is concerned with behaviourally based treatments. In some physical illnesses, such as diabetes, there is no known cure. All patients who have diabetes can do is to manage their disorder, by behavioural control of some kind. Health psychologists help people to do this, by looking at aspects of behaviour such as diet control, lifestyle and how people monitor their own health.

By now it should come as no surprise to discover that one of the most important factors in managing diabetes, as well as other behaviourally based disorders, is for people to have a sense of control over their own health. People who see their illness as not under their own control are more likely to suffer, and to do things which will make the situation worse, than people who see what happens to them as the outcome of their own actions. A passive approach to an illness like diabetes has demonstrably worse outcomes than an active management of the problem. So health psychologists are also involved in training people in techniques for managing their own stress levels, and the like.

Health education

Another aspect of health psychology is in health education programmes: public campaigns which are designed to encourage people to take up healthy behaviours and to minimise risks. Anti-smoking campaigns, AIDS avoidance campaigns, and, more controversially, advice about what constitutes a healthy diet, are the kinds of areas in which psychologists have been involved.

Persuading people to take up healthy lifestyles is not as easy as it may sound. Simply giving people information does not really do, because there is often quite a difference between what we know and what we do. We may be aware that something is risky, and yet do it anyway. And there are also social factors involved, which can influence what we actually end up doing.

For example, there is a big discrepancy between the number of young people who are aware that they should use a condom when they are having sex, and the number who actually do. Even though the risks of AIDS are high, and the consequences of contracting HIV can be tragic, many people still engage in extremely risky behaviours.

Psychologists studying this area have identified a number of factors which maintain this risky behaviour, such as the belief that sticking to one partner will minimise the risk — even though the partnership later breaks up and the person then enters another relationship — or the idea that using a condom detracts from the spontaneity of the experience, and makes it seem too 'planned'. There are questions of habits: many older people are reluctant to adopt condom use because they have established sexual habits without them. And there is also, of course, the question of a power imbalance between men and women, since many men oppose the use of condoms and many women do not feel confident enough to insist on their use.

It is these kinds of factors which show how complex the problem of risk-avoidance really is. It goes much deeper than simply providing people with information, and an awareness of human psychology is necessary to explore the complexity of the issues. As we have found so often, health care and the promotion of healthy behaviour involves understanding the human being on a number of different levels. It is far from being simple and obvious.

12

PSYCHOLOGY AND THE ENVIRONMENT

This chapter is about environmental psychology, which is the study of the way that our surroundings and circumstances influence how we act and how we feel. It is not just physical surroundings which are important in this: environmental psychologists study the social environment too, in terms of the other people who are around us and how their presence makes a difference.

Our environment can affect us in more than one way. For example, it can act as a confining or restricting force. We adapt our behaviour to our surroundings, and those surroundings sometimes only allow certain kinds of actions. If you are a patient in a hospital, for instance, there are only a certain number of possibilities for action, partly because the environment only allows you to do certain things. The kinds of behaviour which are possible for someone out walking in the hills are entirely different from the kinds of behaviour which are possible for a mother at home with a small child.

Environments also have the power to produce particular kinds of behaviour from us. How a patient in a hospital acts is to a very large extent determined by the hospital environment: it is not just that it restricts the possibilities, it is also that we realise that certain kinds of behaviour are expected from us and so we act accordingly. We tend to speak in hushed tones in a church or holy place, even if we are not personally very religious, because just being in that environment produces that behaviour.

Another way that the environment affects us is that it can motivate us to act in certain ways. Different types of environment encourage us to do different things. Think of going on holiday, for instance. When we are away from home, we often find ourselves exploring new places, or trying out new foods — behaviours which we would not be nearly as likely to do at home. People are also sometimes motivated to stay in a particular part of the country, even if it means adapting to a less well-paid kind of work; or to live in a particular kind of house, even if it means hard work and struggle to get there.

———— Proxemics and privacy ————

Human beings are very conscious of space and places: it seems to be one of those things which is built deeply into our awareness. For example, we automatically seem to use distance as a type of **non-verbal communication**, which says something about the relationship that we have with other people. The usual distances are different from one culture to the next, but in all societies we stand closer to people that we like than we do to people that we do not like; we stand further away when talking to a stranger than to a friend, and we conform to cultural standards about what is the usual, or acceptable, distance for certain kinds of interaction.

Personal space

The area of psychology which is interested in personal space and the distances which we keep between people is known as **proxemics.** Everyone seems to be surrounded by a little 'bubble' of personal space, and we only allow people inside this space if we know them well enough. But, as I have already said, different cultures have different ideas as to how big that bubble is. What is a comfortable conversational distance for someone from a Middle Eastern country will often feel too close to a European, so if the two are in conversation, it is easy for tensions to arise. The European will feel tense and crowded, because they feel that their personal space is being invaded; while the Middle Eastern person will feel that the other is being distant and hostile, and not particularly friendly.

Zones of personal distance

Hall (1966) proposed that we have four zones of personal distance, which are listed in Table 12.1. When we are looking at this table, though, we have to remember that the distances which Hall provided as examples are drawn from Europe, Britain and the United States — and do not represent all of the subcultures in those societies, either. We also need to bear in mind that one category can sometimes shade into another — our personal distance zones are not really as rigid as they might seem from this description.

TABLE 12.1 ZONES OF PERSONAL DISTANCE

(i)	Intimate	(0 – 45 cm)	for lovers, very close family (such as mother and child), or very close friends
(ii)	Personal	(0.5 m – 1.2 m)	for friends, or family members
(iii)	Social	(between 1.2 m and 3.5 m)	for a business conversation, or a discussion with a stranger
(iv)	Public	(between 3.5 m and 7.5 m)	for public meetings and ceremonies, with speakers and audiences

---

It is not just the distances themselves which vary. Even when people are very close, the amount that they actually make contact with one another depends on their culture. Jourard (1966) observed couples at pavement cafés in various parts of the world, and observed how often they touched hands, or made body-contact in some other way. London had the lowest number: many couples did not make any contact at all during the period in which Jourard was conducting the observations. Puerto Rico, on the other hand, had the highest, with as many as 180 contacts between couples in the course of a single hour.

Often we try to protect our personal space by using markers like shopping bags or newspapers. You will often find, for example, that people reading in libraries will mark out a small area around themselves using bags or coats — establishing a kind of temporary 'territory'. In 1966, Felipe and Sommer conducted a study in which the researchers deliberately went and sat down too close to people working in libraries (it is interesting, isn't it, that we all have an idea of what 'too close' means?). Only one of the 80 people involved actually asked them to move, but the others all indicated that they were uncomfortable with the situation. Some people piled up papers and books to form a barrier; others used body posture to separate themselves, by turning away from the intruder and hunching their shoulders or putting an arm around their work; but most simply packed up their things and moved away.

Protecting privacy

Incidentally, this study is another example of the kind of research which psychologists used to do, but which would not be considered ethically acceptable nowadays. People are entitled to their privacy, and to be allowed to work undisturbed, and it is important that modern psychological studies should not cause anyone to feel discomfort or distress. So a study which deliberately intruded on someone's privacy would not be permitted by a psychology ethics committee, unless there was a very good reason indeed for doing it, and unless the people themselves had agreed to co-operate.

The concept of **personal privacy** is an important one for environmental psychology, although it is a hard one to define. Privacy means different things to different people. Some people see privacy as being entirely alone; others see it as being just with friends or family; others, as in the library study, see it as being left undisturbed to get on with what they are doing even if there are other people around. Personal privacy is closely linked with social respect, and we saw in Chapter 5 how important that can be for us. So even if it just takes the form of respecting personal distance, it is important to respect people's privacy.

This may seem to be a relatively unimportant point, until we remember that there are some situations in which people lose all right to personal privacy. One of the reasons why people find it so disturbing to be in hospital, for instance, is because hospital patients are placed in a situation where all of the normal social markers for privacy and personal space have disappeared. Nurses and other people can enter freely what would normally be an intimate zone for the person, and make bodily contact; and everyday actions become far more public than they were before. Sommer and Dewar (1963) discussed how this invasion of personal space and personal privacy is a serious source of strain for a hospital patient.

We protect out privacy in other ways, too. For example, even an ordinary family house has certain areas which are 'public', such as the sitting room, but other areas which are entirely private. In the normal run of things, a visitor to someone's house would not expect to see the bedrooms, for example. And even the public access is restricted to certain people: strangers are excluded carefully, by physical barriers such as fences and locks, and the part of ground which represents the territory is carefully marked out. Protecting personal privacy is so important to us that, for most people, what is really upsetting about being burgled is not so much what has been lost, as the knowledge that their personal territory has been invaded by a stranger who has no respect for them or what is theirs.

Defensible space

Newman (1972) suggested that having some kind of **defensible space** is important in minimising urban stress, and even crime. From studying the incidence of vandalism on different housing estates, Newman found that most of it happened in public places, and not in areas which were clearly 'owned' by a resident or small group of residents. The most extreme amounts of vandalism happened in public areas which were also enclosed or hidden from view, like lifts or stairwells.

Newman argued that housing developments ought to recognise the concept of 'defensible space' — the idea that the people living in housing projects should have areas which were clearly marked out as theirs, and which they could look after. By doing so, Newman asserted, it would be possible to reduce the amount of vandalism. When existing housing estates were looked at, Newman argued, some of them seemed to have been designed almost to encourage vandalism, because of the way that they used the space.

Newman identified four principles for developing areas of defensible space. The first was that there should be clearly defined territories, which people could see as 'owned', like individual gardens and entrances. The second was surveillance: it is important, Newman said, that an area should be overlooked, so that other people can see what is going on in it. The third is image: a building should look secure and well-protected, because that would reduce the number of opportunistic crimes. A building which seemed to be an easy target would attract people who were ready to take advantage of any opportunity, like an open window; whereas one which looked secure would not attract them so much in the first place. And the fourth principle was that the surrounding environment should also be open and easily surveyed. There is not much point in a well-designed housing development which can only by reached along dark, lonely roads!

Meeting strangers

A different facet of privacy is concerned with how we respond to the people around us. In modern industrial society, crowds are an ordinary part of everyday living. Yet this is a relatively recent development. For most of our history, human beings have tended to live in small village or nomadic communities, consisting of 100 to 200 people, so everyone would be known as an individual. In that situation, encountering a stranger is a rarity, so anyone new would automatically be an object of interest.

The problem is that we have kept many of our biological adaptations to meeting strangers: we respond differently to strangers from the way we do to friends, and in a way which is more aroused and tense. Yet in city or town life in modern Western societies, we meet strangers all the time. So mechanisms which are adapted for a life in which most people are known and familiar become overloaded and stressed, because they are continually being activated.

It is for this reason that so many people find crowds stressful. In a crowd, we are unable to maintain our usual personal space, and this is a source of tension. People sometimes even bump into us, which we find even more stressful, and we often perform quite complicated dodging manoeuvres when walking down a crowded pavement, in order to avoid bodily contact with strangers. We are also liable to make eye-contact with strangers, and eye-contact is one of the most powerful signals of all.

Eye-contact — looking directly into someone's eyes while they are also looking at you — is not a kind of signal that we take lightly. Prolonged eye-contact is a signal of intense interest in the other person. At its extremes, it can signal love — or its opposite, hostility and threat (there is no chance of confusing the two, because the muscles around the eyes are arranged quite differently). We look at someone who is speaking to us, which is a signal that they have all of our attention. We look away from someone if we do not want to disturb them, or make them feel self-conscious.

So even fleeting eye-contact, of the sort we have with strangers, is stressful when it happens often enough. In situations where prolonged eye-contact might happen because the same strangers have to remain close by, like in a lift or a tube train, we tend to look upward, or out of the window in order to avoid it, which is why advertisements tend to be placed high up. City-dwellers learn to cope with this type of stress, of course, but it is present in the background nonetheless.

Crowding can produce stress in other ways, as well. In a well-known study in 1962, Calhoun showed that laboratory rats which were allowed to breed freely and become overcrowded became much more aggressive, even killing one another as part of the competition for living-space and food. Since this behaviour would normally be totally alien to these animals, it showed how much stress the crowding had created.

There are indications, too, that human beings become much more aggressive if they are crowded. Loo (1979) studied young children in a day nursery, and found a strong link between bad temper and crowding. The more children there were, the more quarrelsome the youngsters became. Similarly, McCain *et al.* (1980) showed that prison riots and also suicides were much more common when prisons were overcrowded than when they held their intended number of prisoners.

In another study, Kelley (1982) showed that there was a strong link between the density of the population in 175 American cities, and the amount of crime. Even the types of areas which were relatively low in crime showed more crimes as the population increased — and that included all sorts of crimes, ranging from car theft to murders. Kelley drew the implication that population density, in and of itself, is one source of environmental stress, which shows itself in increased crime rates — although there are other factors which influence crime as well, of course.

— Sources of environmental stress —

Most of us have had the experience of being in an environment which calms or soothes us. For many people, being out in the country is a particularly restful and relaxing experience. For others, being in a bustling, busy market can be an experience which lifts their spirits and makes them feel happy. But environments can have the opposite effect too. Our surroundings can make us feel tense, or anxious, or can simply represent an increased strain as we go about our day-to-day lives.

Some aspects of our environmental experience, then, can be relaxing or uplifting. In 1982, Herzog *et al.* surveyed a large number of people about which features of cities they found most pleasant. Trees, grass and water were popular, as was distinctive architecture which was in harmony with its surroundings. Old, untidy settings like factories and alleyways were considered to be the least pleasant of all.

Noise

Other types of environmental experience, though, can be deeply stressful. Whether we are aware of it or not, we are taking in information from the world around us all the time. If a stimulus is continuous, though, we become habituated to it, so that we are no longer aware that it is happening. You will probably have noticed this if you have a 'fridge which hums. You do not consciously hear the humming, but when it stops you become aware that it was there in the background before.

Background stimulation, like this, can be much more intense than we realise. People who live in small towns or in the country often find it difficult to sleep when they are visiting a large city for the first time, because they find the continual traffic activity too noisy. People who live in the city do not notice it as much, but their senses are still registering it. The continual background noise of traffic, machinery and household equipment is a source of minor, but continual, stress.

Loud noise is even more stressful. People who live close to airports often have to have special sound insulation to protect them from the noise of the aircraft taking off and landing, and those who live close to motorways often need a sound screen, like a thick row of trees, to baffle the noise. Loud noise at work can cause people to go deaf, which is why operators of noisy machinery are expected to wear ear defenders; but it is a source of stress too.

A high level of noise at work affects our level of arousal (see Chapter 3) so that we feel 'keyed up', and often irritable. It also makes it difficult for us to communicate with other people, which is also stressful. This affects some kinds of work more than others: in an investigation of the effects of work noise, Poulton (1976) found that it was skilled jobs, which require concentration or rapid action, which are most affected by work noise.

Not all noise is stressful, though. The noise level at a music concert can be extremely loud, but does not produce serious effects — although it might, perhaps, if we were trying to do a skilled task which required concentration. For the most part, though, the fact that we have chosen to listen to it, and also the fact that it is musical rather than simply noise, makes a lot of difference to our reactions.

Control and stress

As we have seen so often, if we feel we have some **control** over the stimuli around us, then we do not find them nearly as stressful. And that can apply to loud, unpleasant noises too. Glass and Singer (1972) asked people to solve a set of problems, while a loud, harsh noise occurred from time to time. Half of the people in the study were able to press a button which would stop the noise, at least temporarily, but they were asked not to use it unless they really had to. The others did not have any way of stopping the noise. The first group, who could have stopped the noise if they wanted to, did not stop it at all, but they performed much better on the problem-solving task than the others. It seemed that just knowing that they could control it if they wanted to was enough to remove the stressful influence of the noise.

There are other studies which also show how important a sense of control can be in reducing stress. Lundberg (1976) investigated the levels of stress experienced by male passengers on a commuter train. The more people there were on the train, the more stress the passengers experienced, even though there were always enough seats for everyone. Lundberg also found that people who were first on the train, or who joined it at an early stage in its journey did not experience as much stress as those who joined the train later, even though they had a much longer journey.

What seemed to be important in the passengers' experience of stress was whether they could choose their own seats or not. People who joined the train early had more choice in where they sat, and were more likely to be able to choose a favourite seat. It seems that feeling that they had some kind of control over their commuting experience made a considerable difference to the amount of stress which they felt.

Temperature

Temperature can be a source of environmental stress, too. People working in an atmosphere which is too cold or too hot find it difficult to concentrate on their work, which is a source of frustration. But we have to be a bit careful when we are looking at temperature as a source of stress, because there is quite a big difference between external high temperatures — warm weather — and an indoor hot stuffy environment.

Baron and Ransberger (1978) looked at weather reports and civil disturbances in America, and found that riots were most likely to happen when the temperature was hot — although not when it was unusually or extremely so. That does not mean, though, that rioting is caused by hot weather. As Smelser (1962) and many other researchers have shown, riots are sparked off by perceived social injustice, not simply because people feel like rioting. But in hot weather more people are out on the streets, and so unfair or unjust events are more easily noticed and more easily communicated to others.

Pollution

We also respond more strongly than we realise to levels of pollution in the environment. Pollution represents a source of physical stress for our bodies, because they have to cope with semi-toxic substances, such as lead or nitrous oxides, as well as trace amounts of real toxins, such as those in commercially grown vegetables. But it can produce mental effects as well. Rotton *et al.*, in 1978, showed that when people were experiencing high levels of air pollution, they felt less happy, and also were more likely to dislike other people, and to see the negative side of things that happened to them.

On a more specific level, too, Bleda and Sandman (1977) showed that cigarette smoke could produce depression and anxiety in non-smokers. So it seems that environmental stresses of various kinds, whether it be noise, crowding or chemical pollution, can make a lot of difference to how we live our lives.

Disasters and accidents

Experiencing ongoing environmental stress is one thing: experiencing a disaster is quite different. From time to time, events happen which have massive implications, both for the people who are involved in them but also for the smooth and safe running of society as a whole. The nuclear explosion at Chernobyl, the Hillsborough football stadium disaster, the Zeebrugge Ferry disaster, the Kings Cross fire, and many others were traumatic events of such magnitude that they affected the lives of thousands of people: not just those who were directly involved and their families, but many others as well.

Systems and errors

Psychologists studying how these disasters have happened find, repeatedly, that they show a similar pattern. In each case, a large number of minor problems have occurred fairly regularly, but these are overlooked or tolerated because they are part of a much more complex system, because they would be awkward or expensive to correct, and because the chances of them escalating into a serious problem are considered to be low. But eventually these ignored minor problems combine, to produce tragic and disastrous consequences.

These problems are often a direct result of ignoring psychological factors in the situation. As we have seen in this book, psychological factors are many and varied, and so are the ways that they manifest themselves in complex systems. The shiftwork practices in the ferry company, for example, meant that the people who were operating the Herald of Free Enterprise were unlikely to be functioning at their most alert, which of course was a major factor in how the error took place. As we saw in Chapter 4, people work better with some kind of shift systems than with others, and this needs to be taken into account in any complex system.

Similarly, there are some kinds of design which are likely to reduce errors, and some which make them more likely to happen. Ergonomic psychologists investigate the best possible locations for warning and alert signals, and also which types of signals are most needed. The lack of alert signals on the bridge to indicate that the bow doors were still open was another factor which led to the Herald of Free Enterprise disaster. It might seem a trivial factor in itself, but combined with the other factors involved, it made all the difference.

The important thing about these kinds of factors is that they make the whole system more vulnerable. People do not act like robots: sometimes they make mistakes. So any type of complex system has to be able to allow for the occasional mistake on the part of its human operator, and has to be designed in such a way that these mistakes are less likely to happen. Having a shiftwork system which means that people on duty are over-tired and less alert makes mistakes more likely; having a ship control system which does not point out vital information such as whether the bow doors are closed also makes mistakes more likely.

The kinds of mistakes which people make are not random: they are ones which can be taken into account when complex systems are being put together. Reason (1990) performed a number of studies of everyday errors and mistakes, and found that they tend to fall into three categories: those to do with skills, those to do with knowledge, and those to do with the rules that people are working by.

Skill-based errors

Skill-based errors are often concerned with the way that actions become so automatic that we do not need to pay conscious attention to them (see Chapter 7). This means that sometimes we fall back on habitual routines when really we intended to be doing something else. You have probably done something like this yourself, such as turning down your usual route to work or school instead of going in a different direction, because you were not thinking about it.

Since this is quite a common type of human error, Reason argued that it needs to be taken into account when a complex system is being designed. If that sort of mistake would be serious, then it is important to make sure it does not happen, by making sure that the kinds of routines which people are asked to follow in different circumstances are different enough from one another, so that people do not just slip into automatic routines and habits. If two systems involve similar patterns of activity, then this sort of mistake is much more likely to happen.

Knowledge-based errors

Most kinds of knowledge-based mistakes come from the fact that sometimes people simply do not have the knowledge that they need in order to take effective action. An operator who has only been trained in doing one particular job, and hasn't had special training for what to do in an emergency, can easily make a mistake, simply because they do not know what the best thing to do is. So if the failure of effective action could result in a disaster — no matter how unlikely — it is important that people should be aware of how to deal with it.

Rule-based errors

Rule-based mistakes are often associated with tackling problems which have not arisen before. Usually people will try to deal with these by applying rules or principles which they have met before. As we saw in Chapter 6, we use our existing mental schemas to direct what we should do in new situations. Sometimes, though, the rule will be inappropriate, with serious consequences.

Another kind of rule-based mistake happens when we are simply applying an inappropriate rule. To return to the Zeebrugge ferry disaster, Reason showed how the way that the directors of the company saw their job was an example of people working within an inappropriate rule. They defined their primary task as being to keep their shareholders happy, rather than as being to ensure that the ferries ran safely on a day-to-day basis. This led to the adoption of practices which were cheap, but not safe.

This point may need a little explanation, because it is not saying that the company's finances do not matter. Ultimately, of course, a company which does not make a profit will not be able to run. But most similar companies would see running the ferries safely as their primary objective, on the grounds that it would ensure confident passengers and more profitability in the long run. The directors of the ferry company, though, aimed for profitability at the expense of safety and efficiency. As the outcome of the disaster showed, it was an ineffective policy in the end. But it is a clear example of applying inappropriate rules for the situation.

Post-traumatic stress disorder

Whenever we are involved in any kind of sudden loss or bereavement, we experience grief. Grief is an extremely disabling emotion, which can last for a very long time and has a number of complex elements. Ramsay and de Groot (1977) identified some of the main components of grief, and these are listed in Table 12.2. As anyone who has experienced the loss of someone they love or were fond of knows, the complexity and intensity of the experience can be overwhelming at times.

TABLE 12.1   COMPONENTS OF GRIEF

1.	**Shock**	A feeling of numbness and unreality
2.	**Disorganisation**	Being unable to perform even simple, routine tasks
3.	**Denial**	Refusing to admit that it has really happened
4.	**Depression**	Feelings of pining and despair
5.	**Guilt**	Blaming oneself for the death, no matter how unrealistically
6.	**Anxiety** and/or **panic attacks**	A frightened response to being overwhelmed by emotions
7.	**Aggression**	Hostility and anger at the unfairness of the bereavement, sometimes targetted at medical staff or relatives
8.	**Resolution**	Accepting the fact of the bereavement as the worst of the grief dies down
9.	**Re-integration**	Beginning a new life without the dead person. Many people find it hard to do this straight away, but begin to manage it after a couple of weeks.

For people who are involved in major disasters of this kind, though, the experience is even more severe. In addition to the grief which they experience as a result of the death and loss involved in the event, there is also the shock of the experience itself. This is often deeply traumatic, and can have lasting effects. Clinical psychologists working in this area have identified a syndrome known as post-traumatic stress disorder, or PTSD, for short. Although it has been known about for some considerable time, it is only recently that PTSD has become acknowledged as a clinical problem in its own right.

Post-traumatic stress disorder happens in people who have experienced severe emotional traumas of one sort or another. It occurs in people who are engaged in prolonged and dangerous fighting, in people who have experienced torture, and in those who are involved in major disasters. If the stress is serious and continuous enough, it seems that most people will be affected in the end. Swank (1949) in a study of 4,000 survivors of the Normandy campaign, found that all soldiers experienced what was then known as shell shock (but is now recognised as PTSD) if three-quarters of their companions had been killed, no matter how resilient they seemed to be.

Emergency workers who have to deal with major disasters can also experience post-traumatic stress disorder. Taylor and Frazer (1982) studied the people who helped out in 1979 when a DC10 aeroplane on a tourist flight crashed into a mountain in Antarctica. All of the 257 passengers and crew were killed, and it took ten weeks to recover and identify the bodies. Several of the workers who had been helping to recover the bodies experienced persistent images of the disfigured corpses or experienced nightmares of air crashes.

Symptoms of PTSD

There are three main groups of symptoms in post-traumatic stress disorder. The first involves **re-experiencing** what happened. People suffering from PTSD often have recurrent nightmares of the event, and may also experience vivid memories of it during the waking day, which are extremely distracting for them as well as distressing. The second group of symptoms occur as the mind attempts to cope with the trauma, and they are known as **avoidance** or numbing reactions: people often feel detached or estranged from others, and distant from everyday life. The third group of symptoms seem to be to do with the increased **arousal** level of the body, so they include inability to sleep or to stay asleep for very long, irritability, and a tendency to outbursts of anger.

These symptoms are similar to those which people would be likely to experience after any disturbing event, but what makes them distinctive in post-traumatic stress disorder is how strong they are, and how long they last. Although sometimes the symptoms do not appear until some time after the event, they can go on for several months, or even years. They can also disappear for a while, and then reappear. Archibald (1963) found that 15 years after a traumatic event had taken place, two-thirds of survivors still showed symptoms of PTSD.

Often, though, people do not recognise that what they are experiencing is actually post-traumatic stress disorder. Mitchell (1992) described how doctors were trying to treat the residents of the Scottish village of Lockerbie for some time after an American airliner exploded above the village, causing deep trauma and shock among the residents. However, the doctors were not aware of PTSD, and so were at a loss for how to proceed. When the residents received insurance leaflets describing the symptoms of PTSD, the local doctors were able to realise that what they were treating was actually a specific and recognisable syndrome, rather than just a collection of individual reactions.

It matters whether the disorder is recognised, because it is possible to organise therapy which helps people to get over it — but only if people know what is happening. Some clinical psychologists specialise in this type of therapy, working with the victims of disasters to help them to overcome the problem and return to normal living. Although the symptoms do not disappear altogether, it seems that having therapy does help people to get over the most severe problems a little more quickly, and to cope with it better.

We can see, then, that psychology can be usefully applied, not just in understanding how disasters and accidents take place, but also in helping people to recover from the worst of their effects. The most important message, though, is the one which becomes apparent when we look at how these disasters happen in the first place: that if we take full account of psychological factors in the design and management of complex systems, disasters are much less likely to happen. That does not mean that they absolutely would not happen, of course — nobody could promise that — but it does minimise the risk. And when the consequences of failure are so very extreme, anything which minimises the risk of a disaster is worth while.

13

PSYCHOLOGY — THROUGHOUT LIFE

In this chapter we will be looking at a branch of psychology which is to do with how we develop throughout our lives. Lifespan developmental psychology is not just concerned with children. It is concerned with the experiences of adulthood and ageing, and with the idea of continuous development, throughout the lifespan.

The lifespan approach

The lifespan approach is quite a contrast to the old, traditional type of developmental psychology. For the first seventy years of the twentieth century, both psychologists and society in general tended to assume that almost all of our development happened while we were children or teenagers. By the age of 21, it was thought, the significant parts of development were largely over.

Nowadays, though, we see development quite differently. People continue to grow and change all of their lives: we are quite different at 30 than we are at 20, at 40 we are different again, at 50 we have changed even more, and so on throughout our whole lives. So developmental psychology now defines itself as being concerned with development throughout life, and not just with child development.

It is not just a matter of thinking about these extra years, either. When we start looking back over psychological research into ageing and development, we find that often the evidence which seemed to suggest that people do not change much as they get older was seriously flawed in the way that it was interpreted. When we look at the same things again more carefully, we find quite different outcomes.

Intelligence and ageing

For example, for many years people 'knew' that various abilities, including intelligence and physical strength, reached their peak in the very early 20s, and then declined steadily from then on throughout a person's life. This knowledge was based on a series of studies, reported by Miles, in 1931, which involved measuring various human characteristics in people of different ages. When they plotted the results of these measurements on a graph, Miles found a steady decline: the older the person was, the less strong, or intelligent (as measured by IQ tests) or able they were.

Other researchers found similar results, so for a great many years there was a strong belief in an inevitable decline with age. This belief is still held by a great many people, including some doctors and social workers. But when we look more carefully at the evidence, what we find is actually quite a different picture.

Cross-sectional methods

The problem was that all of these studies were done using a **cross-sectional method**. That is, the researcher tested several different groups of people of different ages. But someone who was 60 in 1930 had experienced quite a different upbringing and lifestyle than someone who was 20 at that time. Their schooling was quite different, their life experiences were quite different, and their standards of living were different too. The same thing applied to other cross-sectional studies that were conducted later on in the century: they failed to take account of the very major differences in education and health care which had taken place.

So it was not surprising, for example, that older people did badly on intelligence tests in the 1960s, when they had experienced an education which consisted largely of learning large chunks of information off by heart. Younger people, on the other hand, had experienced a form of education which stressed reasoning and mental skills, and so they naturally performed much better on IQ tests.

Longitudinal methods

When psychologists actually began to look at how individual people developed, following them up through their lives, a very different picture emerged. Obviously, **longitudinal research** like this is quite hard to do, because a researcher, or a group of researchers, needs to follow it up over many years. So there are fewer longitudinal studies of lifespan development than there are cross-sectional ones.

But there are some. For example, in 1966, Burns reported on a study of intelligence and ageing which had begun in the 1920s with a group of teachers who were just emerging from their training colleges. The researchers tested the teachers' intelligence throughout their career, and found that, contrary to what the cross-sectional research showed, their IQ scores had actually increased as they had become older. The apparently inevitable decline with ageing was not inevitable at all!

What was even more interesting was what the researchers found when they looked at the particular scores which the teachers had obtained on their IQ tests. The tests assessed intelligence in two parts: **verbal intelligence**, which was to do with the use of words and knowledge of vocabulary, and **numerical intelligence**, which included the use of symbols and logical reasoning as well as arithmetical abilities.

When the researchers looked at these scores, they found that the 'arts' teachers, who taught subjects like English and history, showed an increase in their verbal intelligence scores, but a slight (though not very great) decline in numerical intelligence. The science teachers, though, showed an increase in their numerical intelligence but a slight decline in their verbal intelligence scores.

What this clearly implied was that, more than anything else, it is the amount of practice which we have which is most important in whether we are likely to improve our intelligence as we get older or not. If we adopt a passive mental approach to living, just receiving information passively and not bothering to learn new things unless we absolutely have to, it is likely that our intelligence would decline. Our muscles waste away if we do not use them, and our intelligence is likely to decline if we do not use that as well. But if we remain active in our thinking, and ready to learn new things or to challenge our previous assumptions, then we are likely to retain our intelligence, and even increase it. The more we use a skill, the better we get at it.

This is only one example, but both psychologists and doctors are finding, more and more, that getting old has almost as much to do with lifestyle and practice as it has to do with the number of years that we actually carry. Everybody gets older, of course, but ageing does not mean an inevitable steady decline from age 20, as people used to think.

Memory and ageing

The problem, though, is that we all have our own beliefs about ageing, and sometimes these can become self-perpetuating. For example, most people believe that your memory inevitably declines as you get older. Because they believe that, they notice each time they fail to remember something, and take it as 'proof' that their memory is really getting worse. Their belief becomes a **self-fulfilling prophecy**, because they become convinced that there is less and less point in trying to remember things because they will not manage it anyway. So they do not remember things, because they do not make any effort to store the information.

Harris and Sunderland, in 1981, decided to put this idea to the test. They obtained a group of people aged between 20 and 36, and compared them with a group of people aged between 69 and 80. When they tested their memories for events in everyday life, they found that the younger people in the study actually experienced more memory failures than the older people!

It was possible, of course, that the younger people forgot more simply because they had more going on in their lives. After all, the older group were all retired. So Harris and Sunderland repeated the study, this time with a group of people who were still working, aged between 50 and 60. This time, they found an even stronger difference between the two groups. Again, the younger people were much more forgetful than those who were older, even with information that they were trying to remember.

So why is it that older people are so convinced that their memories are poorer now than they were when they were young? It is possible, of course, that they really did have better memories when they were younger, and that for some reason the younger generation studied by Harris and Sunderland did not have very good memories at all – after all, this was a cross-sectional study. But what seems more likely is that it is much more to do with motivation and attention.

Attention and motivation

Young people, by and large, do not worry too much about their mental abilities. Older people, though, sensitised by society's belief in an inevitable decline in mental ability with ageing, do worry about it. So when a younger person forgets their key, or cannot remember someone's name, or forgets what they came into the room to do, they hardly notice it because it simply does not matter to them. When an older person does the same thing, though, it sticks in the mind, because they are always wondering if it is a sign of age.

So where the younger person simply shrugs off everyday forgetting, the older person worries about it, and notices it much more. This means that when older people look back on their own earlier lives, they do not remember being worried about forgetting things at all when they were younger, and they come to the conclusion that they simply had better memories. This reinforces the belief that their own mental abilities are declining, and so becomes a circular process.

Principles of lifespan psychology

As a result of these, and many other studies, developmental psychology nowadays has become increasingly concerned with lifespan development, our personal beliefs, and how we interact with other people, and with society in general. Sugarman (1986) identified four central ideas in lifespan developmental psychology. The first of these is the idea that development always needs to be seen in its **social context**. How people develop is influenced by their society, their family, their social class, and their culture, and social influence can come from many other sources as well. So we cannot really study development without taking these into account.

The second idea which Sugarman identified is to do with the fact that social influence is not just a one-way process. People influence one another, and are influenced by others — it is a two-way process, which we call **reciprocal influence**. This influence is not static, either – it changes all the time. We are influenced by family members and by changes happening within the family, as well as by changes among our friends and working colleagues. And we exert our own influence on these changes as they develop.

Reciprocal influence is important, but it is far from being the whole story. We are also active **agents** in our own lives, making our own choices and decisions. In that sense, we are all active in shaping our own development – and how we understand what is going on is an important aspect of that. For example, as we saw earlier, we know that mental abilities do not inevitably decline with age. But someone who believed firmly that they did decline would tend to 'take it easy' and avoid challenging situations as they grew older, because they would not think it was worth trying. And because of that, they would decline faster than someone who understood lifespan development in a more positive way.

Another fundamental principle that Sugarman identified in lifespan psychology is that of **complexity**. Essentially, this is the same principle that we have encountered so often throughout this book. People are not simple beings, and no one single approach is going to be enough to tell us about human beings. We have to take into account different levels of explanation, and to explore connections and issues which arise from them, if we are to get any useful awareness of what human beings are really like.

In the rest of this chapter, we will take a brief look at some of the areas studied by lifespan developmental psychologists. We will begin by looking briefly at child development and adolescence, before going on to look at some of the psychology of adulthood and old age.

—— **Childhood and adolescence** ——

Throughout this book we have looked at different aspects of child development. In Chapter 2, we looked at the way that the young infant is primed to be sociable, almost from the first moment that it is born, and in Chapter 7, we saw how it learns through interacting with other people and with the world around it. These are fundamental aspects of the child's social and personal development, which form the foundation for later, more complex forms of social learning during childhood.

We have also explored several different aspects of the young child's cognitive development. In Chapter 6, we saw how children develop different kinds of mental representations as they grow older and their worlds become more complex. In Chapter 5 we saw how self-efficacy beliefs are important in the young child's learning, and this also connects with the influence of parents' and teachers' expectations during the child's school experience, which we looked at in Chapter 11. And there have been many other examples of child psychology which have come up throughout the book.

Play

Because we have already looked at child development in some detail, then, we will not go into it at length here. But we will look at one special aspect of child development, which is very important to the child's psychological development — play. There are several different kinds of play, and the main ones are listed in Table 13.1.

TABLE 13.1 TYPES OF PLAY	
Physical play	e.g. running, jumping about, skipping, etc.
Pretend play	e.g. imagining situations, characters, scenes, etc.
Play with words	e.g. puns, rhymess, riddles
Play with objects	e.g. playing with toy cars, dolls, household objects
Social play	e.g. ring o'roses, competitive games, role play

Physical play

Each of these types of play serves its own function. Physical play, of course, helps the child to develop a strong body through exercise, and improves the child's general physical health. But it also encourages the child to develop a positive body-schema, so that it becomes aware of physical capabilities and develops better co-ordination. Physical confidence is not everything, of course, but it can be quite an important source of self-efficacy beliefs, and we have seen how important those are. Although it is often overlooked in modern Western societies, or relegated to the limited arena of school sports, physical play is a very important foundation for later adulthood.

Physical play is sometimes a purely individual activity: most children will simply enjoy developing the physical skills involved in swinging on a bar, or clambering around a climbing frame. Indeed, the urge to climb on things seems to be very powerful among small children, and may easily represent a strong internal drive to develop our physical skills to the full. Some physical play, though, is social — rough-and-tumble play between children, or between adults and children, is also something which children evidently enjoy a great deal.

Pretend play

Pretend play, on the other hand, is about a different sort of learning. It allows the child to explore its social world and the possibilities which it offers. So it is no accident that children's pretend play tends to begin by acting out simple domestic situations. Pretend play allows the child to practise different social roles, and to develop an awareness of the wider social world.

Pretend play also encourages the child to develop its imagination, and many children do this to quite a high degree. It is not uncommon, for example, for a child to develop an imaginary playmate which accompanies the child and becomes the focus for its exploration of the world. These imaginary playmates may be human, or they may be humanised animals, like a lion or horse. Although parents sometimes worry when their child begins to talk to someone who is not there, there is no evidence at all that it is harmful. Some psychologists have even collected evidence that many particularly high-achieving scientists and public figures had imaginary playmates when younger, which might suggest that exercising the imagination in this way is actually a positive thing for a child to do. But it is hard to obtain evidence for this idea one way or the other.

Play with words

Children also enjoy playing with words. Indeed, as anyone who has heard a toddler babbling will know, they seem to enjoy playing with speech sounds before they even have words, and this urge to experiment continues throughout early childhood. Many children talk constantly to themselves as they play, and this type of talking, known as **egocentric speech**, does not actually seem to have anything to do with communication. According to Vygotsky (1962), when a child is using language like this it is actually thinking aloud: the language is a kind of running commentary on what the child is thinking about. As the child grows older, that kind of way of using language becomes internalised — we think it to ourselves, but do not say it out loud (unless we are used to being on our own).

But children also engage in sociable playing with words. Opie and Opie (1969) went round children's playgrounds collecting the word-games which children used, and found an enormous range of rhymes, riddles and puns, which amounted to a kind of verbal culture, passed on from child to child. The popularity of these word-games also implied that they formed an important part of how children learn to interact with one another, and help children to develop an understanding of how subtly words can be used. It does not just stop at playgrounds, either: the fascination with 'double-meanings' shown by young adolescents who are just learning about sex is another example of the many different ways that people play with words.

Play with objects

Children also play with toys, although, as we have seen, most of their play does not actually involve toys at all. But some does. Even from quite a young age, an infant will play with an object, holding it, sucking it, and show interest in it. Lowe (1975) discussed how play with objects becomes more sophisticated as the child grows older and its social awareness develops. Lowe's stages are presented in Table 13.2.

Toys which attract curiosity and interest in children seem to be more positive than toys which are simple representations of objects. Hutt (1966) suggested that exploratory play is strongly linked with both mental and emotional development in children, so it seems like a good idea for a child to have toys which encourage it to explore and to be curious. In one set of studies, Hutt used a 'supertoy', which was a wooden box with wheels, buzzers, bells, counters, pedals and levers. Playing with different combinations of levers and pedals would produce several different outcomes —

TABLE 13.2   STAGES IN PLAYING WITH OBJECTS

Age of child	Activity
9 months	The child will hold, wave, bang and suck objects
12 months	The child looks at things before sucking, waving, banging them about
15 months	Familiar objects are used as if in everyday life e.g. 'pretend' drinking from a cup
21 months	The child uses more than one thing e.g. 'feeding' a doll from a toy bowl
24 months	The child's play with objects is becoming increasingly realistic, mirroring everyday life e.g. driving toy cars along marked-out 'roads'
30-36 months	The child begins to get toys to 'act' for themselves e.g. a doll may put the other toys to bed

noises would sound, and counters would be covered up or revealed. Children enjoyed playing with the supertoy, and would play with it for longest if it was set to maximum complexity.

More interestingly, Hutt observed 2- to 3-year-old children playing with the supertoy, and then saw the same children four years later. The children who had been most interested in exploring the supertoy were more confident and more social, and also had higher IQ levels, than the children who did not explore it much. Nobody is suggesting from this that playing with the supertoy produced these differences, of course, but it does suggest a strong link between an inclination to explore, and later development. And this in turn suggests that toys which encourage exploration and curiosity in children would be likely to be of positive benefit to them.

Social play

Social play is another category of playing which has been studied by psychologists, although, as we have seen, the other kinds of play are also social, at times. Essentially, there are three main kinds of social play: **free play**, which is worked out by the children themselves as they go along; **formal play**, which has clearly defined rules and procedures, like skipping games or card games;

and **creative play**, in which children develop a new game together, perhaps involving imaginary characters or entirely new rules.

Early research into children's play tended to focus on children in playgroups, and so was all to do with how children of the same ages played together. But, of course, most social play actually takes place between members of the same family — brothers, sisters, parents and other relatives — so it is generally between people of different ages. Cohen (1987) used a diary method for recording the play of his two young sons within the family, and found that even from a very early age children would initiate different favourite games with different members of the family.

Garvey (1977) found that when pre-school children are left to play with someone of the same age, they often begin a kind of dramatic play, involving familiar scenes and stories. Younger children, for example, often play games about mothers taking care of babies; while older children are more likely to play games which reflect their growing awareness of a wider context, like doctor–nurse games or acting out fairy stories.

We can see, then, that children's play is quite varied, and can take many different forms. Through playing, children develop skills and engage in exercising both their mental and physical muscles in preparation for adult life. What is very striking, though, is how much of children's play is social in character. Even if the child is not actually interacting with other people directly, it is often rehearsing social roles or expressing its social awareness as it interacts with toys. The psychological study of play, like so many other aspects of psychology, shows us just how powerfully we are influenced by other people and our social worlds.

Theories of adolescence

Adolescence is often thought of as a turbulent period — a period of upheaval and rebellion from parental authority. It is an image which was very popular with Hollywood from the 1950s on, and it has passed into our everyday consciousness. But it is questionable just how realistic this impression of adolescence is. Although some people, undoubtedly, do have a turbulent time in this period of their lives, others pass through adolescence quite smoothly, and without major upheavals. These differences have been reflected in psychological theories, too. Cockram and Beloff (1978) identified four major perspectives on adolescence, which are manifest in psychological theorising.

Adolescence as 'storm and stress'

This view sees the adolescent as inherently rebellious, rejecting the authority of parents or other representatives of 'the establishment', and looking only to the peer group for social influence. Adolescents in the 1950s and 1960s were portrayed as moody and emotionally unstable, and as implicitly difficult for adults to interact with. Various explanations were put forward for this phenomenon, including the idea that it was a throwback to the animal passions of an evolutionary past, that it resulted from the hormone imbalances of puberty, and the psychoanalytic notion that it was an emotional reworking of early childhood sexual conflicts.

Some anthropologists and psychologists, such as Margaret Mead (1972) and Bronfenbrenner (1974) argued that it arose as a result of the alienation of young people from adult culture, in Western capitalist societies. In non-technological societies, Mead argued, adolescents were fully participating members of their communities, and so were not left to their own devices and regarded as a separate culture. Even in Soviet Russia, Bronfenbrenner argued, young people were more integrated into their society than they were in America, and showed fewer signs of alienation.

All of these theorists, however, were working on the assumption that a turbulent adolescence was the normal state of affairs for young people in Western societies. But, gradually, this view was challenged, as psychologists such as Bandura (1972) began to study 'normal' adolescents, rather than adolescents who were attending clinics or courts because they were disturbed or troublesome. Bandura found that most adolescents did not particularly oppose their parents' values, or show hostility or rebellion. Rather, for many people, adolescence was a period in which they developed a more trusting and positive relationship with their parents, rather than the reverse.

Research by other psychologists confirmed Bandura's arguments, and the 'storm and stress' model of adolescence became increasingly regarded as one which only had a limited usefulness

— appropriate for some adolescents, but not for most. Accordingly, different models of adolescence were put forward.

Adolescence as role transition

One of the most popular of these alternative models was the idea that adolescence can most usefully be seen as a period of role transition — a time when people are changing how they interact with society in general, and with the other people around them. Moving from school to work, or from school to higher education, involves adopting different social roles, and these in turn can produce changes as different sides of the personality emerge.

There are several different aspects to the changing roles of adolescence. Sometimes we retain the same roles, but how we are expected to perform those roles changes. Someone might still be an older sister, for instance, but we would expect a 10-year-old older sister to act differently from a 16-year-old elder sister. But there are entirely new roles, too, which appear during adolescence, and these have to be learned. A Saturday job in a shop, for example, involves learning a way of interacting with people that is different from the styles that we adopt with family or friends.

Part of being an adolescent, then, involves balancing out the different demands of the social roles that we are called on to play. Sometimes these result in widely differing expectations: someone might be regarded as a responsible adult in their Saturday job, as a child by members of their family, and as an irresponsible teenager by their schoolteacher. Each of these will bring different 'selves', or aspects of the personality, to the fore, so balancing these different demands is something which takes a little bit of learning.

Adolescence as a developmental stage

A third way of looking at adolescence identified by Cockram and Beloff was to see it as a developmental stage. This idea is based on Erikson's theory of life-long development (Erikson 1968), which identified a number of different conflicts which each individual has to resolve as they pass through life. Erikson identified eight major conflicts, which are listed in Table 13.3. The early conflicts, he argued, formed the foundation for the successful resolution of later ones, so all were important stages in the person's psychological development.

TABLE 13.3 ERIKSON'S THEORY OF DEVELOPMENT
THROUGH THE LIFESPAN

EARLY INFANCY — trust/vs/mistrust
The infant has to strike a balance between trusting people and risking disappointment, or being mistrustful and unable to relate to other people fully.

LATER INFANCY — autonomy/vs/shame and doubt
The toddler has to develop a sense of personal agency and control over behaviour and actions, rather than mistrusting its ability to do things.

EARLY CHILDHOOD — initiative/vs/guilt
The child has to develop a sense of personal responsibility and initiative, rather than simply feeling guilty and uncertain.

MIDDLE CHILDHOOD — industry/vs/inferiority
The child has to learn that systematic effort will overcome challenges, rather than just giving up and accepting failure.

PUBERTY AND ADOLESCENCE — identity/vs/role confusion
The adolescent needs to develop a consistent sense of inner self, rather than being swamped by the range of roles and choices available.

YOUNG ADULTHOOD— intimacy/vs/isolation
The young adult needs to learn to develop intimate and trusting relationships with others, rather than avoiding relationships because they can become threatening and painful.

MATURE ADULTHOOD — generativity/vs/stagnation
The adult needs to develop a productive life, recognising their personal achievements and abilities, instead of stagnating psychologically.

LATE ADULTHOOD — integrity/vs/despair
The older person needs to be able to look back on their life positively, rather than to feel that it has been meaningless and futile.

The particular conflict which needed to be resolved during adolescence, Erikson argued, was that of identity versus role confusion. In a sense, this relates to the perspective on adolescence that we were just looking at — the way that the adolescent needs to come to terms with the many new social roles that it is expected to play. In terms of the individual's own psychological development, Erikson argued, it was important that the adolescent could accept the fact that they had a single, integrated identity, despite the fact that they played so many different social roles and acted differently in each one.

Only by maintaining, or developing, a coherent sense of identity, Erikson believed, would the adolescent form a firm foundation for a later productive adulthood, and for mature and satisfying relationships. If the different role demands which they experienced were too stressful, the person would experience what Erikson called a state of **identity diffusion**, in which they would have difficulty forming relationships with other people and would also find it difficult to make coherent plans for the future, and work towards achieving them. Without a clear sense of who we are, such things would be very difficult, and yet adolescence is often an important time of preparation for adult life, and can involve a considerable investment in work, effort and planning.

The lifespan approach to adolescence

The fourth type of theory of adolescence described by Cockram and Beloff is the lifespan approach to adolescence. This model presents the adolescent as an active agent in their own lives — unlike the other ones, which tended to see the person as passive, merely suffering or experiencing all these different demands. But adolescents are very active in interacting with their own environment, and can shape what happens to them to quite a high degree.

Lerner (1985) argued that adolescents interact with their environment in three ways. The first of these is that they act as a stimulus to other people, and people respond to them. Adolescents also process information, mentally: they think about what they are experiencing, interpret it, and respond accordingly. And thirdly, adolescents act as active agents in their own lives, making their own choices, and deliberately influencing what is likely to happen. All of these combine to mean that the adolescent is much less passive than the older psychological models implied.

So what can we conclude from all of this? Essentially, it seems, that there is no single way of looking at 'adolescence' which will explain what everyone experiences. There are a lot of role-changes which take place during adolescence, and a great many major life-changes too. But each person will cope with them in their own way, and according to the awareness and understanding that they have developed as a person in their own right. Throughout this book, we have been looking at mechanisms which influence people, and which give us clues to understanding why people are like they are. They apply just as much to adolescents, too!

——— Adulthood and ageing ———

It is only relatively recently that psychologists have begun to study adulthood in its own right. Of course, psychology is about people, and so the various aspects of how human beings function which we have looked at earlier in this book are relevant to understanding adulthood. In that sense, psychology has always studied both adults and children. And work psychology, which we looked at in Chapter 9, has a long history too — and that is entirely about adult life. But the idea that the period of life which we know as adulthood might also be worth studying in its own right is a relatively new one. To date, much of this research has been concerned with looking at the various phases which people pass through in the course of their adult life — charting what happens to us — or at least to many people in Western industrial societies — in those years as we grow older.

Life-transitions

Gould (1978) developed the idea that adult life consists of a series of transitions, or **life-changes**, which occur at different times in our lives. The first of these is that of adjusting to the responsibilities of being independent and living away from parental care. Looking after ourselves without someone in the background is quite different from the kind of independence which occurs when living as part of a family group, where there is always someone to fall back on, or to look after you if you fall ill.

That transition, Gould argued, takes place usually between the ages of 16 and 22. Then there is another one, which takes place during the 20s, in which the person develops their own competencies and autonomy, and chooses their own rules to live by, rather than simply conforming to their parents' rules and principles. A third transition, according to Gould, happens between 28 and 34, as the person comes to know themselves better, and learns to come to terms with aspects of their nature which they were not really aware of before. And the final transition, in Gould's model, is that of accepting that life is not going to last for ever — developing a sense of our own mortality. This, Gould argued, happens between 35 and 45.

There are some big problems with this type of approach to studying adulthood, of course. One is that it is very culturally specific — it is probably fine for describing the lives of middle-class white North American men, but may be rather different for people of different backgrounds. And the other, of course, is that it does not account for individual differences. Some people do not leave home until much later in life; some people do not experience a lengthy period of independence but marry from their family home; and some come across these transitions at very different ages.

If there are so many problems with this type of model, why put it forward? Well, mainly because it is a start. By identifying the kinds of things that are missing from a model like this, we can move towards developing better ones. Psychology does not have all the answers: it is continually changing, and trying to improve its theories and ideas. When a new area of thought first opens up, the theories which are produced are often quite limited, but they do provide a useful basis for developing a deeper understanding of people.

And sometimes even if a theory is a little bit limited, it can still be useful. For instance, Duvall (1971) developed a model of the different stages of marriage, which has been criticised because it does not take account of the experiences of single parents, or of divorce. But it can still help us to understand how a consistent long-term marriage does go through different phases, which actually involve different behaviour on the part of the couple, and different assumptions about what they are actually doing.

The family life-cycle

Duvall identified eight different stages of marriage. The first of these is the **honeymoon period**, in which the married couple are learning to live together, without having children. At this time, they are getting to know each other and setting foundations for later life. Statistically, a couple whose honeymoon period lasts for two years or more before children come along are much more likely to stay together in the long term than those who only have a brief interval before starting a family, and that may partly be because they know one another as people much better.

The second period in Duvall's model is the **nurturing period**, when the oldest child is less than 2 years old, and the couple are learning to cope with being new parents. It can be a stressful time for people, not made easier by lack of sleep and anxiety about how the child or children are progressing. So at this time, the couple are likely to need to give one another quite a high level of both practical and emotional support

The third stage is what Duvall referred to as the **authority period**, in which the family have pre-school children with the oldest between 2 and 5 years old. Essentially, the parents have to train their pre-schoolers to behave in a socially acceptable way, and not act like tyrannical little monsters! This, too, can be a deeply demanding phase for the parents.

Things often ease up a little when the family enters the **interpretive period**, in which the oldest child is between 5 and 13 years old, and at school. (The reason why Duvall categorises these stages from the age of the oldest child is mainly because this signals the need for the parents to learn new behaviours. They have already learned most of the behaviours they will need for younger children — although each child is different, of course.)

The fifth period in the family life-cycle is the **interdependent period**, which consists of families with teenagers. At this time it becomes possible for the teenagers to take more of a share in the emotional and physical aspects of the family, and the relationship between parents and child can become a two-way, interdependent one rather than a simple, one-way, dependent one.

Then there is the sixth period, which Duvall refers to as the **launching period**, as the young adults emerge to become independent in society. Typically, this period involves some degree of support from home — perhaps providing a home for a child who is away at college during term-time, or providing help with furnishings or a regular Sunday lunch for a young adult who is independent and working. This period lasts from the time when the first child leaves, to when the last child leaves home.

The seventh is the **empty-nest period**, when all of the children have left and the parents are together at home. This can be quite a difficult adjustment for some families, particularly if the children have been the exclusive focus of attention. Some couples, though, find it a pleasant relief, because it means they can simply enjoy one another's company again. They often engage in co-operative activities, such as redecorating, or travelling together.

The final period in the family life-cycle which Duvall described is the **retirement** period, in which those members of the partnership who were working are now retired. This, too, can be a period of re-adjustment, particularly if one of the couple has been accustomed to having the house to themselves for most of the day.

We can see, then, that each stage of the family life-cycle involves different adjustments and new forms of learning. Although, inevitably, it does not fit every single family, identifying the different stages in this way has proved to be very useful for marriage guidance counsellors and other people who are either trying to help people to adjust to changes in their relationships, or who are trying to do the adjusting themselves.

Ageing

As we saw at the beginning of this chapter, a psychological decline with ageing is not nearly as inevitable as it once appeared to be. If we use our mental abilities, we are more likely to improve them than to lose them, at least until the very final years of our life. For people who lead full and active lives, and do not hesitate to make efforts or to stretch themselves a little, it seems that they can retain their abilities almost to the end of their lives, with only a relatively sudden decline in the last five years of old age, rather than a continuous steady one.

But, of course, your system responds to the demands that you make on it — which is why sports doctors and physiotherapists know how important it is to exercise injured muscles as soon as healing has begun. Simply resting means that the muscles adapt to the limited demands, and become weaker. It is the same with ageing: people who believe in a continuous decline, and do not push themselves to make an effort, naturally become more and more frail and feeble, because they are never stimulating their bodies or minds to become stronger. There are limits to this, of course, but not ones which normally occur in most people's lives.

But there's another dimension to ageing, which is just as important as the question of physical decline — some would say, more so. That's the social side of ageing. Despite the fact that, in Western industrial societies at least, old people are the largest group in the population, they tend to be much less visible than people of other ages. We see older people around, of course, but not nearly as many as we might expect. And this takes some explanation, because not everyone is housebound or too weak to get about.

Disengagement theory

Cummings and Henry (1961) put forward a biological explanation for this. They proposed that, as people grow older, there is a kind of inherited biological mechanism which encourages them, gradually, to withdraw from society. They have fulfilled their evolutionary function in bringing up families and so helping their offspring to survive, and now, Cummings and Henry argued, evolution has no place for them. As a consequence, they become less and less involved in social affairs, leaving decision-making and social organisation to younger people and becoming increasingly withdrawn into their own lives.

This rather gloomy process is known as **disengagement**, on the idea that there is an innate tendency to disengage from society with age — a bit like an animal creeping away to die in private. It reflects a tendency of psychologists at that time to look for biological explanations for all human behaviour. But there are many problems with this model. For one thing, the relative lack of social involvement of older people is not anything like an animal creeping away to die, because the period of being 'an old person' or a pensioner is so very long. Nowadays, it is not uncommon for people to live for 30 years or more after they have retired, and that's quite different from an animal's day or so of being ill and weak before dying.

Activity theory

An alternative explanation for why older people do not seem to take as active a part in society as they might was put forward by Havighurst, in 1964. Havighurst attributed it to the relatively few opportunities which older people have to play meaningful roles in society. When a person is active and working, they play a large number of different social roles. These include various roles at work as well as roles to do with the family. In other words, as Havighurst put it, their **role-count** is high. But when someone retires from work, their role-count drops dramatically, because all of the social roles that they played which were relevant to work — even ones as simple as being a commuter — vanish. All that is left are the ones to do with family and home.

In other words, Havighurst was arguing, people become less visible in society when they retire simply because they do not have as many opportunities to play a part in everyday social living. And this had personal consequences, as well as social ones, because the person could easily come to feel apathetic and useless as a result. The way to counteract this, Havighurst argued, is for the person deliberately to replace their lost social roles by adding new ones: joining clubs and societies for older people, or working for organisations like Oxfam, who employ people over conventional retirement age. Keeping up one's role-count, in this model, is the way to ensure a positive experience of old age.

Social exchange theory

In 1975, Dowd proposed a different way of explaining this question. Dowd suggested that retirement is actually a sort of social contract, which the person makes with society. They obtain increased leisure time, and an 'honourable discharge' from the idea that all responsible members of society ought to work as hard as possible — the Protestant Work Ethic — and in return they give up their involvement in how society's affairs are run. This **social exchange** is seen, according to Dowd, as a fair trade, both by society and by old people.

Dyson (1980) interviewed a large number of people about their experiences of retirement, and challenged the idea that people see it as a fair exchange. At least, they saw it as fair for old people in general, but not in their own personal case. The retired people who Dyson interviewed felt that, for the most part, society had thrown them on the junk heap too early, and that they were still perfectly capable of making an active and useful contribution to society. For other old people, though, they saw it as a generally fair exchange.

Social labelling

Dyson's research gave some interesting hints about the emergence of a new perspective on ageing, which developed during the 1980s. This view sees the lower visibility of older people in society as a product of **social labelling**. We live in an ageist society, in which stereotypes of old people are very strong — even though most people are personally acquainted with individuals who do not fit that stereotype at all. This makes it very difficult for someone to break through the social stereotyping, and be regarded as an intelligent person with something useful to contribute, because they are simply seen as someone who is old, and therefore useless.

The stereotypes about old people are particularly unpleasant. They are often regarded as sick, stupid, or even dirty. Because a minority of old people become confused, or suffer from mental disorders such as Alzheimer's disease, it is assumed that any old person is likely to become mentally incapacitated — although, as we have seen, the evidence is very different. Because of this, the positive contributions which older people can make to social events and processes is often overlooked, or simply ignored. Recently, a number of organisations and individuals have begun to challenge these stereotypes about ageing, and there is some indication that attitudes are beginning to change. But there is still a long way to go.

14

PSYCHOLOGY AND EVOLUTION

Throughout this book, we have looked at psychology as the study of the human being. We have looked at many different approaches to understanding people, and seen how each may contribute to developing an overall picture. But there is one level of explanation which we have not yet explored, but which also contributes to psychology. That is the biological level: the level of explanation which says that human beings are, evolutionarily and physically speaking, animals, so looking at other animals may help us to understand what we are like.

This particular branch of psychology is known as **comparative psychology**, because it is all about comparing different species to identify underlying mechanisms of behaviour and development. Comparative psychology is not just concerned with comparing animals with human beings: it is also about comparing one species of animal with another, in an attempt to understand how and why different types of animals act as they do. For example, in a comparative exploration of dolphin cognitive abilities, Schusterman, Thomas and Wood (1986) drew on studies of the behaviour of many different species, including parrots, elephants and chimpanzees. By comparing what is known about, say, learning in one species with learning in another, very different type of animal, it is sometimes possible to identify general laws or principles about learning, which might help us to understand something about how human beings learn, too.

---------------------------- **Evolution** ----------------------------

Comparative psychology is firmly based on the idea that all animals, including human beings, have evolved from primitive common ancestors. Essentially, the theory of evolution, as put forward by Charles Darwin in 1859, proposes that there has been a continuous process by which different animal species have changed and developed. This process is brought about by the species gradually adapting to the demands of its environment, through a gradual genetic change. It may need a little bit of explanation, and since it is so important to psychology in general, as well as to comparative psychology, it is worth going into here.

The genetic basis of evolution

Inside each of our body's cells, there is a complex substance known as **DNA** (desoxyribonucleic acid, to give it its full name). This subtance consists of long strands of molecules, with two strands

Figure 14.1 The double helix

running side-by-side, and arranged so that the molecules on the two strands are linked together in pairs, a bit like a zip fastener. These strands are twisted so that they form a spiral-like shape known as a helix. Because there are two strands, the end result is a **double helix** — like a very twisted ladder (Fig. 14.1).

Genes and chromosomes

There are four kinds of DNA molecules, and different combinations of these occur all the way along each double helix. Together, they spell out what is known as the **genetic code** — a tremendously complicated set of instructions, which gives instructions to the cells in the body, so that they will know how to develop. As a result of these complex instructions, we develop specialised liver cells, heart cells, hair cells, skin cells, and all the other different types of cells which make up a body. Sections of DNA — known as **genes** — also give instructions about when different types of cells should develop, and whereabouts in the body they should be.

The strands of DNA in our cells are grouped together into larger units, known as **chromosomes.** These, too, are arranged in pairs, and, for the most part, each pair of chromosomes is very similar. The genes on each chromosome all have a matching gene, known as an allele, on the other one, except for one special pair of chromosomes known as the X and Y chromosomes, where the Y chromosome is much shorter and so does not have a full matching set. These particular chromosomes are the ones which determine which gender we will have.

When we, or any other living thing, reproduce ourselves sexually — that is, by combining sperm from one parent with ova from another — we do it by producing special cells which only have half of the chromosomes: one of each pair. These combine with special cells from the other parent to form a complete set, which can then develop into a new individual. In this way the new individual inherits some characteristics from each of its parents.

Mutations

Sometimes the new combination of characteristics is particularly beneficial: the individual may have inherited the very best from each parent, and so may be stronger, or healthier. Sometimes, too, there are slight mistakes made in the copying, when the special reproductive cells are made, and these can result in the new individual being different in some way. These are known as **genetic mutations**. Although most of the time mutations are not particularly helpful, they can sometimes be beneficial. It is when these beneficial changes occur that evolution happens.

Any individual, whether it is a plant or an animal, exists in the world and needs to survive in it. That means that it needs to obtain enough nutrients, and whatever living space or other conditions it needs to keep it alive. It also needs to have some way of combining reproductive cells with another member of the same species, if it is to reproduce by sexual means. And in doing all this, it will often be in competition with other animals or plants, which are also trying to survive.

So anything which helps an organism to get an edge over the competition will be useful. And slight physical changes, like the ones which can sometimes be produced by genetic mutations, can sometimes give an organism just that edge that it needs, by helping it to become better adapted to its environment. That means that it will more able to survive and reproduce than other members of its species.

Natural selection

One of the examples of evolution which is often described is that of the finches on the Galapagos islands. When Darwin reached these islands, on the voyage made by the famous ship HMS Beagle, each island had a slightly different kind of finch living on it. But when the different finches were examined, it was apparent that, at some time in the past, they had all developed from just one species of finch which had originally colonised the islands. But because each island presented a slightly different environment, **natural selection** had meant that the birds had gradually adapted to their particular island, and so become different from those on other islands.

Imagine, for example, an island in which the main source of food for the birds was seeds, with thick, strong shells. If a finch had inherited the genes for a slightly thicker, stronger beak — perhaps as a result of a genetic mutation — then it would have an edge over the competition. It would be able to get to its food more easily, and using less energy, than the other birds. So it would be likely to grow to be strong and healthy. When it mated, some of its offspring would also inherit the gene for a thick strong beak, and they too would become stronger and healthier than the others.

Survival of the fittest

So if something happened which made the food supply scarce — perhaps a drought, or some other natural change — these would be the birds which survived. They would be less likely to die of starvation, because they were healthier and better fed in the first place, and they would be more likely to be able to get at particularly tough seeds which the other birds could not manage. So in the end, over thousands of years, it would be their descendants which occupied the island.

On another island, though, where the main food supply was insects which hid under stones, a thick strong beak would not be much help. Adaptation to that particular environment would produce a different kind of physical form. Natural selection is all about the **survival of the fittest** — and the fittest animal is the one which is best adapted to its environment.

Adaptation and development

This continuous process of adaptation and development has produced a vast diversity of living organisms, ranging from plants and yeasts to mammals and birds. These can be roughly organised into general groups, one of which is the order known as **primates**, which includes monkeys, lemurs, apes, and human beings. And when we look at different species, we can trace part of our evolution. For example, Fig. 14.2 tells us something about the evolution of the largest part of our brain, the cerebrum

But although it is quite common, it is a mistake to think of evolution as a straight-line development leading up to the human being. That is only one out of many different branches of evolution. There are lots of different groups of animals, each of which has adapted to their environment in different ways. We often think of a shark's brain as being quite primitive, for instance: it is not really up to much in the way of learning or intelligence. But a shark is most superbly adapted to its environment, and in many ways represents a triumph of evolution. It would be hard to design a more efficient and better adapted animal to fill the ecological role which the shark

Figure 14.2   Evolutionary development of the brain

plays. In a sense, every animal which is alive nowadays is the outcome of a battle for survival which has been going on for millions of years, so none of them can really be regarded as inferior, or inefficient.

Biodiversity

The most important part of the whole evolutionary process is the fact that the animal is able to pass its genes on to its offspring. And evolution has meant that this has been achieved in a vast number of different ways. Natural selection favours an animal which can make sure that its offspring will survive. A species might do that, as frogs do, by having hundreds of offspring, so that at least a few will avoid being eaten by predators and grow up to become mature frogs. Or a species might do it by having just one or two young ones, but nurturing them carefully in family groups until they are old enough to look after themselves.

When we actually look at what plants and animals do, we find a tremendous range of different behaviours and options. The principle of **biodiversity** means that there are examples of almost every different kind of activity that we could think of, somewhere in the animal kingdom. In many species, for instance, it is the fathers which rear the young rather than the mothers — after all, they too have invested their genes in their offspring. In some species, males hold territories; in others, females do. The more we look, the less there seem to be general rules about what is an optimal strategy for survival.

Sociobiology

Sometimes even, we find that an animal helps its genes to survive by laying down its own life. The sociobiologist E. O. Wilson, from his studies of ants (1975), showed how it was often an evolutionary advantage for a single animal to die to protect its relatives, since they too shared the same genes. Moreover, it was also sometimes an advantage for an individual animal not to have offspring directly, but instead to devote its life to taking care of siblings or cousins, which again shared the same genes. In this way, ultimately, that animal's own genes would survive and be perpetuated.

Wilson used this argument to explain how ant societies, and similar insect communities in which very few individuals reproduce directly, could have evolved. In these societies, altruism, or self-sacrificing behaviour, could sometimes become an evolutionary advantage: survival of the fittest did not necessarily mean the survival of the biggest and strongest, but of the one which was best able to make sure that its genes were perpetuated.

Wilson, and also Dawkins (1976), then went on to draw a number of parallels between the sociobiological processes which he had observed in ant societies, and things which happened in human societies, but these were much more controversial. Partly, this is because human beings use a rather more direct method of perpetuating their genes, by caring for their children and helping them to survive to maturity. But mainly it is because there are really quite a lot of other differences between human beings and ants: parallels like this may appear attractive on the surface, but do not really stand up to scientific scrutiny.

The main objection to the sociobiological version of evolution as applied to human beings was not really the ideas themselves, but the sociobiologists' claims that human behaviour was essentially determined by these biological mechanisms. As we have seen throughout this book, what human beings do needs to be understood on a number of different levels, including cultural, social and interpersonal ones. We may be influenced by our evolution, but that's not at all the same thing as being determined by it. There are any number of other factors which influence what we do, and all of them make a difference.

Coevolution

Of course, evolution is not just a one-way process. Animals do not just adapt to their environments, they also change those environments by living in them. Even an amoeba, which has only one body cell, secretes chemicals into the water that it swims in, and so changes that water. And more complex animals often exert quite a strong influence over their environments, so that the environments also evolve with the animals.

This process is known as **coevolution**, and it is something which has often been overlooked when people have talked about evolutionary processes. Often we have assumed that the relationship between animals and their environment is just a one-way thing: that animals use their environment to live in, but do not really affect it, except to use up its resources. A number of large-scale ecological problems have arisen from this rather simplistic view of the world.

When the first white settlers arrived on the American Prairies, for instance, they found it teeming with buffalo, and also with the small animals known as prairie dogs. When they exterminated the buffalo and introduced cattle, they also systematically wiped out the prairie dogs. Since these ate grass, they reasoned, they would be in competition. But more recently — and almost too late, because the prairie dog was nearly extinct — biologists have found that the prairie dog's activities did not use up the grass at all — rather, they enriched it, so that it grew more lushly and provided more foodstuffs, for the buffalo and everything else.

Similarly, Trevor (1992) reported on a 30-year-old experiment in Tsavo National Park, in Kenya. In other national parks, the elephant population was culled when it seemed to be growing too large for the park's resources; but in Tsavo they decided to let nature take its course, and see what happened if the elephants were allowed to multiply unrestrictedly. Although this led to some heartbreaking scenes in the short-term, by producing a country virtually stripped of vegetation and the deaths of a large number of elephants through starvation, in the longer term the country became richer and more lushly vegetated than even before. The elephants' activities had spread the vegetation more widely, for example, they had scraped out new water-holes during the drought, and all the other species had benefited too, over the 30-year period.

These examples of coevolution show how animals and their environments interact — and there are some similar examples with human societies, too. The Native Australians, for instance, managed the Australian bush by using fire, systematically, for many thousands of years. They lived from the land, but also managed it, and the plants and animals also adapted to this management. And this process also meant that the environment changed, as well. Australian plants burn easily, but their seeds and roots are well protected, and they regenerate from fire very quickly indeed.

In some sanctuaries in Australia which have been set up by white people, and protected from fire for many decades, the native plants often develop serious diseases. They have not evolved natural resistance to plant disease, as European and American plants have, because they did not need it. Under the Native Australians' management, regular fires wiped out the diseased plants, and sterilised the soils, so that the new plants grew up more healthily than before.

Coevolution, then, is a significant part of the evolutionary process, for people as well as for animals and plants. We have all evolved in order to be well adapted to our environments. But animals do not just adapt to their environments: their environments also adapt to the animals. It is this two-way relationship which we need to bear in mind when we are looking at what the study of animals can tell us about animal, or human, psychological processes.

Animal learning

In Chapter 7 we looked at some of the basic forms of learning, and much of that research was undertaken with animals. From these studies, comparative psychologists in the first half of this century were able to learn about association learning, and the way that animals can learn new behaviours and complex tasks by using different kinds of reinforcements for learned associations. That is very much the kind of training method which we use if we are teaching tricks to pets, for instance, or training performing animals — although there is a certain amount of debate as to whether the animals are really responding as mechanically as all that, or whether they are simply going along with their trainer because they enjoy it.

But comparative psychologists who are concerned with investigating animal behaviour in the natural environment — an approach which is known as **ethology** — have identified a number of other interesting aspects of animal learning, some of which may also be relevant as mechanisms in human learning too.

Imprinting

Some of these mechanisms became apparent as a result of research into **imprinting**. Imprinting is how young farmyard birds become attached to their mothers. Anyone who has seen young ducklings following their mothers around, or young chicks with a mother hen, will probably have been struck by how close the young birds stay to her, and how they scurry to catch up if they have been left behind.

Researchers exploring this attachment found that these young birds engage in a special, very rapid form of learning not long after they are born. This learning begins with a period of following around the first large moving object that they see. After they have followed the object — which in the farmyard, of course, is normally their mother — for a few minutes, the young birds become firmly attached to it, and will become distressed if they are separated from it at all. This is the mechanism which is known as **imprinting**.

Because imprinting is a special kind of learning, that means that the young birds can sometimes become attached to animals which are not their mothers. People living on farms, of course, have known this for centuries: ducklings which have lost their mother while still unhatched have been 'fostered' very successfully with hens, and people who have hand-reared ducklings have found that for the next couple of months they were constantly followed by a little procession of young birds. This special kind of learning is particularly interesting, partly because of how it happens, partly because of why it happens, and partly because of when it happens.

How imprinting happens

Unlike, say, the way that a young kitten learns to hunt, imprinting happens very quickly indeed. There is a kind of inherited 'readiness' to learn the attachment. Moreover, as soon as imprinting has happened, the young bird avoids other large moving objects — as if the inherited 'readiness' has switched itself off.

It appears that the young animal inherits genetic instructions which make it ready to learn at the proper time, and which end as soon as the learning has taken place. It does not inherit an image of its parent, but it is born ready to learn in just the sort of way which makes it most likely that it will imprint on its parent and nobody else. And in order to strengthen the probability that it really will imprint on its parent, and not something else, the duckling is also influenced by what it hears while it is still in its shell.

By hiding microphones in nest boxes, Hess (1972) found that the mother clucks gently to her eggs as she is sitting on them. When they hatch out and have become strong enough to leave the nest box, the mother takes up a position outside, and clucks to the chicks, who go towards her (Fig. 14.3). By calling gently to a set of unhatched eggs, Hess showed that the sound of his voice served as a similar attraction to a group of young ducklings when they hatched out.

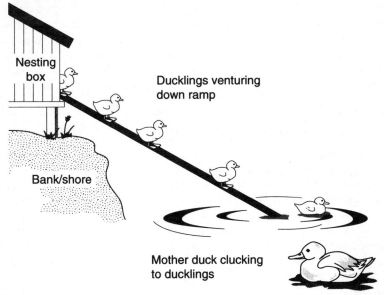

Figure 14.3 The imprinting process

Imprinting is interesting, then, because it shows us how genetic instructions can work to 'shape' the kind of learning that we are most likely to do. Human beings, too, seem to be genetically prepared for certain kinds of learning. As we saw in Chapter 7, we learn very quickly to avoid any food which has made us sick, and we continue to avoid it for the rest of our lives, pretty well. Like imprinting, it is a rapid form of learning which evolved because it helped us to survive.

Why imprinting happens

For a long time, psychologists believed that all attachments between parents and young happened by imprinting, and some went on to develop dire theories about the damage that could happen if a young infant was not with its mother all the time. But as we saw in Chapter 2, it gradually became apparent that young human infants develop their attachments in a rather different way — they develop them gradually, through the social interactions which take place between the infant and older people.

So why would a rapid, powerful form of attachment like imprinting evolve? As with anything else, it evolved because it helped members of the species to survive and adapt to their environments. And when we compare attachment mechanisms in animals of different species, we find that the ones which form an imprinted bond — a rapid, powerful attachment soon after birth — are the ones which have **precocial** young. Precocial animals are ones which can move about freely soon after they are born. Young horses, for example, can run around about an hour after birth, and so can lambs and goats. They, too, imprint rapidly on their parents.

So imprinting is nature's way of making sure that a young animal which is capable of getting around freely does not just run off and get lost, or eaten by the first predator that it meets. By developing a strong, rapid attachment to its mother, it stays close to her until it has learned a bit more about its world and how to survive in it. Human beings, which are much more helpless for some time after they are born, do not need to develop an imprinted bond with their caretakers. Instead, they have time to develop a relationship more gradually, through interaction with other people.

When imprinting happens

The other thing which is particularly interesting about imprinting is when it happens. There is a particular period — between about five and 25 hours after birth, for ducklings — when imprinting is most likely to take place. At first, researchers investigating imprinting believed that this was the only time it happened, and so they called it a **critical period**. A critical period is a time when a particular kind of learning absolutely must take place, or it will never happen.

Comparative psychologists soon found that critical periods also occurred with other kinds of development. Marler and Tamura found that young white-crowned sparrows had a critical period while they were young, for learning to sing a full adult song, complete with the regional 'accents' that all these sparrows have. Even though this period occurred way before the birds were old enough to sing themselves, they had to hear an adult bird singing at that time. If they did not, then when they grew up, they would only sing a very basic version of the song, without any of the full trills and embellishments that wild birds produced.

With imprinting, though, it became apparent after a while that the period when it usually happened was not absolutely critical — even though it was undoubtedly the strongest period for that type of learning. If a young duckling was kept in isolation, and away from any other kinds of moving objects, even small ones, then it was possible for it to imprint even once the normal learning period was over. So researchers came to regard it as a **sensitive period** — a period when development was most likely to happen — rather than an absolutely critical one.

Critical and sensitive periods are also interesting because they suggest that there can be times when genetic influences make us more ready to learn things than we are at other times. Lenneberg (1967) suggested that childhood is a critical period when human children have to learn to speak, and which ends at puberty. If children do not learn by then, Lenneberg argued, they never will.

Fromkin *et al.* (1974) challenged this view, by describing a case study of a girl called Genie, who had been brought up in virtual isolation and not discovered until after puberty. Although she was unable to speak when she was discovered, because she had never heard human language before, Genie did learn to talk. But she learned a little bit differently from ordinary children, and researchers concluded that childhood is probably a sensitive period for learning language, even if it is not a critical one.

The idea of childhood as a critical period for language learning led to a number of experiments with teaching children foreign languages. In the early 1970s, for instance, a project was set up which involved teaching the French language in state primary schools in Britain. The project was eventually abandoned by Government decree, on the grounds that the children concerned did not seem to be doing much better in secondary school French than those who had not learned it. More recently, though, there is some evidence that those children — who, of course are now adult — are much more likely to speak conversational French when they are travelling in Europe than most other British people are, and so the project may have been on the right track after all.

So even though, on the surface, it might seem as though there is not all that much that the study of ducklings can tell us about human beings, when we look at the underlying mechanisms more closely, we can see that it can give us quite a few insights which might help us to understand ourselves a bit better. But that does not, by any stretch of the imagination, mean that what human beings do and what ducklings do is exactly the same. As we saw, human beings develop their attachments in a quite different way from ducklings. But discovering the underlying mechanisms for that kind of learning can be useful.

Learning by instinct

We have already seen how human beings and animals can have an inherited predisposition to learn some things very quickly indeed. Avoiding foods which have made you sick is not confined to humans — it is something that most animals will do. But it goes further than just avoiding foods which have been associated with unpleasant experiences. Avoidance learning seems to be shaped, so that we are ready to associate some things together and avoid them, but not others. In other words, we are ready for learning which will help us to survive.

Learning for survival

For example, in one study in 1966, Garcia and Koelling looked at how rats respond to different unpleasant experiences. They began by showing how the animals quickly learned to avoid salty water, if they had been given an injection to make them sick soon after drinking it. But rats who drank salty water and were then given an electric shock did not learn to avoid the water. They did not learn to connect the two stimuli at all. On the other hand, they learned to connect the electric shock with a light or a clicking sound very easily indeed.

In other words, these rats had been ready to learn some connections, but not others. They could associate shocks with lights or sounds, but not with tastes. And they could associate sickness with tastes, but not other unpleasant happenings. It is easy to see, I think, how this type of learning fits with the idea of evolutionary adaptation. In real life, you would be likely to be able to hear or see something which was about to cause you pain; but you would taste something which was about to poison you. So it makes sense for any animal to be ready to learn those kinds of associations.

Pretty well all animals, it seems, are more ready to learn some things than others. Honey bees, for instance, find it very easy to learn to recognise particular smells. If a bee is fed with food that has been scented with a distinctive smell, such as lavender, then it begins to select lavender scents, and to go to those for food even if other food is available. They make the association between smell and food very readily.

But they do not associate other stimuli with food as easily. Menzel and Erber (1978) showed that a honey bee can learn to link smell and food 90 per cent of the time after just one learning session, as long as it is a flower scent which is being used. They take longer to learn smells which are not of flowers. And they take even longer to learn stimuli which are not smells at all. For instance, although they will learn to go to a particular colour for food, it takes them three or four learning sessions, not just one. And it takes them five or six learning sessions to go to a particular shape. They can learn it in the end, but they are not nearly as quick to learn as they are with smells.

There are some stimuli, too, which bees simply will not learn at all. For instance, they do not learn to associate light with food, no matter how many learning sessions they are given. It simply does not form an association. Yet bees are very sensitive to light: they detect polarised light and use it in navigation. Evidently, as far as bees are concerned, foraging for food and finding your way home are two entirely unconnected skills!

What we find, then, when we look at this kind of animal learning, is that it is not simply a matter of random associations between stimuli. Evolutionary pressures have 'shaped' both animals and humans to be particularly ready to learn certain things rather than others. We have seen a human application of this principle already, when we looked at how strongly the human infant is pre-programmed for social interaction with other people, and how readily human children learn by imitating others. Gould and Marler (1987) discussed how this evolutionary 'shaping' of the capacity to learn applies across many different species, and seems to be a fundamental feature of learning.

Novelty and curiosity

The examples we have looked at here have been mainly about a readiness for very specific kinds of learning: imprinting on a parent, being sociable with one's caretakers, or seeking out or avoiding food. But some animals have inherited a predisposition for a more general kind of learning. They will explore places, or be curious about new objects. And sometimes, too, they seem to be ready to learn entirely new forms of behaviour.

Rats and monkeys, for example, will generally explore new situations, and will investigate strange objects that they come across — unless there is some good reason to avoid them. And this exploration, too, can be an evolutionary advantage. In one study, Blanchard, Fukanaga and Blanchard (1976) put experimental rats in a box with a cat — separating them by a clear screen. If the rats had been in the box before, and so had explored it, they crouched down and remained immobile, to avoid attracting the cat's attention. But if they had not had a chance to explore the box, they ran around looking for a way to escape.

In other words, rats use the knowledge that they obtain from their natural tendency to explore new places, to tell them what to do in the case of a potential threat. If you know that you are in a place with no escape, then the best thing to do is to try not to attract a predator's attention. If you do not know, then the best thing to do is to try to find a way out. But it is better to know, so exploring anywhere new is a good way of surviving.

Learning and brain development

As we saw in Fig. 14.2, the cerebrum of the brain is much larger and more highly developed in some species than it is in others. That part of the brain is the part which we use for learning and thinking, and those animals which have the largest and most highly developed cerebrum also seem to be those animals which are able to pick up on a wide range of different opportunities for learning. As far as land animals are concerned, human beings have the most highly developed cerebrum of all. And we are also capable of learning more than any other land animals.

But this does not really apply to sea mammals, such as dolphins. A dolphin's cerebrum is even larger and more convoluted than a human being's, but we do not really know what that implies, since a dolphin's experience is so very different from ours. Almost from the first time that human beings can co-ordinate their muscles, we are manipulating objects, changing them and shaping our environments. Although dolphins play with objects too, their experience is much more to do with living in and experiencing their environment: they do not manipulate it at all. That's very different, and it is not at all clear whether we actually have any common ground for understanding what constitutes dolphin intelligence.

It is apparent to anyone who works with dolphins that they are intelligent, but it is unlikely that intelligence means the same thing in a dolphin as it does when we are talking about a human being. What we do know, though, is that dolphins are very ready to learn all sorts of things, including entirely novel kinds of behaviours. Moreover, they give every sign of enjoying doing so. Pryor, Haag and O'Reilly (1969) trained a dolphin to perform a new type of action each day, by giving her a reward when she did something she had not done before. By the end of the study, the dolphin was producing many entirely new actions, including tail-walking and back flips, and some actions which were so elaborate that the researchers found it hard to describe them!

We can see, then, that when we are talking about animal learning being shaped by the demands of adaptation to the environment, we are not just talking about learning simple responses. If an environment is constantly changing, it makes evolutionary sense to be prepared for new kinds of learning. A species which can live in different environments may need to be able to learn very different behaviours to survive. Human beings live in all kinds of conditions, from arctic wastes to tropical forests — so it would be inappropriate for us to be genetically prepared for dealing with a particular physical environment. Instead, we are genetically prepared to interact with and learn from other human beings, and that's what allows us to survive.

There is, of course, a great deal more to comparative research than we have been able to look at here, and much of it is extremely fascinating. This book has only really been able to give you a very superficial 'taste' of modern psychology. But I hope that you have found it an interesting one. It is an intriguing area of study, and one which can give us a lot of insights into why we are like we are. I, personally, have always enjoyed the study of psychology. I hope you have enjoyed this brief taste of it, too.

— FURTHER READING —

If you are interested in taking your exploration of psychology a bit further, you could try one of my two general texts:

Hayes, N., *A First Course in Psychology* (3rd edn. Nelson 1993)

— — and S. Orrell, *Psychology: An Introduction* (2nd edn. Longman 1993)

or, if you would like something rather more advanced:

Hayes, N., *Foundations of Psychology* (Nelson 1994)

There is also a dictionary which explains many of the psychological concepts which you will have come across in this book:

Stratton, P. and N. Hayes, *A Student's Dictionary of Psychology* (2nd edn. Edward Arnold 1993)

Alternatively, if you want to read more specialised books in psychology, these would probably be a good place to start:

Argyle, M., *The Psychology of Happiness* (Routledge 1991)

Baddeley, A. *Your Memory: A User's Guide* (Penguin 1984)

Bakker, F., *et al., Sport Psychology* (Wiley 1990)

Burr, V. and T. Butt, *Invitation To Personal Construct Psychology* (Whurr 1992)

Duck, S., *Relating to Others* (Open UP 1988)

Harris, P., *Children and Emotion* (Blackwell 1988)

Reason, J., *Human Error* (Cambridge UP 1990)

Shackleton, V., *Business Leadership* (ITBP 1995)

Turner, J., *Social Influence* (Open UP 1991)

The full academic references for *Access to Psychology* are available on the Internet at http://www.hud.ac.uk/schools/human+health/behavioural_science/staff/nicky/Teachref.html

INDEX